W9-BKM-329

American Cooking:
The Eastern Heartland

LIFE WORLD LIBRARY
LIFE NATURE LIBRARY
TIME READING PROGRAM
THE LIFE HISTORY OF THE UNITED STATES
LIFE SCIENCE LIBRARY
GREAT AGES OF MAN
TIME-LIFE LIBRARY OF ART
TIME-LIFE LIBRARY OF AMERICA
FOODS OF THE WORLD
THIS FABULOUS CENTURY
LIFE LIBRARY OF PHOTOGRAPHY
THE TIME-LIFE ENCYCLOPEDIA OF GARDENING
FAMILY LIBRARY
   THE TIME-LIFE BOOK OF FAMILY FINANCE
   THE TIME-LIFE FAMILY LEGAL GUIDE
THE AMERICAN WILDERNESS

Foods of the World

American Cooking: The Eastern Heartland

New York · New Jersey · Pennsylvania · Ohio · Michigan · Indiana · Illinois

by

José Wilson

and the Editors of

TIME-LIFE BOOKS

photographed by Richard Jeffery,

Enrico Ferorelli, Constantine Manos,

John Robaton and Brian Seed

TIME-LIFE BOOKS, NEW YORK

THE AUTHOR: José (pronounced Josie) Wilson was born in England and worked for women's magazines there before coming to the United States in 1951. Here she has worked for the *Ladies' Home Journal* in Philadelphia and for *House & Garden* in New York, and was editor of *House & Garden's New Cook Book* (1967). Now a freelance writer, Miss Wilson has contributed to many magazines and co-authored three home-decorating books; she writes a syndicated column and—with James Beard—teaches cooking classes.

THE STUDIO PHOTOGRAPHER: Richard Jeffery, who made the studio photographs and the cover, has contributed to many volumes in this series. The still-life materials for his pictures were selected by Yvonne McHarg.

THE CONSULTANTS: James A. Beard *(far left)*, special consultant, is the leading authority on American regional foods. His many books include *How to Eat Better for Less Money*. The late Michael Field *(left)*, consulting editor for FOODS OF THE WORLD, was a noted teacher, lecturer and writer on culinary subjects. Among his own books is *All Manner of Food*.

THE CHEF: John Clancy *(below)* heads the kitchen staff that tested the recipes for this book as well as for other volumes in the FOODS OF THE WORLD Library. He also teaches cooking classes in Manhattan and on Long Island.

THE FIELD PHOTOGRAPHERS: Among the photographers who took the field pictures for this book are Constantine Manos, a Boston-based freelance whose work appeared in *American Cooking: New England;* Enrico Ferorelli, an Italian lawyer turned photographer who divides his time between Rome and New York; John Robaton, a native of Hershey, Pennsylvania, who is with Camera 5 Agency; and Brian Seed, a London-based freelance who was field photographer for *African Cooking* in this series.

THE COVER: Both funnel cakes *(top)*, a kind of deep-fried cruller served with molasses, and *fastnachts,* square sugared doughnuts, are popular Pennsylvania Dutch treats at coffeetime. They are listed in the Recipe Index.

TIME-LIFE BOOKS

FOUNDER: Henry R. Luce 1898-1967

EDITOR-IN-CHIEF: Hedley Donovan
CHAIRMAN OF THE BOARD: Andrew Heiskell
PRESIDENT: James R. Shepley
CHAIRMAN, EXECUTIVE COMMITTEE: James A. Linen
EDITORIAL DIRECTOR: Louis Banks

VICE CHAIRMAN: Roy E. Larsen

EDITOR: Jerry Korn
Executive Editor: A. B. C. Whipple
Planning Director: Oliver E. Allen
Text Director: Martin Mann
Art Director: Sheldon Cotler
Chief of Research: Beatrice T. Dobie
Director of Photography: Melvin L. Scott
Associate Planning Director: Byron Dobell
Assistant Text Directors: Ogden Tanner, Diana Hirsh
Assistant Art Director: Arnold C. Holeywell
Assistant Chief of Research: Martha T. Goolrick

PUBLISHER: Joan D. Manley
General Manager: John D. McSweeney
Business Manager: John Steven Maxwell
Sales Director: Carl G. Jaeger
Promotion Director: Paul R. Stewart
Public Relations Director: Nicholas Benton

FOODS OF THE WORLD

SERIES EDITOR: Richard L. Williams
EDITORIAL STAFF FOR AMERICAN COOKING: THE EASTERN HEARTLAND:
Associate Editor: Harvey B. Loomis
Picture Editor: Iris Friedlander
Designer: Albert Sherman
Staff Writers: Gerry Schremp, Gerald Simons
Chief Researcher: Sarah B. Brash
Researchers: Joan Chambers, Marjorie Chester, Rhea Finkelstein, Barbara Ensrud, Lyn Stallworth, Mollie E. C. Webster
Test Kitchen Chef: John W. Clancy
Test Kitchen Staff: Tina Cassel, Leola Spencer
Design Assistant: Anne B. Landry

EDITORIAL PRODUCTION
Production Editor: Douglas B. Graham
Quality Director: Robert L. Young
Assistant: James J. Cox
Copy Staff: Rosalind Stubenberg, Eleanore W. Karsten, Florence Keith
Picture Department: Dolores A. Littles, Joan Lynch
Studio: Gloria duBouchet

The text for this book was written by José Wilson, recipe instructions by Michael Field and Gerry Schremp, other material by Eileen Hughes and the staff. Valuable assistance was given by the following individuals and departments of Time Inc.: Editorial Production, Norman Airey, Margaret T. Fischer; Library, Peter Draz; Picture Collection, Doris O'Neil; Photographic Laboratory, George Karas; TIME-LIFE News Service, Murray J. Gart.

© 1971 Time Inc. All rights reserved.
Published simultaneously in Canada. Revised 1972.
Library of Congress catalogue card number 70-150960.

Contents

The Recipe Booklet that accompanies this volume has been designed for use in the kitchen. It contains more than 135 recipes, including all of those printed in this book. It also has a wipe-clean cover and a spiral binding so that it can either stand up or lie flat when open.

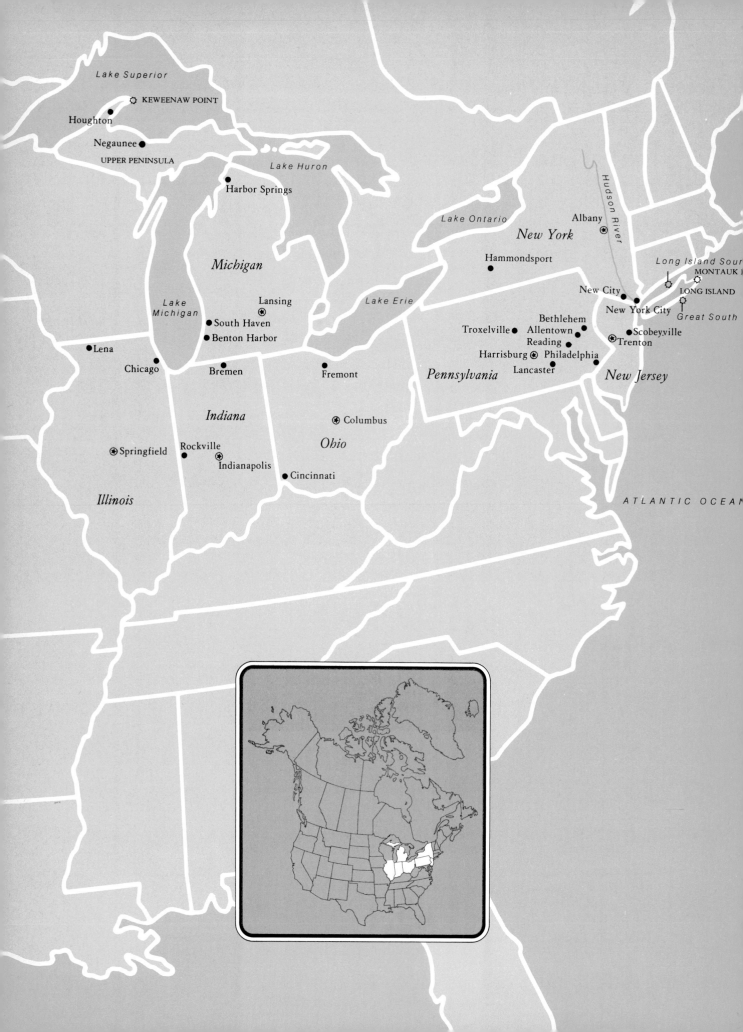

Lake Superior

⊕ KEWEENAW POINT

Houghton

Negaunee ●

UPPER PENINSULA

Harbor Springs ●

Lake Huron

Lake Ontario

Albany ⊕

New York

Hudson River

Hammondsport ●

Long Island Sound

MONTAUK

New City ●

New York City

LONG ISLAND

Michigan

Lake Erie

Great South

Lake Michigan

Lansing ⊕

Bethlehem ●

South Haven ●

Troxelville ● Allentown ●

Scobeyville ●

Benton Harbor ●

Reading ●

⊕ Trenton

Lena ●

Harrisburg ⊕ Philadelphia

New Jersey

Chicago ●

Bremen ●

Fremont ●

Pennsylvania

Lancaster ●

Indiana

⊕ Columbus

ATLANTIC OCEAN

⊕ Springfield

Rockville ●

Ohio

⊕ Indianapolis

● Cincinnati

Illinois

Introduction: Christening a Region

The grouping of states that we visit in this book may strike you as unusual, yet it is also logical. We have gathered together New York, New Jersey, Pennsylvania, Ohio, Michigan, Indiana and Illinois—comprising less than 10 per cent of the country's land and more than 30 per cent of its people—because they enjoy a common culinary tradition. We have christened the region the Eastern Heartland, and someday even the geography books may follow suit.

A great many of the people who settled the more westerly states of this region came from, or at least paused in, New York, New Jersey and Pennsylvania long enough to absorb and carry westward with them, via the waterways or overland, the strong patterns of cooking and eating that the original Dutch, English and German colonists had established. All across this area the men and women of the frontier depended on the fish and game they found in abundance, and the incredibly productive farms and orchards they planted; and their cooking was soon enriched by the diverse styles and tastes of the new waves of immigrants who followed them. All these elements have combined to give us what I regard as archetypal American food, or what in France would be called the country's *cuisine bourgeoise.* Eastern Heartland cooking is stick-to-the-ribs stuff, more plain than fancy, given to substantial meat dishes, dumplings, breads, pies. It does not have the austere background of the New England style, or the glamorous background of some of the Southern style; but it is hearty, appetizing, often exciting and always good.

I have visited or lived in most of the Eastern Heartland, and I have delighted in the range of foods to be found in the region, from the seafood and shellfish native to Long Island's waters, to the corn-and-pork sturdiness of the Pennsylvania Dutch, Indiana and Illinois farm kitchens, to the wonderful fish and game of Michigan's forests. It is a region where country cooking flourishes at its most impressive—but it is also the region that through the influence of two of its cities, Quaker Philadelphia and polyglot New York, taught the entire country how to enjoy the finest sophistications of the table.

José Wilson, the author, is an Englishwoman who has come to know the food and cooking and the very soil of America and loves it all. She and I have worked together for years, first on *House & Garden* and more recently in my cooking classes, and we have shared our feelings about what constitutes good food. Long before this book was thought of, we were devoted to much of the food in this region (though we did not have a name for it then) and her research for the book has given her all the more zest for the subject. In exploring the culinary joys of the Eastern Heartland she has tasted well and reported well.   —*James A. Beard*

I

The Joys
of Discovery

When I came to the United States from England some 20 years ago, I had a clear mental picture of what I would be eating here. Like many Europeans, I had visualized American food in terms of those glossy magazine ads—mountains of hamburgers and hot dogs dripping with ketchup and mustard, thick steaks, ice cream and apple pie. I was also vaguely aware of some quaintly named outdoor feasts known as clambakes and barbecues (this was before England had enthusiastically embraced the barbecue grill without, unfortunately, importing the climate to go with it).

I was soon to discover, with gluttonous delight, how much more there is to American cooking than the clichés. My initial encounter was with the marvelous food to be found along that part of the Atlantic seaboard where I first lived, in New York City and in Philadelphia.

I arrived in New York in April, the season for shad and shad roe, and got my first taste of it when I was taken out to lunch and told to forget everything else on the menu. Since then the flavor of this incomparable fish that spawns in the Eastern rivers has marked for me that longed-for, imperceptible turning point when winter yields to spring. When I walk down Manhattan's Second Avenue and spot shad in the windows of the fish stores and big bundles of early asparagus on the vegetable stalls, I look forward to a month or two of vernal self-indulgence. I prefer to cook both simply so that the flavors have a chance to come through; the asparagus steamed until barely bity-tender, the shad broiled for the minimum time with butter and lemon juice. This with a glass of white

Opposite: Dried ears of corn make a familiar kitchen decoration in the Eastern Heartland, where corn in its many variations is an agricultural and culinary staple. The plump wine-red "strawberry corn" and the short yellow ears hanging in this Indiana window may be popped and eaten. The multicolored ears, generally known as Indian corn, are grown mainly for show.

8

wine constitutes for me the perfect spring meal, the more welcome because these are seasonal foods to be savored during their heyday.

Wherever and whenever I encounter shad, I can't resist it. I've had it broiled to perfection at a New Jersey shad bake *(Recipe Index)* and eaten it in the open air from paper plates, and have also enjoyed the sautéed roe elegantly couched on a bed of sorrel purée *(Recipe Index)* that I've had in one of New York's best restaurants.

In Philadelphia I had my first taste of that local delicacy, scrapple, a savory mishmash of ground-up pork and cornmeal flavored with herbs and cooked in a loaf pan. There are numerous variations on this theme, but originally it was a thrifty way to use up leftover scraps of pork—hence the name—by mixing them with cornmeal or oatmeal. The more meat the better the scrapple; but when the pork had to be stretched, the amount of meal was increased, which probably explains another name by which scrapple was known in some parts of the country: poor-do.

There is a world of difference between freshly made scrapple and the canned variety, although most scrapple lovers today, even out in the country, buy it fresh from their butcher rather than making it themselves. The scrapple I had for breakfast was packed with meat and pungent with sage. It had been cut into half-inch slices and fried with the merest dab of shortening until the outside was a crisp brown while the inside was still moist and soft. Philadelphians often eat it with syrup, for breakfast; in the countryside they love to dribble rich dark molasses over it and serve it with home fries or a jacket potato for a more filling meal. For some, scrapple is an acquired taste; but I loved it at first bite, and still do.

Actually I was on home ground here because pork, in all its forms, has always been one of my favorite foods. My native county of Cumberland, in the northwest of England, is noted for its hams and sausage, as is Pennsylvania. So when I found in the little town of Strasburg, in Pennsylvania Dutch country, a local butcher who made fresh pork sausages, I had another orgy of indulgence; this time it was sausage-and-mashed, a childhood passion that is to me the essence of comforting food. There is absolutely nothing to it and I can't say why it always tastes so good, just a plump coil of sausage spurting its luscious fat over the creamy mashed potatoes, topped with a melting mound of golden butter the way I and the Pennsylvania Dutch like them. I always bake the sausage slowly in the oven on an enameled plate, as my mother did. The skin takes on a glossier, crisper brown than if you fry it in a pan on top of the stove.

Every time I go to the Pennsylvania Dutch country it offers new and fascinating discoveries. In summer, at the annual Kutztown Fair, I have watched sunbonneted women spiraling batter into hot fat for one of the specialties of the region, funnel cakes *(Recipe Index)*. At Christmas time I have bought bags of clear toy candy—edible figures of reindeer, birds, horses and dogs—with which I once decorated a tree for my godson.

There were many more foods I grew to know and hunger for. Plump, juicy blue point oysters, littleneck and cherrystone clams, the magnificent striped bass and swordfish and tender little bay scallops of Long Island, soft-shell crabs and deviled clams, clam chowder and oyster stew, big bowls of blueberries smothered in sour cream, and corn on the cob—no

Opposite: A page from an 1859 issue of *Harper's Weekly* shows how shad were caught in New York Bay and the Hudson River more than a century ago. This kind of fishing still goes on and still calls for "rough and ready customers" to work the boats and handle the nets *(following pages).*

SHAD FISHERY—VIEW OF SHAD FISHING IN NEW YORK BAY AND HUDSON RIVER.—FROM A SKETCH BY OUR OWN ARTIST.

THE SHAD FISHERY.

AT about this season of the year, sometimes a little earlier, a large number of men are actively employed in the shad fishery around the shores of Long and Staten Islands, and up the river as far as Albany. Large numbers of men and youths migrate from the higher waters of the Hudson, and waking from the half torpid state of inactivity in which they have passed the winter, set to work with a zeal and energy worthy of the highest cause.

Rough and ready customers are these men, and not perhaps over refined, but boisterous and jolly on the approach of spring, their harvest time, the rest of the year being spent in a more monotonous manner, varied occasionally by a trip to the deep sea fisheries.

The shad is a member of the family of Clupeidæ, a family which, though not numerous in species, includes a series of fish of the highest importance in an economical point of view. The herring, anchovy, pilchard and sprat belong to it, as does also that favorite of London epicures, the whitebait. All of these fishes have small mouths, and either very small teeth or none at all, and they are therefore but ill adapted to prey on other fishes, and are mostly obliged to find their subsistence in the myriads of minute animals diffused throughout the waters of the ocean, or lurking among the weeds at the bottom. They are all of them eminently migratory in their habits, traversing at different seasons, the entire ocean, and performing their journeys in immense schools, to which fact one of them, the herring, owes its name, it being derived from the German word *heer*, signifying army. Cuvier separated the shad from the Clupeidæ proper from the circumstance of there being a notch or emargination in its upper jaw, not observable in the other branches of the family, and assigned to it the name Alosa. In other respects the generic characters are identical in both. The shad is found in Great Britain and Europe as well as in this country, but is by no means so great a favorite there as here.

The English shad is a coarse and insipid fish, but there is a peculiar species caught in Scotland called the Alice shad, which is much esteemed.

The shad is sometimes called in England mother of herrings, and sometimes rock herrings, the first of which names may, perhaps, be intended for mother of herrings, shad having a disagreeable habit of feeding upon the small individuals of their own class when crustacea, of which they are most fond, are not readily available. With regard to the young shad, there has been much doubt manifested as to what manner of fish they were, and until the year 1828 it was supposed in England that the whitebait and the young shad were identical. Yarrell demonstrated the incorrectness of this supposition, and decided the whitebait to be an independent species, which

THE SHAD.

it has ever since continued to be, to the great satisfaction of certain corporations of the city of London, who repair annually to the towns of Greenwich or Blackwall, on the Thames, to partake of a whitebait dinner.

Little is known of the habits of the shad beyond the fact of its periodical migrations to the fresh-water rivers for the purpose of depositing its spawn, in which respect it differs from the herring and pilchard, which spawn on the coast, in salt water, and seldom ascend rivers above the mean line of separation between salt and fresh water. Like the salmon, it lingers some time in brackish water before ascending into the fresh—an important fact in its natural history. It is well known that the water at the mouths of rivers is usually warmer, by several degrees, than that of either the river or the sea in those neighborhoods, owing to the want of compenetration of the two liquids, on account of their different densities. The shad finds it necessary to resort to this warm water for the development of its spawn, and accordingly several weeks usually elapse between the time of its first appearance in the bay and its arrival at the spawning place. It is at this time that its flesh is in best order for the table, and it deteriorates rapidly as the roes mature and spawning time approaches.

In the English species, according to Yarrell, the operation of spawning is attended with some degree of difficulty, and is accompanied by a violent lashing of the tail, as though they required powerful muscular exertion to disencumber themselves of the matured roe. The noise produced in this manner, it is said, may be heard at a considerable distance in still weather.

SHAD FISHERMEN MENDING THEIR NETS.—FROM A SKETCH BY OUR OWN ARTIST.

more than 10 minutes from field to pot—slathered with butter and sprinkled with salt. If I knew anyone coming to this country for the first time, these are the things I would insist they try, prime beef notwithstanding. They are among the native foods the first settlers found, and they are still an integral part of the cooking of the states that make up the territory this book stakes out as the Eastern Heartland—New York, New Jersey, Pennsylvania, Ohio, Michigan, Indiana and Illinois.

I became aware of this culinary continuity as I left the sandy strands of the Atlantic coastline and traveled through the varied terrain of the region. From the mountainous, lake-dappled landscape of upper New York State I journeyed south to the rolling farm lands and placid countryside of New Jersey and eastern Pennsylvania. Crossing the Alleghenies to Pittsburgh, as the pioneers once did, I followed the long surge of the Ohio River through Cincinnati and into Indiana and Illinois, and then left this rich, verdant landscape to head north through flat fields and farm lands to the industrial Great Lakes cities of Cleveland, Detroit and Chicago. Finally, I reached the majestic wilderness of Michigan's Upper Peninsula, a stone's throw from Canada, and at that point had encompassed the farthest points of the Eastern Heartland.

Throughout this broad territory I encountered a style of cooking that I think of as being unequivocally American or, as James Beard describes it in his introduction to this book, "the *cuisine bourgeoise* of America." While it is essentially country-style cooking, it harmoniously embraces, along with the simple substantial meals of the farming people, the richer and more lavish foods of the old landowning families and the city dwellers. In the Pennsylvania Dutch region, for instance, the cooking of the German farmers who migrated to this land in great numbers during the 18th Century has remained pure, almost unchanged, while in nearby Philadelphia the culinary tradition is based on the elegant, luxurious dishes introduced by the English Quakers.

The Eastern Heartland's cooking draws heavily on the limitless resources of its waters and forests, from the plentiful shellfish and shad of New York to the fresh-water fish and abundant woodland game of Michigan. It is soundly based on the produce of the fertile farm land that stretches from New Jersey to the Mississippi River, and makes liberal use of the fruits from the orchards that bloom over the entire region. In the rural areas it has traditionally been embellished by an intriguing assortment of drinks made from the indigenous foods—fruits, flowers, berries, even weeds—that grow wild in splendid profusion.

That so many different and, in some ways, heterogeneous localities can share a characteristic cooking style is due to the fact that historically the whole region owes a debt to a culinary tradition that was nurtured in the early Middle Atlantic colonies of New York, New Jersey and Pennsylvania. The origins of this tradition lie in three national cuisines of Northern Europe—the Dutch, the English and the German—that united in colonial America to form a food pattern that has passed into the mainstream of American cooking. It is a pattern in which ham and other pork products, yeast breads and coffeecakes, pancakes, waffles, doughnuts, cakes, cookies, pies, preserves and pickles all figure prominently.

                                                Continued on page 17

At sundown, in sight
of the George Washington
Bridge and Manhattan
Island, two Hudson River
fishermen haul in their
catch of shad. The business
has changed little since the
sketches on page 11 were
made. Every April, long
hickory poles are driven
into the river bottom about
30 feet apart. Twice daily,
when the tide is low, the
fishermen stretch their
long gill nets between the
poles. The shad, heading
upriver to spawn, swim
headfirst into the nets and
are trapped. They are
harvested at high tide,
packed with ice in boxes
and sent to market.

Off Manhattan the Shad Run Still Draws Fishermen with Their Poles and Nets

The Hudson River (along with the Connecticut and the Delaware) is one
of the favorite spawning grounds of the American shad, the largest member
of the herring family, known scientifically as *Alosa sapidissima,* or "most
delicious shad." Every year, from April until June, fishermen on the Hudson
catch shad as their predecessors have done for 300 years—netting the fish
swimming upriver to spawning grounds on the flats near Kingston, where
they were born four or five years earlier. The female, or roe, shad, some
weighing 12 pounds, cost more and are much preferred to the male, or buck,
of the species, because of their highly prized eggs. The shad harvest fluctuates
enormously between the all-time high of nearly 4.5 million pounds in 1889
and the record low of 40,000 pounds in 1916. Recently the catch has been
about 100,000 pounds, but the market for Hudson shad has fallen sharply
too. Polluted waters have contributed to the decline of the shad runs and
given some of the fish a slightly "off" taste. Those caught in the lower
Hudson still make good eating, however, and when and if the pollution
problem is solved, the fish may regain its reputation as a most delicious shad.

13

Every spring when the shad run, shad bakes are as popular in some Hudson River towns as clambakes are in New England. The cooking technique *(opposite)* is copied from a method used by the Indians. A 25-foot-long bed of 500 pounds of charcoal is lit about three hours before the boned shad fillets are to be cooked. While the charcoal burns to hot ashes, the fillets, seasoned with salt and pepper, are nailed skin side down to greased hardwood boards *(left)*. Slices of bacon provide extra flavor and help keep the fillets moist and tender. The planks are placed at a slight outward angle to ensure even cooking—which takes half an hour or more. At this bake, held in Edgewater, New Jersey, shad dinners were prepared for 700 appreciative people.

In the home version of a shad bake *(Recipe Index)*, the fillet is butter-basted and broiled. It is then planked on a hardwood board, ringed with a piping of potatoes *duchesse* and briefly put under the broiler again. The spring months when shad is to be had is also asparagus time in the Eastern Heartland, but today's fresh produce knows no season and you may serve the fish with whatever other fresh or frozen vegetables you fancy. Here it is embellished with a medley of cherry tomatoes, green beans and peas.

The cooking of the Middle Atlantic colonists was good and substantial, born of what they brought, what they found, what they raised and what they learned from the Indians. It formed a sturdy connecting wedge between the austerity of New England, restricted by harsh weather, poor land and rock-bound shores, and the leisurely, aristocratic living of the South, favored by climate and fostered, to be sure, by slave labor.

Most of those first settlers of the Middle Atlantic states were farmers, and the structure of their meals reflected the life of a predominantly agricultural community—the huge breakfasts, "dinner" at noon and supper in the early evening that still persist in many of the rural areas of the Eastern Heartland. These settlers had fortuitously come upon some of the most productive farm land in the world and were further blessed by great stretches of river, lake and ocean where fish grew to prodigious size, by towering forests that harbored game, and by sheltered bays that lured wild fowl on their migratory flights from Canada to Mexico. Like any colonists, they quickly adopted the local foods—oysters, clams, venison, wild turkeys, watermelons and muskmelons and the corn dishes of the Indians. Yet they were not so gullible or foolhardy as to arrive empty-handed or ill-equipped. Within 10 years after the establishment of the first Dutch trading post of New Amsterdam in 1614, settlers were landing from ships bulging like Noah's Ark with horses and cattle, sheep, hogs and poultry. They brought with them the seeds and grains for planting fields of wheat and rye, vegetable gardens and orchards.

Records of New Netherland show how cannily the Dutch husbanded their resources. Not for them the hard, grinding, hungry winters that the Virginia and New England settlers so painfully survived. Each autumn set off a flurry of activity, with the farmsteads taking on the appearance of small food-processing plants. Meats, fish, vegetables and fruits were smoked, salted, spiced, dried or otherwise preserved. Apples were pressed for cider and vinegar, or stored "down cellar" in bins along with root vegetables. After weeks of backbreaking work the larder was safely stocked with corned beef and salt pork, hams and bacon, stone jars of lard, pickles and preserves. Even oysters and clams were stored for the winter, buried in beds of sand mixed with cornmeal and watered twice a week—although how many people suffered stomach qualms from this rather dubious method of preservation is not known.

From the beginning, New Netherland was a well-fed colony, prosperous enough to import spices, wines, brandy, rum and molasses. Some of the landowners were men of great wealth; to stimulate colonization the Dutch West India Company had allowed them to take possession of huge tracts of land along the Hudson on the condition that they pay the costs of transporting and settling at least 50 colonists within four years and underwrite the expenses of running the estate. Under a kind of sharecropping arrangement, the tenant farmer in return had to pay the owner, or patroon, a tenth of the produce raised on his *bouwerie,* or farm, an annual rent of 500 guilders (about 200 dollars), give three days' service a year with his horse and wagon, cut firewood and maintain the roads and buildings. This enabled the patroon to live like a king on a holding that was often more like a small province than a private estate.

Opposite: Shad roe on a bed of sorrel is the ultimate spring treat for seafood lovers on the Atlantic Coast. The fresh roe is available from April through June, a time, happily, when sorrel is young and tender. Both are at their best cooked quickly and simply. The sorrel is finely chopped, boiled, then sauced with egg yolks and cream. The shad roe is seasoned, dusted with flour, and fried lightly in butter. Traditionally, the roe is served on the sorrel, with lemon and boiled new potatoes *(Recipe Index).*

When the British took New Netherland from the Dutch in 1664, re-christening it New York, they saw no reason to change a system so eminently satisfactory to the landed gentry. Until the start of the Revolutionary War, the Hudson River's banks from New York to Albany were lined by the estates, some of them hundreds of square miles in size, of Dutch and English lords of the manor—the Livingstons, Van Cortlandts and Van Rensselaers.

A Dutch cookbook of 1683, *The Wise Cook and Housekeeper,* seems to have been the culinary bible of the Hudson Valley ladies, and the recipes did not skimp on luxuries. There is an apple custard made with "Rhenish wine," and a sauce for partridges or pigeons that includes saffron. A recipe for ox tongue calls for stewing it in broth and red wine with butter, cloves, pepper, ginger, cinnamon and sugar, and ends with the assurance, "It is good," which it might well have been.

They were hearty trenchermen, those Dutch, and their greatest pleasures were those of the table. Washington Irving's description of a Dutch tea in "The Legend of Sleepy Hollow" makes one hungry just to read it:

"Such heaped-up platters of cakes of various and almost indescribable kinds, known only to experienced Dutch housewives. There was the doughty doughnut, the tender 'olykoek' and the crisp and crumbling cruller; sweet cakes and short cakes, gingercakes and honeycakes and the whole family of cakes. And then there were apple pies and peach pies and pumpkin pies; besides slices of ham and smoked beef; and, moreover, delectable dishes of preserved plums, and peaches, and pears, and quinces, not to mention broiled shad and roasted chickens, together with bowls of milk and cream, all mingled higgledy-piggledy, with the motherly teapot sending up its clouds of vapor from the midst."

That kind of glorious, heart-warming afternoon meal has long since gone from the American scene, but many of the foods remain. Seventeenth Century Amsterdam looks over our shoulder every time we sit at a lunch counter munching a doughnut or eating cole slaw with a sandwich, for these most taken-for-granted of American foods were the *oliebollen* and *kool sla* of the Dutch settlers; and the pancakes and waffles a Dutch housewife baked for teatime have been absorbed into our breakfast menu.

Breakfast in America always fascinates me. It is a unique repast that seems to have come into being naturally, born of the pioneer dishes and the indigenous foods. I can find no close resemblance to this morning meal in the European countries from which the settlers came; you couldn't say there was anything Dutch or German or Swedish or French or even English about it. I am not talking here about the convenience breakfast of frozen orange juice and packaged cereal, or the drugstore-hotel monotony of half a grapefruit with a maraschino cherry on top, with eggs and bacon, toast and coffee. I don't consider that kind of meal to have any national identity. To me the quintessential American country breakfast is the strange (to a European) and unforgettable mingling of sweet and meat—of syrup-saturated pancakes with sausage, waffles with bacon, ham and eggs with hot breads and sweet breads, all manner of coffeecakes and muffins, doughnuts and even pie.

I have grown to like most of these things, but I still eat them in my own way. The nuttiness of buckwheat cakes tastes so good with coarse, well-seasoned country sausage that I leave the syrup in its pitcher and ask for extra butter instead. Or if I order blueberry pancakes with blueberry syrup, I don't have bacon. These breakfast foods—bacon, ham and sausage, breads and hot cakes, syrups and preserves—form the links with the past of farms and frontiers, and no matter where you travel in the Eastern Heartland you find them cropping up again and again.

Not all the culinary traditions of the region originated with the first colonists. During the mid-19th Century, a great wave of immigrants arrived to man the nation's factories and mines, its steel and lumber mills, and to build the railroads and towns that girdled the body of America. With them came a great diversity of cuisines to enrich and enlarge the repertory of the past and a new approach to the everyday routine of eating.

For one thing, the rapid industrial growth of the nation brought fortunes to those with the luck or acumen to cash in on the boundless opportunities, and these industrial tycoons and merchant princes—the Vanderbilts, Carnegies, Morgans and Mellons—cultivated a taste for the finest foods, the most ornate table appointments, the most punctilious service. To meet their demands there arose something new in America, a restaurant culture. The cradle (and today still the capital) of this culture was New York, where in an astonishingly short time restaurants developed by skilled European chefs and restaurateurs matured into epicurean establishments that challenged the best of Europe.

By the late 19th Century, the cult of the restaurant had spread across the Eastern Heartland, as far as newly booming, brash Chicago. Here it joined forces with another new phenomenon, the steak. It was at this time that America became beef-conscious, and Chicago gained fame for the quality of its steaks and roasts from the Western steers railroaded by the thousands to the city's stockyards.

Situated at the lower tip of Lake Michigan, Chicago was strategically placed at a point where railroads from east, west and southwest converged. Emerging phoenixlike from the Great Fire of 1871, the city had rebuilt, expanded and prospered until it was the acknowledged metropolis of the prairies. Young and vigorous, magnet for the region's new money, the city flaunted visible proofs of its wealth: the expensive shops in the Loop, the magnificent mansions of Lake Shore Drive and the cosmopolitan cuisine served in the Palmer House and Ambassador Hotels.

Now the stockyards that lay behind the glittering façade are mostly gone and steak is no rarity but a national staple, yet Chicago, with more than 500 "steak houses," still deserves its reputation as the city where the quintessential meal of middle America—steak and potatoes—is to be found at its best.

Other Eastern Heartland cities reflected the new spirit that was abroad in America, the spirit of immigrants with nothing to lose and everything to gain, the people who had left the villages and city slums of Europe to seek their fortunes in the land of opportunity. Among them were hundreds of thousands of Germans from Bavaria and the Rhineland, many of whom surged into the young town of Cincinnati during the 1830s and 1840s; their culinary influence, mingling with that of the South (Ken-

Continued on page 24

19

Using a swirling motion, Mrs. Brown funnels the wafflelike batter into hot lard.

Pennsylvania: Odd Delights of Country Cooking

A trip through the fertile eastern counties of Pennsylvania offers the traveler an opportunity to sample such rural specialties as funnel cakes, clear toy candy and animal cookies. On these pages Mrs. Kitty Brown is shown cooking funnel cakes *(Recipe Index)* on a coal-fired stove in her kitchen in Marietta. The vital utensil is a large tin funnel *(left)*. The flow of batter is regulated by a deft forefinger applied to the bottom of the spout. At right, surrounded by her collection of mid-19th Century cooking utensils, Mrs. Brown arranges a platter of the spiral-shaped cakes. Funnel cakes once were staple fare at the hefty midmorning meals the early-rising farmers of the area ate before returning to work in the fields.

Here she flips the cake over to cook the other side. The golden fried cakes are dipped in hot molasses and served with sausage.

The clear toy candy castings below and the animal cookies on the opposite page are favorite Christmas treats for children, intended to enchant the eye as well as the palate. Charles Regennas of Lititz, shown pouring liquid candy into molds at right, learned the craft from his grandfather and is now teaching it to his sons. During the Christmas season Mr. Regennas, a mail carrier, prepares as much as 400 pounds of candy for sale in a small shop near his home. The candy is made by boiling a mixture of glucose, granulated sugar, water and food coloring until it reaches 290°. It is then poured into oiled molds and allowed to set. Mr. Regennas owns about 300 of the metal molds, all lovingly fashioned long ago to bring holiday cheer to children.

In her kitchen in Bethlehem, Mrs. Janette Turner strings "fish" together from a batch of freshly baked cookies. Traditionally, these wafer-thin molasses cookies are made in huge quantities, both to eat and to use as decorations.

tucky lies just across the Ohio River) has been a lasting one. At the house of Cincinnati friends recently I was handed with my cocktail a strip of something crisp and darkly brown that I couldn't identify at first. This was a local specialty, a curious combination of salt and sweet that tasted surprisingly good—thickly sliced country bacon sprinkled with brown sugar and broiled until the sugar caramelized.

Just as Chicago meant beef, Cincinnati meant pork. Hog killing was the foundation of the city's fortunes and earned it the nickname of Pork-opolis. In some years in the latter half of the 19th Century as many as half a million hogs were slaughtered there, and famous Cincinnati hams were served in the country's best restaurants and hotels and even, it is said, at the White House.

The old section of the city where the Germans settled in the 1840s is still known as Over the Rhine, and there, in a huddle of run-down houses and tiny stores, is a celebrated old German restaurant established by August Grammer in 1872. Once a hangout of sportswriters and politicians, Grammer's retains a wonderful, masculine *Gemütlichkeit;* the room where I had lunch, fronting on Walnut Street, has one wall of leaded, frosted glass, a tiled floor, tin ceiling, huge mahogany bar and walls hung with steins and painted with delightfully corny murals of Bavarian castles and landscapes. The current owners, Carl and Dick Mohaupt, obviously love the place and wouldn't think of changing anything about it, including the menu, which is comfortably padded with old-fashioned German dishes like *Schmierkäse* (cottage cheese) salad, sauerbraten with noodles, homemade sauerkraut and smoked country sausage, schnitzel, potato pancakes and German fried potatoes. I had the potted pork chop, a thick cut of the loin slowly cooked with sauerkraut; then, although it meant piling cabbage on cabbage, I ordered another Cincinnati dish, hot slaw—shredded cabbage with a dressing of hot bacon fat, vinegar and a bit of sugar with crispy pieces of bacon scattered on top, a perfectly complementary mélange of flavors and textures.

The Germans, of course, were not the only national group to leave their mark on American cooking. You have only to think of a typical luncheonette menu with its Danish pastries, Swedish meatballs, Italian spaghetti and French omelets to realize how all-embracing the range of American food has become. There are other national dishes that flourish mainly in places with a strong, persistent ethnic tradition, yet they should also be counted as part of the American culinary tapestry. Among them I would put the pasty *(Recipe Index),* which has established its own little beachhead in the lovely wild stretch of Michigan's Upper Peninsula between Lake Michigan and Lake Superior. If Italian pizza and Mexican *tacos* can become all-American favorites, why not Cornish pasties?

I grew up with pasties; strictly speaking, they belong to Cornwall in the extreme southwest of England, but like many foods that make good functional sense they are cooked and eaten all over England. Originally the midday lunch of the Cornish tin mines, the pasty (pronounced *passtee)* is a large pastry turnover filled with finely cubed beef, potato, turnip and onion seasoned with salt and pepper and sometimes just a touch of mixed herbs (parsley, thyme and marjoram). The firm, sturdy crust encases this juicy mingling of meat and vegetables, a meal in a shell. One of the great merits of the pasty, which gives it an edge over other types of snack food, is that it will stay hot for hours if wrapped in a napkin and newspaper the minute it is baked and popped in a pocket or lunch pail. Over the years this has endeared it not only to miners but also to hunters and fishermen who otherwise would go without the pleasant sustenance of something warm and filling.

When Cornishmen moved into the Upper Peninsula in the 1870s and 1880s to mine iron and copper, the pasty caught on with every other national group around. Now there is a fine rivalry among the Finns, Italians, Germans, French, Swedes and Poles in Michigan as to who makes the best pasties. Some cooks make a suet-and-lard crust, others a regular piecrust with a little baking powder in it. While classicists insist on using only beef, others combine the beef with half pork or half liver. There is argument about the vegetables, too—most people throw in a little rutabaga with the potato and onion, while others include carrots as well. No matter what goes into them, everyone agrees on what goes with them, and in the best American tradition that is ketchup and dill pickles.

In summertime, the Upper Peninsula buzzes with tourists, but I was there in early fall when the air had a crisp edge that touched the sumac with flame. The lodges and cabins, and the roads that cut through the Marquette and Hiawatha National Forests, were almost deserted. Ever since crossing the Mackinac Bridge that links the Lower and Upper Peninsulas I had been thinking of pasties; but I had been advised to avoid the first roadside stands advertising "Pasties to Go" and to head farther west toward the copper country of Keweenaw County, a claw of land digging into Lake Superior, if I wanted to taste the real thing. This is the mining region where the Cousin Jacks and Cousin Jennies, as the Cornish were nicknamed locally, had made their homes.

I left Marquette in a drizzling rain and, if I had not been told to look out for Madelyn's Pasty Shop on the way to Ishpeming, I might have passed right by, for it hardly looks like a pasty paradise from the outside, or on the inside either. A small, unassuming roadside café, it has a counter, three Formica-topped tables, a rack of postcards and a refrigerated case of soda pop and milk, and that's about all, except for a kitchen in back. The pasties, though, were superb. With such a simple food, the excellence depends on the ingredients, and there was no skimping, padding or other commercial chicanery here, just the right proportions of meat and potato and onion and rutabaga, with the meat tender sirloin strip, cubed by hand. Every pasty is made and baked on the spot and emits a little whiff of savory steam when the fork goes in—and all it cost was 80 cents.

My praise of the pasty is in no way intended as a slight to the culinary contributions of the Finns, the Swedes, the Italians, the Germans, Poles and French. The pasty speaks to me of home, and the flavor of home is something you carry with you no matter how far you travel, and however many new foods you find and come to love. What the Cornish and all their fellow immigrants have managed to achieve in their kitchens is the best of both worlds, Old and New, and it is this felicitous combination that gives Eastern Heartland cooking its strength and substance.

A pasty is a sort of portable potpie without the pot. Its history is a venerable one. French and English chroniclers mentioned it as far back as the 14th Century, and in the 17th, Shakespeare wrote about a hot pasty in *The Merry Wives of Windsor* but omitted the recipe. The pasty came to America in the mid-19th Century with immigrant Cornish miners who settled in Michigan's Upper Peninsula to work the rich iron and copper deposits there. Mining methods have changed since then, but the pasty is still going strong. At left 68-year-old Frank G. Matthews, a former miner who runs a mining museum in Negaunee, the peninsula's iron-ore center, demonstrates the proper way to eat a pasty. The nine-inch pie is consumed end to end to prevent too much of its savory meat-and-vegetable juice from dribbling out. This one is wrapped in a crib bag, an all-purpose cotton mesh pouch that miners used before the introduction of lunch pails to help keep their freshly baked pasties warm and crisp. Other nationality groups of the Upper Peninsula have embraced the pasty and created many variations, but the pasties in these photographs are the traditional version. As the cross section at the upper right shows, a crust of dough, tightly crimped down the center, encloses generous layers of meat, turnips, onions and potatoes, seasoned with salt and pepper. At lunchtime, in the old days, a miner removed his pasty from the crib bag and reheated it on a shovel *(right)* over the candle he wore attached to his canvas hat. Washed down with a flask of hot tea, the pasty provided a complete home-cooked meal in the cold, damp underground regions. For pasty recipe, see next page.

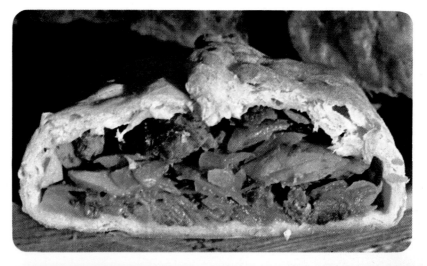

To make six 9-inch pasties

4 cups unsifted flour
2 teaspoons plus 1 tablespoon salt
1½ cups lard (¾ pound), chilled
　　and cut into ¼-inch bits
10 to 12 tablespoons ice water
2 pounds top round steak, trimmed
　　of fat and cut into ¼-inch cubes
5 medium-sized boiling potatoes
　　(about 1½ pounds), peeled and
　　coarsely chopped
3 medium-sized turnips, scraped
　　and cut into ¼-inch cubes
　　(about 1½ cups)
1½ cups finely chopped onions
1 teaspoon freshly ground black
　　pepper

To serve 4

1 pound fresh sorrel
10 tablespoons unsalted butter, cut
　　into ¼-inch bits
3 egg yolks
¼ cup heavy cream
A pinch of sugar
Salt
Freshly ground black pepper
2 pairs shad roe
½ cup flour
1 lemon, cut into 4 wedges

Pasties, Michigan Style

In a large chilled bowl combine the flour, 2 teaspoons of the salt and the lard. Working quickly, rub the flour and fat together with your fingertips until it looks like flakes of coarse meal. Pour in 10 tablespoons of ice water, toss together, and gather the dough into a ball. If the dough crumbles, add up to 2 tablespoons more water, a teaspoonful at a time, until the particles adhere. Divide the dough into 6 equal balls, dust them with flour and wrap in wax paper. Refrigerate for at least 1 hour.

Preheat the oven to 400°. Combine the beef, potatoes, turnips, onions, the tablespoon of salt and the pepper in a bowl and stir them together.

On a lightly floured surface, roll out one ball of dough at a time into a rough circle about ¼ inch thick. Using a plate or pot lid about 9 inches in diameter as a guide, cut the dough into a round with a pastry wheel or sharp knife. Place about 1½ cups of the filling mixture on the round, and fold and shape the pasty as shown below. With a large spatula, carefully transfer the pasty to an ungreased baking sheet. Then repeat the procedure to roll, fill and shape the remaining pasties.

Bake in the middle of the oven for 45 minutes, or until the pasties are golden brown. Serve them hot, or at room temperature.

Shad Roe on a Bed of Sorrel

Wash the sorrel under cold running water. With a sharp knife, trim away any blemished spots and cut off the white stems. Stack the leaves together a handful at a time, roll them into a tight cylinder and cut it crosswise into fine shreds. Drop the sorrel into enough lightly salted boiling water to cover it by at least 1 inch and boil briskly for 2 or 3 minutes, until the shreds have wilted. Drain the sorrel thoroughly in a sieve.

Melt 4 tablespoons of the butter bits over moderate heat in a heavy 8- to 10-inch skillet. When the foam subsides, add the sorrel and stir it about to coat the shreds evenly. Then reduce the heat to low. Beat the egg yolks and cream together with a wire whisk and pour the mixture slowly

PUTTING A PASTY TOGETHER
Roll out all of the pasty dough and cut it into 9-inch rounds. For each pasty, spread 1½ cups of the filling in a strip across the center of the round *(left)*. Fold one side of the round up over the filling. Then turn up the other side of the round and press the edges of the dough together snugly at one end *(below)*.

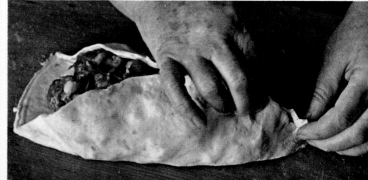

over the sorrel, stirring continuously. Add the sugar, 1 teaspoon of salt and a liberal grinding of pepper and stir for 1 to 2 minutes. Do not let the mixture come anywhere near a boil or the egg yolks will curdle. Remove the pan from the heat and cover to keep the sorrel warm.

With scissors or a small sharp knife, slit the membrane connecting each pair of roe. Sprinkle the roe with salt and a few grindings of pepper, dip them in the flour to coat both sides and shake off the excess. Melt the remaining 6 tablespoons of butter in a heavy 8- to 10-inch skillet. When the foam subsides, add the roe and fry them for 5 to 6 minutes on each side, regulating the heat so that they brown evenly without burning.

Spoon the sorrel onto 4 individual heated plates, dividing it evenly among them, and place the roe on top of each portion. Garnish with lemon and serve at once, accompanied if you like by boiled potatoes.

Funnel Cakes

Preheat the oven to its lowest setting. Line two large baking sheets with paper towels and place them in the center of the oven. Pour vegetable oil into a heavy 12- to 14-inch skillet to a depth of about 1½ to 2 inches and heat the oil until it is very hot but not smoking.

Meanwhile, combine the flour, sugar, baking powder and salt and sift them together into a deep bowl. Make a well in the center and pour in the eggs and 1 cup of the milk. With a large spoon, gradually incorporate the dry ingredients into the liquid ones and stir until the batter is smooth.

To make the cakes, ladle ½ cup of batter into a funnel with a tip opening ½ inch in diameter. Keep the spout closed and control the flow of batter with the forefinger of your other hand. Dribble the batter directly into the hot oil, moving the funnel in a circle to build a snaillike coil of 3 or 4 rings about 6 inches in diameter. Form 2 or 3 cakes and deep-fry them for about 2 minutes on each side, turning them once with a slotted spatula. When the cakes are brown, arrange them side by side on the paper-lined pans and keep them warm in the oven. Repeat the procedure 4 or 5 times, using ½ cup batter for each batch. If the batter becomes stiff, add up to ¼ cup more milk a tablespoon at a time.

Serve the cakes warm, accompanied by molasses or maple syrup.

To make about 12 six-inch cakes

Vegetable oil for deep frying
2 cups unsifted flour
1 tablespoon sugar
1 teaspoon double-acting baking
    powder
¼ teaspoon salt
2 eggs, lightly beaten
1 to 1¼ cups milk

Starting from the sealed end, press the two edges of the round together to encase the filling securely and form a double-thick band of dough about ½ inch wide along the seam *(below)*. With your fingers, crimp the band into a decorative rope or scalloped fluting. When it is ready for baking, the shaped pasty should resemble the ones shown at right.

Moravian Sugar Cake

Bring the water to a boil in a small heavy saucepan, drop in the potatoes and boil briskly, uncovered, until they can be easily mashed against the side of the pan with the back of a fork. Drain the potatoes in a sieve set over a bowl, pat them dry with paper towels and return them to the pan. (Measure and reserve 1 cup of the potato water.) Then mash the potatoes to a smooth purée with the back of a fork. (You should have 1 cup of purée.) Beat in 8 tablespoons of the butter bits and cover the pan to keep the purée warm.

When the reserved potato water has cooled to lukewarm (110° to 115°), pour ¼ cup of it into a shallow bowl. Add the yeast and 1 teaspoon of the granulated sugar. Let the mixture stand for 2 or 3 minutes, then stir well. Set the bowl in a warm, draft-free place (such as an unlighted oven) for about 5 minutes, or until the yeast bubbles up and the mixture almost doubles in volume.

Combine 6 cups of the flour, the remaining cup of granulated sugar and the salt in a deep mixing bowl, and make a well in the center. Drop in the potato purée, the yeast mixture, the eggs and the remaining ¾ cup of potato water. With a large spoon, mix the ingredients together and stir until the dough is smooth and can be gathered into a soft ball. Place the ball on a lightly floured surface and knead, pushing the dough down with the heels of your hands, pressing it forward and folding it back on itself. As you knead, sprinkle flour over the ball a tablespoon at a time, adding up to ½ cup more flour if necessary to make a firm dough. Continue to knead for about 10 minutes, or until the dough is smooth, shiny and elastic, and gather it into a ball.

With a pastry brush, spread 1 tablespoon of softened butter evenly inside a deep mixing bowl. Place the ball in the bowl and turn it around to butter the entire surface of the dough. Drape the bowl loosely with a kitchen towel and put it in the draft-free place for about 1½ hours, or until the dough doubles in bulk.

Brush the remaining 2 tablespoons of softened butter over two 16-by-11-inch jelly-roll pans. Punch the dough down with a single blow of your fist and divide it in half.

On a lightly floured surface, roll each half into a 16-by-11-inch rectangle about ½ inch thick. Place the dough in the buttered pans and set it aside in the draft-free place to rise again for about 45 minutes, or until it has doubled in bulk.

Preheat the oven to 350°. Stir the brown sugar and cinnamon together in a bowl. With your forefinger, make parallel rows of small indentations in the top of each cake, spacing the indentations about 1½ inches apart and pressing down almost to the bottom of the pan. Drop the remaining 8 tablespoons of butter bits into the indentations and fill the holes with brown-sugar mixture. Scatter the rest of the brown sugar over the surface of the cakes, dividing it evenly between them.

Bake in the middle of the oven for 25 to 30 minutes, or until the topping is golden brown and crusty. Transfer the Moravian sugar cakes to a platter and serve them warm or at room temperature.

To make two 16-by-11-inch cakes

2 cups water
2 medium-sized boiling potatoes, peeled and quartered
16 tablespoons butter, cut into ½-inch bits, plus 3 tablespoons butter, softened
1 package active dry yeast
1 teaspoon plus 1 cup granulated sugar
6 to 6½ cups unsifted flour
1 teaspoon salt
2 eggs
2¼ cups light brown sugar (1 pound)
2 teaspoons ground cinnamon

For Christmas, Moravians festoon the tree with fancy home-baked cookies and ply guests with sugar cake *(left)* and frosted slices of half-moon cake.

II

Feinschmecker Country

Of all the regional cooking styles in America today, perhaps the most enduring and distinctive can be claimed by the Pennsylvania Dutch, descendants of the German religious radicals who began emigrating to America at the end of the 17th Century to join William Penn's thriving young colony for "schismatical, factious people," his "Holy Experiment" in religious tolerance. The cooking of this frugal, industrious and enterprising people—farmers then and farmers still—has changed little over the years.

Despite the industrial-age pressures that have pushed the cost of prime farm land to around $2,000 an acre, the part of southeastern Pennsylvania settled by the "Dutch," as they call themselves (the word is a corruption of *Deutsch,* meaning German, and has nothing at all to do with Holland), has remained to a large degree agricultural and unspoiled. Against the hazy backdrop of the densely wooded Blue Mountains to the north, the landscape seems to have come from a scene by Andrew Wyeth or an American primitive painting—trim white-sided, black-roofed farmhouses and barns, well-fed black-and-white Holstein and Jersey cattle outlined against fields glowing in every shade of green.

Even along much-traveled Route 222, which links Reading and Lancaster, the two principal towns, the air is fresh with the scent of honeysuckle and the moist fragrance of warm earth in the neatly furrowed fields of grain, corn and tobacco that border the road. Throughout the area roadside stands and hand-lettered signs in front of farmhouses offer for sale the seasonal produce—strawberries and sugar peas in June;

Personification of a simpler past, this patriarchal Amishman lives and dresses in exact accord with Biblical injunctions to till the soil and shun worldly vanities, yet he eats as well as any man. The Amish, strictest of the Pennsylvania Dutch sects, avoid such newfangled amenities as automobiles, telephones and life insurance, but good wholesome cooking they are not against.

33

tomatoes, corn and squash in late summer; melons, pumpkins, apples and cider in the fall.

Almost everything the Pennsylvania Dutch eat comes from the land they live on: they grow their own vegetables and fruits, butcher their own steers and hogs. From this treasury of raw materials they have evolved an enormously rich and varied range of dishes that would do credit to a small country, although their style of cooking flourishes within a severely limited region: a rectangle about 80 miles long and 35 wide, with Lancaster at its southwest corner and Allentown, some 55 miles north of Philadelphia, at its northeast corner.

From the late 17th Century onward this region became a sanctuary for thousands of German Protestants of many diverse sects whose homeland in the Rhine Valley had been ravaged first by the Thirty Years' War and then by the armies of Louis XIV. The Mennonites, members of a sect founded by Menno Simons in 1561, were the first and most important group of Deutsch to arrive in Pennsylvania, followed by a multitude of others—Crefelders, Amish, Dunkards, Schwenkfelders, Seventh-day Adventists, Moravians and strange minor cults with names like New Born, Mountain Men and the Society of the Woman in the Wilderness. Under the sheltering wing of William Penn, who offered them land at 10 cents an acre, they settled down, increased and prospered. In 1763 there were approximately 280,000 Germans in the state, and their neighbors were highly impressed with their industry. Wrote Benjamin Rush, an influential Philadelphian of the day: "A German farm may be distinguished from the farms of other citizens by the superior size of their barns, the plain but compact form of their houses, the height of their enclosures, the extent of their orchards, the fertility of their fields, the luxuriance of their meadows, and a general appearance of plenty and neatness in everything that belongs to them."

This still holds true, although the original welter of religious splinter groups can be narrowed down to two divisions—the "Plain People," Amish and Mennonites, who worship at home or in plain meetinghouses, and the more liberal and worldly members of the Lutheran and Reformed Churches (among them, the Moravians), often called the "Gay Dutch" or "Fancy Dutch" or "Church People."

Although the Fancy Dutch are scattered throughout the area, they are to be found in large numbers in the Oley Valley, near Reading, where you see their red barns decorated with flamboyant designs—six-pointed stars, whirling swastikas—the so-called hex signs that are no longer intended just to ward off the evil eye, but are a part of the colorful, decorative tradition of the Pennsylvania Dutch, or, as they would say, "chust for pretty." The Fancy Dutch themselves are indistinguishable from their non-Dutch neighbors in outward appearance; but to drive through the peaceable, pastoral valleys of Lancaster County where most of the Plain People live is to be transported to a vanished age. Here are women demurely clad in ankle-length dresses fastened down the front with straight pins instead of buttons, their hair skinned back and tucked under white net caps and bonnets; patriarchal men in somber black with wide-brimmed hats and long flowing beards (you can tell the married men from the unmarried because the latter are clean-shaven); barefoot, straw-hatted boys with rosy roguish faces, their trousers hiked up by suspenders, looking like Tom Sawyer; horse-drawn buggies clip-clopping serenely along, lighted at night by two flickering oil lamps.

These are the Amish, who in the 1690s began to break away from the Mennonites because they felt the latter were becoming too lax. The Amish live in tight-knit old-fashioned farming communities, eschewing such modern vanities as telephones and electricity, tractors and automobiles. Some of the Mennonites, too, cleave to the old order and the unautomated life. These "horse and buggy" or "hook and eye" Mennonites, as they are called, are very like the Amish in manner and mode of dress, but the men are usually clean-shaven. Then there are the "black bumper" Mennonites, who feel that it is all right to drive cars as long as they are painted black, and others, even more liberated, who dress and live very much like other farm people.

Plain or Fancy, the Dutch are united by two bonds. One is their common language, compounded of the old south German dialect of their forefathers interlarded with English and their own highly individual idioms (when a Dutchman says, "The bread is all," he means all gone, and of anything strange he will remark, "It wonders me"). The other is their gargantuan appetites. These are people who love to eat, in their own expressive phrase, *feinschmeckers,* which, roughly translated, means those who know how good food should taste and who eat plenty of it.

The cooking of the Dutch has remained remarkably intact, not only in Pennsylvania but also in other states where the Plain People settled during the westward migration—Ohio, Indiana, Iowa, Illinois and as far north as Kitchener, Ontario. Like their language, their cooking is an amalgam of the foods of their ancestors and the food they found or grew in their new country. Truly German is the emphasis on hams, sausages and dishes made from every part of the pig, from ears to tail and feet (even the cleaned stomach, or hog maw, is regarded as a delicacy when stuffed with sausage meat and diced vegetables and then baked). Similarly, the use of cabbage and sauerkraut and slaw, the yeast-dough *kuchen* (or coffeecakes) and the orgy of cookie baking that goes on around Christmas when the traditional *lebkuchen* and sand tarts *(Recipe Index)* appear are all reminders of this German past.

Native grains such as corn and buckwheat figure in this hearty pattern of eating, and fried cornmeal mush or buckwheat cakes with syrup or molasses are the accompaniments for sausage or fried ham—especially at those prodigious breakfasts that give farmers the stamina to turn out on dark frosty mornings when the ground rings hard as iron.

Main-dish soups, thick with dried beans, peas and vegetables, are an important, sustaining part of the cuisine, and there is always ample starch in the form of bread or hot cakes, potatoes in every guise, dumplings and noodles, and every kind of pie imaginable.

From the apples in the orchards that are everywhere in the region comes that distinctively Pennsylvania Dutch preserve, dark, thick apple butter *(Recipe Index)* made from sliced apples cooked—with cider, sugar and sometimes spices—for hours and hours in a huge kettle, constantly stirred with a wooden paddle. The cider is even more important in its own right because it is fermented into vinegar, which is a leitmotif of all Dutch cooking. Specifically, vinegar is the essential preserving ingredient in the pickles and spiced fruits that go to make up the traditional "seven sweets and seven sours" of the Dutch table.

These sweets and sours are perhaps the most characteristic aspect of Pennsylvania Dutch cooking, the mainstay of the table, served in a great number of bowls and plates to augment and accompany the main dishes of meat and potatoes. Actually there do not have to be seven sweets and seven sours; a housewife picks from all the pickles and preserves and fruits and relishes on her shelves the ones that go best with the main dishes she is serving. Salty meats like ham need the sweetness of spiced watermelon rind or cherries; beef, on the other hand, can take the less delicate contrast of some spicy bread-and-butter pickles *(Recipe Index)*. The more meats served, the more sweets and sours go on the table, and it is the mark of a good hostess to provide something for everyone.

In fact, you might say that providing something for everyone, and plenty of it, is one of the chief aims and glories of Pennsylvania Dutch cooks. There is one thing for sure at a Dutch meal, you never go hungry. A local saying goes, "Better a burst stomach than wasted food," and some of the ample figures tend to support this. Seldom have I seen so many hefty, solid, well-fed men and women as in Pennsylvania Dutch country—*feinschmeckers* indeed.

To appreciate the natural riches of Dutch cooking you have only to pay a visit to the marvelous Central Market in Lancaster. I have learned that the best time to go there is on a Friday morning—as early as you can make it—when the stall holders bring in the pick of their produce.

From the outside the market, a large nondescript building in the center of town, gives no hint of the delights within. Once in the door, though, one discovers half a dozen long aisles lined with neat, immaculate stalls presided over by the farmers and their wives and children and laden with locally grown produce and home-baked pies, breads and cookies, homemade pickles and preserves. Each stall has the owner's name and the location of his farm neatly lettered on an overhead sign and if the names alone—Shenk, Funk, Wenger, Shank, Enck—did not proclaim this is a true Dutch farmers' market, the perfection and dewy freshness of the vegetables would.

Farmers' markets have always been part of the Pennsylvania tradition and the foods they sell are those the farmers themselves like to eat. A roving eye can spy some fascinating, unfamiliar treasures. One mild morning in June, among the baskets of sugar peas and tiny new potatoes no bigger than a quarter, I chanced upon bunches of a vegetable so pretty it was almost a sin to think of eating it—frail pale-pink stalks topped with yellow-green leaves, no more than ¼ inch in diameter and 6 to 8 inches tall. These were tender young poke shoots, also called "poor man's asparagus"; I found out later that when cooked briefly in salted water they do taste rather similar, although with a simpler, wilder flavor.

The air on that early summer morning was heady with the sweet earthy scents of lettuce and spinach, celery and asparagus that had only a few

Continued on page 46

A Life Style Not Subject to Change: Hard Work and Simple Pleasures

Amish shoppers inspect a display of cabbages at the Green Dragon Market, said to be named after a tavern that stood on this site near the town of Ephrata. Cabbage, served up as crisp slaw or briny kraut, is standard year-round local fare.

Some sects of the Pennsylvania Dutch have changed little since colonial times, when a traveler summed them up as "the most early-rising, hard-working people I ever saw." Now, as then, their industry and fertile farm lands bring forth rich harvests, making it clear to all that their austere ways are a matter of choice, not necessity. They remain a plain, reverent, family-centered folk who take their few simple pleasures—among them the pleasure of eating very well—with innocent gusto. Among their institutions is market day, usually held on Friday in a scattering of pleasant country towns. Here the farmers' wives gather to gossip as they shop. Rows of neat stalls offer such merchandise as dyed eggs and daffodils, sausages and shoofly pies, pickled pig's feet and plucked fowls with their innards arranged on beds of parsley. Though the strict Amish rarely mix with strangers socially, the stall owners are cordial and informative to any visiting *auslanders*. One may tell a tourist where to get the first sauerkraut of the season. Another will discourse proudly on the local apples—Fanny, Ewalt, Blue Mountain, Paradise. But, she may add with a knowing wink, the best ones for pies are the Yellow Transparents.

The famous Dutch-country auctions are the place to go for anything from crockery to harnesses to simple enjoyment. The important auctions, such as the New Holland horse sale *(left and below)* and the Green Dragon cattle auction *(right)*, bring out farmers from miles around. Would-be buyers—bearded Amish or clean-shaven Mennonites—come early to get good seats and, as their sons watch from hay bales or horseback, they punctuate the auctioneer's spiel with shouted bids or prearranged signals, such as pulling an earlobe. Even those who merely come for the show go home refreshed by a day spent among old friends—and, at some auctions, satisfied by a free dinner.

Content with life at a horse-drawn pace, a young Mennonite takes a buggy ride through the quiet countryside near Kutztown.

Rachel and Netta Zimmerman, already veteran workers in their teens, roll out one of their family's six buggies for a washing.

Edwin Jr., 11, takes time out from milking to play with the pets.

Down Kutztown way, Mennonite Edwin Zimmerman counts his blessings in good round numbers: he owns a 150-acre farm and has 10 children to help him run it. All of them work—not just to do the day's chores but as on-the-job training for a lifetime. The boys learn farming by helping their father in field and barn, and the girls prepare to become farmers' wives by helping their mother cook, bake and clean the house. Each Friday Rachel and Netta take the week's bread from the oven, and reinforce the lessons that they will someday pass on to their own daughters.

The Zimmermans specialize in dairy farming, but cleave to the old Pennsylvania Dutch tradition of growing everything for their own needs. Edwin Zimmerman even raises tobacco for himself and his grown sons (pipes and cigars are tolerated, but cigarettes are still taboo). Above, he removes a young tobacco plant from a nursery bed to set it out in a field. At right, his daughter Rachel picks rhubarb, to be used in custard and in pies, plain or meringue. Her sister Netta, at left, holds some sugar peas, which are as much appreciated by the Pennsylvania Dutch as by the Chinese. This vegetable with the edible pod is picked just as the peas are forming. The ends and strings are cut off, and the washed pods are boiled until tender, at which point salt, pepper and lots of butter are the only "fixings" that are needed.

hours ago left the embrace of the soil. Mingling with these clean fresh smells was the buttery richness of cookies and pies, the pungency of smoked meats and the horseradish root a woman at one stall was grating for her customers. In among the foods were stalls with bright, tight bouquets of flowers, house plants and bundles of mint and sage for herb teas.

Some of these family-owned stalls have been in the same spot for many decades. Mrs. Shertzer, a smiling apple granny in a dark dress and a white cap who sold me a bag of dried corn ("There's an old man in his seventies who still does it the best way, over steam, and we buy from him," she said), told me that she started to tend market with her father in 1898, when she was 12. Now she helps her son sell his eggs, chickens and vegetables. She advised me which stall holder had the best dried apples and how to keep them from getting too dried out by putting a few drops of water in the bag.

You find this same friendliness and helpfulness everywhere. It is no distraction, but a pleasure, for the stall keepers to take time out to chat or patiently explain their wares to a stranger. At Shenk's cheese stand there were big enameled dishes full of a thick, honey-colored, glossy mixture that turned out to be a local specialty called cup cheese. It is made from sour milk, whose drained dried curds are cooked with butter, baking soda and milk or cream until they form a thick, custardy mass that is poured into cups—hence the name—and cooled. The longer it ripens the stronger it gets. The cheese at Farmer Shenk's stall is made in three strengths, from a mild variety to a strong one that has the ripeness and flavor of a well-matured Camembert or Liederkranz, and I was allowed to taste all three varieties.

Naturally I bought a sample of each from the plump, cheerful woman behind the stand, and then I went on to fill my already heavy shopping bag with goodies from Clyde Weaver's meat stall—pig's-feet souse, tangy with vinegar *(Recipe Index)*; pawnhass (the local name for scrapple); fresh pork sausage; a big dark-red Lebanon bologna with a sweet and smoky flavor and the milder, smaller ring bologna. I just can't resist buying in the Lancaster market; everything has a good honest country taste that is all too rare in this age of the bland, tasteless packaged product designed to appeal to (or, perhaps, not to offend) the national palate.

The same aura of integrity that pervades the food stalls in the Lancaster market invests any authentic Pennsylvania Dutch dining room, whether public or private. I had my initial experience in Dutch eating one September evening when the temperature was hovering in the high 80s. A bowl of green salad and a cool sliver of melon was what I wanted, but I had been urged by a large and friendly Dutchman I'd met in Reading to go to a local hostelry, Haag's Hotel in Shartlesville, which specialized in the traditional dinner with "seven sweets and seven sours."

This turned out to be food for trenchermen, not for finicky eaters. The minute my companions and I sat down at one of the big tables in the plain, workmanlike dining room, a waitress scurried up and, as though a bare spot on the table was anathema, began to cover every inch with dishes of all kinds. We had our choice of a main course, which wasn't so much a choice as a matter of how much food we could cope with—roast

Opposite: "Them that work hard, eat hearty," say the Pennsylvania Dutch, and they disdain dieting. The chicken-corn soup at top left is bolstered with homemade egg noodles. Chicken Stoltzfus *(top right)* is a smooth, creamy stew with baked pastry squares. Chicken potpie *(bottom)* is fortified with the squares of noodle dough known as potpie. All three dishes *(Recipe Index)* flaunt the flavor and golden color of saffron. This precious spice is inseparable from chicken in Pennsylvania Dutch cooking.

A hostess in traditional costume, at top center, serves up potato filling at a dinner prepared by Mrs. Winnie Brendel, a well-known regional cook, in the Country Kitchen, a display cottage at the annual Pennsylvania Dutch Folk Festival in Kutztown. The meal also includes fried sausages, dried corn, red beet eggs, homemade bread and butter, cherry pie, "nothing" crumb cake and coffee. Also offered at the festival, which runs five days in early July, are demonstrations of tinsmithing, candlemaking, basket weaving and other oldtime skills.

chicken alone, or chicken plus fried ham, or chicken, ham and roast beef! With this we helped ourselves, farmhouse style, to whatever our plates or appetites could encompass. With the meat we had sweet potatoes and highly seasoned mashed potatoes, or "filling" *(Recipe Index)*, as the Dutch call the bread or potato dressing that accompanies meat. There was also a bowl of noodles simmered in chicken broth, called potpie —not to be confused with the more substantial chicken potpie *(Recipe Index)*, which in Pennsylvania Dutch country is chicken simmered in broth with squares of noodle dough—along with gravy and stewed dried corn. Then came the collection of sweets and sours—apple butter *(Recipe Index)*, dried apricots, pepper cabbage (cabbage and green pepper in a sweet-and-sour dressing, *Recipe Index*), chowchow (mixed vegetable pickle, *Recipe Index*) and pickled beets.

I have since learned that the sweets at such a meal can include jams, jellies, conserves, sweet preserved fruits and even cakes, cookies and puddings, and that the list of sours is almost endless: spiced and pickled vegetables such as onions, beets, mushrooms, cucumbers, Jerusalem artichokes; chili sauce, tomato ketchup and pickled walnuts qualify, too. Then there are mustard beans, green or yellow string beans flavored with mustard, dilled beans or tomatoes, pickled watermelon rind or spiced cantaloupe—the mind reels and you soon lose count.

It was at this dinner in Shartlesville that I encountered what was to me a new and strange phenomenon—the pudding and cake routine. These

are counted among the sweets. As a matter of course, some kind of pudding (rice, tapioca, cracker, *Recipe Index*) and either cake or cookies are put on the table with all the relishes, to be eaten with or between helpings of your main course.

But if you think this is dessert, as many visitors are apt to, you're wrong. That comes later and it is always pie—apple, pumpkin, rhubarb, peach, coconut, cherry crumb, lemon custard, shoofly *(Recipe Index)*, any one of the vast numbers of pies that Pennsylvania Dutch cooks turn out according to the season or the supplies on hand. As everyone eats pie three times a day, there always have to be plenty of choices. There's a green-tomato pie, a vinegar pie, all manner of custard and crumb pies, a raisin pie *(Recipe Index)*—sometimes called funeral pie—that can be made at any time of year.

Then there are the Amish half-moon pies, or preaching pies, originally made like turnovers so the children could eat them during services without dripping the filling all over the floor. A variation of this is the fried pie, a turnover filled with dried fruit, cooked and flavored with sugar. Children have special little pies of their own, called milk pies, made from the scraps of leftover pastry with the simplest filling of milk, butter, sugar and flour. These are also sometimes called by a family nickname—schlopp, poor-man's pie, grandmother's pie, eat-me-quick pie, promise pie—or, in the dialect, *milich flitche (milich* for milk and *flitche* meaning something put together with a flick of the wrist).

Red beet eggs, a bright sign of summertime in Pennsylvania Dutch country, are made by marinating hard-boiled eggs in beet juice for at least four hours. The longer they marinate, the darker red they get.

Not all of these were offered us by the waitress at Haag's Hotel, of course, but she did present a selection of at least half a dozen pies. I found the choice difficult, but settled for a piece of sugar pie *(Recipe Index),* a local favorite with a sweet, rich filling and a golden pool of melted butter on the top. It was a thoroughly rewarding meal. I did not regret for a moment the light supper I had planned; I had experienced instead a delightful introduction to the culinary traditions of the region.

As I explored those traditions further, I discovered that local cooks take a fierce pride in them: the old dishes persist even though some of the old laborious ways of preparing them have disappeared. In the old days pies, for example, were baked in outdoor "Dutch" ovens, domed stone ovens with a chest-high iron door. First the oven was fired with brushwood, then when the inside was hot enough the ashes were raked out and the oven filled with the pies, loaves of bread, cakes and cookies. After baking, the cooled pies were stored in the pierced-tin pie cupboards you can still find occasionally in antique shops, and then the oven's diminishing heat would be used to dry fruits and vegetables: apples, corn, pears and lima or string beans. Or sometimes these would be preserved by another means—in "dry houses," small buildings just big enough to hold a wood stove with trays built into the walls from the outside. Nowadays dried fruits and vegetables are obtained from local suppliers, but they remain an integral part of Dutch cooking.

Dried corn, stewed or made into corn pudding, still goes with the Thanksgiving and Christmas turkey. Dried lima beans make the Pennsylvania Dutch version of baked beans, cooked in the usual way with salt pork, molasses and mustard. There is an old-fashioned combination of dried string beans with ham and potatoes that I encountered at a small roadside luncheonette in the Oley Valley. In the local Santa Claus language this dish is called *bohne mit schinken un' grumberra, grumberra* (ground pear) being the old name for potato. The soaked beans had been cooked first with the ham and then with the potatoes until they were soft and mushy, in contrast to the firm saltiness of the ham. As a finishing touch, a sassy tweak of vinegar was added to sharpen the flavors.

The advent of freezers has made it easy to preserve a great many fresh foods, but seasonal specialties are still keenly appreciated in the Dutch country. One of the anticipated delights of spring, for instance, is dandelion salad, traditionally eaten on Maundy Thursday in Holy Week. For this, only the first tender young leaves will do; by the time the flowers appear the leaves are too strong and bitter. They are wilted in a cooked sweet-and-sour dressing of bacon fat, vinegar, sugar and egg, sometimes spiked with mustard or smoothed with sweet or sour cream. This dressing, incidentally, is just as delicious on young spinach or curly endive.

Another early vegetable is sugar peas, sometimes called Mennonite pod peas because so many Mennonites grow this rather exotic vegetable as matter-of-factly as they grow sweet corn. This is a special variety of tender flat edible-pod peas, similar to Chinese snow peas and French *mangetout,* that need only to be stringed like a bean, quickly boiled, and enjoyed for their crisp, succulent sweetness. They are sometimes dressed with a sweet-sour sauce, boiled with diced potato, butter, milk and seasoning, or with a little ham and onion for flavor, but to my mind it is heresy to do more than to dribble melted butter over the pods after cooking them for the briefest possible time, or to stir-fry them quickly in oil, Chinese style, add a little chicken stock and let it cook away.

Sugar peas are one of the two vegetables for which Lancaster County is particularly noted. The other is asparagus, which comes in spring and summer, and which the Dutch love simply cooked and served with butter. I also like it when the young shoots are served raw, enhanced by just a dab of the sweet-and-sour dandelion salad dressing.

There are so many riches, so many quirks and unexpected combinations of ingredients, tastes and methods of preparation in Pennsylvania Dutch cooking that it would take a lifetime to discover them all. I have made quite a few trips to the Pennsylvania Dutch country by now, and each time I discover something new and thought-provoking, some further tidbit of food lore and history.

For instance, take saffron. I was much surprised to find that the thrifty farm folk of Lancaster and Lebanon Counties buy a great deal of the world's most costly spice in their markets to use in their chicken and noodle dishes, soups and gravies. They employ many spices of the usual sort for pickling and baking, but their use of so exotic a spice as saffron was something of a puzzlement. Made from dried stigmas of a fall-blooming crocus native to Southern Europe—it takes 75,000 blossoms to make one pound of the spice—saffron has a long history in Europe as a flavoring, dye and medicinal herb. But nowadays you find it mainly in the dishes of countries bordering the Mediterranean—the *paella* and *arroz con pollo* of Spain, Italy's *risotto alla Milanese,* the *oignons monégasques* of southern France, and the many rice dishes of Iran and India. How did it get to Lancaster County?

I was told that the Pennsylvania Dutch once grew their own saffron, and a little historical research confirmed this. Not only were their ancestors of the Rhineland familiar with the spice—cultivation of the crocus had spread to Germany from Italy—but it was so highly prized in mid-15th Century Nuremberg that men were sent to the stake for adulterating it. The precious stuff probably got to Pennsylvania with a group of Silesians known as Schwenkfelders who came to America in 1734. A prominent Schwenkfelder family had owned a saffron warehouse and the immigrants probably brought a supply with them—as well as the recipe for the saffron-flavored yeast cake that was their traditional wedding cake. This still appears in Pennsylvania Dutch cookbooks as Schwenkfelder or Schwingfelder cake *(Recipe Index).*

In such strange fashions do foods migrate, but strangest and most miraculous of all is how and why they survive. Probably this can happen only in regions like the Pennsylvania Dutch country that have kept their culture and character and cooking virtually intact despite the creeping conformism of the 20th Century.

My first encounter with the Pennsylvania Dutch use of saffron remains firmly in my mind because it is associated with my first meal inside a Pennsylvania Dutch home. I had stopped at the farm of a Mennonite farmer named Clarence Herr not far from Lancaster. I was there, actually, to buy

Overleaf: Shoofly pies come dry, moist and in between. This one is the moist "wet bottom" kind that is served at teatime or as a dessert with a dollop of ice cream or whipped cream. Dry shooflies generally appear with morning coffee for dunking. The in-between type of shoofly pie is often paired with stewed fruit—and may be called shoofly cake even though it is baked in a pastry shell. All shoofly pies, however, are made with "barrel" molasses, to which Pennsylvania Dutchmen—and flies—are partial.

Continued on page 54

dried beef, a Dutch specialty of top round that has been cured and smoked until it is as hard and dark as leather. When sliced paper thin, this is the next best thing to the air-dried beef of Switzerland called *viande de Grisons* or *Bündnerfleisch,* and it is far less expensive. I like to serve little rolls of it, instead of prosciutto, with cocktails or with melon or pears. A large piece of the beef will keep almost indefinitely in the refrigerator if you rehydrate it first by soaking it in water overnight, then wrap it in cheesecloth wrung out in cold water and cover it tightly with aluminum foil. Dampen the cheesecloth as it dries out and slice only as much beef as you need at one time with a very sharp carving knife, or even better, on a slicing machine, and you'll have a supply that should last six months or more—if you can manage to restrain your greed.

After I had gone up into the smokehouse loft where the beef was hanging from blackened rafters to pick out the piece I wanted, Mr. Herr and I spent a pleasant half hour discussing the curing and preparation of his dried beef. Then, having learned of my interest in Pennsylvania Dutch cooking in general, he delighted me by asking if I'd like to come and take potluck with him and his family for lunch. A wonderful smell of simmering soup was coming from the kitchen, and with rather impolite speed I accepted and was soon sitting with the farmer, his wife and his brother around the kitchen table. Piled there were all kinds of things begging to be eaten, and almost immediately everyone began reaching for them—a fat loaf of homemade bread with butter, apple butter and *Schmierkäse* (cottage cheese) nearby, plates of sliced dried beef, bowls of red beet eggs (dyed and spiced with the vinegar from pickled beets, *Recipe Index)* and pepper cabbage, bread-and-butter pickles, spiced cherries, shoofly pie and a steaming tureen of chicken-corn soup.

Chicken-corn soup *(Recipe Index)* is one of the most famous dishes of Lancaster County. Unlike many of the local soups it is delicate, subtle and unsurfeiting, just good strong homemade chicken stock with little pieces of chicken meat, noodles and corn cut from the cob floating in it, with chopped parsley and sometimes hard-boiled egg on top—and the whole tinged a glowing gold with saffron. This is similar to corn-and-rivvel soup, another local specialty in which tiny fragments of flour-and-egg dough are rubbed through the fingers into the boiling stock and cooked until they hold their shape and consistency.

The soup Mrs. Herr served was simplicity itself, but as we ate she talked of a long roster of soups more complicated and ingenious. Who else but the Pennsylvania Dutch would think of a pretzel soup, a popcorn soup or a gravel soup (for this, eggs are whisked up, dropped into boiling water until they set into strings, then strained and added to a browned-flour soup)? Then there are all the hefty soups—pepper pot *(Recipe Index),* calf's head, soups of dried beans, peas and lentils, soups made with clams and oysters, with eels, with fresh corn, chestnuts, salsify, lettuce, edible-pod peas, yellow tomatoes. There are even a cider soup and a cold supper soup of bread and milk sweetened with sugar and flavored with fresh berries.

After two bowls of the chicken-corn soup and a plate of dried beef with pickles and a healthy slice of bread, I wasn't sure I could manage pie, but anxious not to hurt the feelings and culinary pride of my hostess, I took a small slice. Shoofly pie isn't my all-time favorite, frankly, because it's too sweet for me, but this turned out to be one of the best I have eaten. There are many versions of shoofly pie, which can be loosely defined as a liquid filling of molasses, boiling water and baking soda in an unbaked pie shell, topped with a crumb mixture and baked. Each version has passionate advocates among the Dutch. There's a rather dry one that is dunked in coffee, a wet-bottom one that is much moister and spicier, and a cakelike kind in which the filling and crumbs are mixed together. No one seems to know, incidentally, how the pie got its name. Logical thinkers tend to the theory that the sweet stickiness attracted flies, but there are various other theories, including one rather unlikely claim that the name came from the French *chou-fleur,* since the crumbs on the surface look like cauliflower. Mrs. Herr had no ideas about the origin of the name of the pie, but she certainly knew how to bake it. Hers was the moist type, and the crust—made with lard instead of butter—was just right: tender, light and flaky.

When we had eaten all we could, the Herrs politely but without wasting a moment returned to their chores, and I took my leave, warmed by their enthusiastic hospitality. As I drove off I felt a pang of nostalgia, for the warmth of that kitchen recalled memories of the one I had spent so much time in as a child. When you grow up in the country you don't learn to cook from a book, but by osmosis, hanging around the kitchen table to watch the bread kneaded, the pastry rolled, picking over the fruit you have gathered for jam and jelly making, then hovering over the black iron kettle and taking a saucer of the cooked jelly to a cool window sill to see if it has started to set.

Dinner on a farm is an event, not a quick and scamped meal put together from whatever is in the freezer, but a big sociable gathering of family and help, with a dozen or more sitting down at the table to some solid, satisfying food. Extra mouths to feed are more than compensated for by extra hands to help—someone to peel the potatoes and shuck the corn, to dress the chicken or roast the beef or make the pie or pudding.

This is the kind of upbringing that makes Pennsylvania Dutch women such superlative cooks. One of the best I have met is Betty Groff, a slim, lively, outgoing woman, supercharged with energy, who is the daughter of Clarence Herr, the man from whom I had bought such fine smoked beef and received such warm hospitality. To Betty (a consultant for this book), cooking in quantity comes naturally. On her father's farm, 10 or 11 members of the family and a couple of hired men would be fed at one big table every day and, when she married, Betty thought nothing of having 32 relatives for Sunday dinner in the traditional round in which the bride and groom are first entertained by all the aunts and uncles and cousins on both sides and then have them all back.

Nine years ago she started cooking special dinners once a month for selected bus tours and groups because, despite helping her husband on the farm, rearing two children and doing all her own canning and cooking (including making 120 pounds of candy at Christmas), she still had time on her hands and was beginning to feel a little isolated from the gregar-

Continued on page 58

The Consuming Importance of the Plentiful Pig

To the Pennsylvania Dutch, there is nothing lowly about the pig. It provides the basic ingredient in their cuisine, and it gets treated with proper respect right from the pigpen to the table. The big porkers—such as Berkshires and Chester Whites—provide lard for piecrusts and deep frying, salt pork for flavoring, and the main event for most meals. Dinner is likely to be built around pork chops, a roast loin or ham cured in the patient old-fashioned way *(above)*, and perhaps appearing in the classic dish *schnitz und kneppe (opposite)*. For breakfast, lunch or in between, the porcine provender includes bacon, sausage, liverwurst, jellied headcheese, and pickled pig's feet. The thrifty cooks let no part go to waste: the little bits end up in scrapple, to be sliced thin and fried crisp.

Clarence Herr, at work above in the smokehouse of his 84-acre farm near Strasburg, cures several hundred hams each winter to sell along with his home-grown melons. He buys the hams from a local butcher in December and rubs them thoroughly with a mixture of salt, medium-brown sugar and saltpeter. Three weeks later he smokes the hams for seven days over hickory logs, using a cold steamless smoke that gives the meat a rich brown finish. Then the hams are hung and dried to cure in time for Easter sales. The butt of a ham is combined with dumplings and dried apples to make *schnitz und kneppe (Recipe Index),* shown at right. When the dumplings are added, the pan is covered tightly and they are steamed for 10 to 12 minutes. If the cover of the pot is lifted during this period the dumplings will collapse, so good cooks always warn, "You dassn't peek!"

ious life she'd known. "I thought of a farm as a place like my father's," she says, "where everyone came and told you what was going on. So when I heard that this organization that ran bus tours was looking for a Mennonite girl to give dinners, I thought how much fun I'd have meeting all those different kinds of people. After all, if I could pass the test with 32 critical uncles and aunts, I could easily cook for 42 strangers who'd never tasted our kind of food before."

Now she and her husband Abe run the business on their own, and it is thriving. He selects and seasons the meats and supervises the carving. With a neighbor, Mrs. Erma Engle, to help and local girls as waitresses, Betty handles an incredible number of meals—which she serves by reservation only. On one particularly busy Saturday evening she served 67 people, offering them a choice of seven almost completely different dinners. "When you make everything fresh for each dinner, it's a challenge to your management," she told me. "People like to come here because I cook in the old style; they say it's just like eating in grandmother's house." To me it was more like being entertained in the home of a country cousin who was a marvelously good cook. The 215-year-old stone farmhouse in Mount Joy near Lancaster is filled with antique furniture and has mellow pine floors and a warm, friendly, lived-in atmosphere, with pots bubbling and burbling on the kitchen stove.

A friend and I with a neighbor of the Groffs, Mrs. Kitty Brown, had

A classic Pennsylvania Dutch family dinner is served *(opposite)* by Abe and Betty Groff of Mount Joy with Betty's 96-year-old grandfather, Jacob Root, as guest of honor and with Betty providing after-dinner music on her cornet. The meal consists of sliced smoked ham, sugar peas, potatoes with browned butter and bread-crumb topping, beets in a sauce with dandelion and potato wines, chicken Stoltzfus, cracker pudding, the ever-present relish tray featuring chowchow, spiced watermelon rind and spiced Persian melon and, for dessert, chocolate cake with caramel icing.

dinner with Betty one day in the fall. The meal began with fresh fruit cup, chocolate cake and a helping of cracker pudding, which is a mixture of milk, sugar and egg yolks thickened with broken saltines and grated coconut; after cooking, vanilla and stiffly beaten egg whites are added *(Recipe Index)*. While pudding and cake are usually eaten throughout the meal, it seems that some people prefer to eat their cake with the fruit cup on the sensible premise that their appetite is bigger at the beginning of the meal. After the fruit cup came one of Betty's specialties, a creation she calls chicken Stoltzfus, a family name common among the Amish. It is a light and delicious chicken pie with a creamy, saffron-flavored sauce and crisp squares of pastry crust on the top *(Recipe Index)*.

With all this came homemade bread, chowchow and spiced Persian melon, with pumpkin pie for dessert. The melon came from Clarence Herr's farm because, Betty explained, the best Persians and Cranshaws are raised on soil with a limestone content; I remembered reading how the early German settlers picked for their farms sites where black walnut trees grew, a sign that there was limestone underground.

After the meal, Betty said she was sorry we had not had a chance to taste the farm's fresh corn—it was a bit late for it. But she told us that since the early days, corn has been one of the mainstays of cooking in her region—at first fresh or dried, now also canned and frozen. It is fried and scalloped, stewed, made into puddings and pies, casseroles and fritters, pickles and relishes, while the cornmeal becomes cornpone, cornbread, corn muffins, hot cakes and mush. Here the American penchant for corn on the cob gives way to corn off the cob. Betty, who freezes more than 600 quarts of sweet corn a year, thinks nothing of gathering 50 dozen ears for her dinners and, between 10 in the morning and 2 in the afternoon, cutting off the kernels by hand. To her it is a labor of love, well worth the time and effort. "There's no flavor like the corn you pick yourself," she says.

When people who love to cook get together, the conversation is always about food. I asked about potatoes, for which I have an inordinate passion. I learned that Pennsylvania Dutch potato recipes alone could easily fill a small book. They come mashed, creamed, roasted, scalloped, fried and hashed brown, in potato cakes and dumplings, potato soup, potato pie, hot and cold potato salads, potato balls and croquettes (these can be made with both sweet and white potatoes) and in that famous specialty of Berks County, potato filling. This is simply mashed potatoes beaten with hot milk, then mixed with sautéed onion, cubed bread, chopped parsley and seasonings and baked in the oven. It is served as a side dish with any kind of meat or poultry, and most of the Pennsylvania Dutch people consider a dinner incomplete without potato or bread filling and its natural partner, gravy.

Mrs. Brown told me about an old custom that made my mouth water. It seems that in the days of coal stoves, when the fire was burning up before being banked for the night and the top of the stove was good and hot, sliced potatoes were put directly on the stove top until they cooked to a brown crisp, to be eaten with butter and salt as a before-bed snack. The slight flavor of stove blacking no doubt added a certain piquancy, just as did the printer's ink from the newspapers in which English fish and chips used to be wrapped.

Mrs. Brown has worked out a modern-stove version of this late-night treat. She washes potatoes, slices them with the peel on, and puts them in a 450° oven, in a single layer, until they brown and blister, then punctures the blisters with a fork and pours butter in the holes (if the slices are recalcitrant and refuse to puff, she advises turning on the broiler). Now that I've made them myself, I agree with Mrs. Brown that there's nothing finer than these crisp buttery potatoes eaten with your fingers.

Potatoes also have played a vital part in the baking at which the Pennsylvania Dutch have always excelled. In many of the old recipes for yeast-raised breads, rolls and crumb-topped *kuchen,* or coffeecakes, mashed potatoes and potato water figure among the ingredients. This undoubtedly dates back to the days when yeast was homemade and chancy. The natural yeasts in the starchy potato water helped to act as a starter, boosting the fermentation that made the dough rise. The mashed potatoes give greater body, moisture and keeping qualities to the finished product and are included in the saffron-flavored Schwenkfelder cake, in *fastnachts (Recipe Index),* or doughnuts, and in the sugar cake *(Recipe Index),* butter *semmel* buns and love-feast buns of the Moravians of Bethlehem. The Moravians who came to Pennsylvania from Bohemia in 1740 held "love feasts" in their churches during hymn singing. Baskets of buns and mugs of coffee were passed around to symbolize the brotherly love of those who broke bread together.

Fastnachts are part of a very old tradition of the Rhineland. Not only are they eaten throughout the year, often dunked in coffee or in a big glob of old-fashioned molasses (the principle of dunking and the word itself originated with the Pennsylvania Dutch), but they have a festival all their own on Shrove Tuesday, or Fastnacht Day, the day before Lent begins. The yeast dough is set to rise the night before and the doughnuts are fried in the morning and served for breakfast. By custom, the last one at table is dubbed a lazy *fastnacht* and gets the least prepossessing doughnut, shaped from the remains of the dough. Supposedly this practice, like the English one of having pancakes on Shrove Tuesday, was intended to use up all the fats in the house before Ash Wednesday, which may also account for the French name for the day—Mardi Gras, or Fat Tuesday.

One wonders how much longer all of these culinary traditions will survive in Pennsylvania, for times are indeed changing and the rising price of farm land is forcing many of the Amish and Mennonite farmers to leave Pennsylvania and settle in the Midwest and Canada. The farmers' wives no longer care to spend time making everything from scratch now that the same mills that press apples for cider will also simmer them into apple butter and turn a load of tomatoes into ketchup or chili sauce.

"I used to make my own butter and sauerkraut, and up until five or six years ago I wouldn't think of buying a noodle, but now I do," one Pennsylvania Dutch housewife told me. "You cook according to the times. Once I canned steak and sausage and beans and peaches, but now I freeze everything instead of canning it."

Probably the last group to cling to the old ways are the Amish. Their deep-rooted sense of thrift and the size of their families make it both more practical and more feasible. An Amish farmer's wife who lives near a friend of mine in Strasburg was proud to show me her cool stone cellar packed with jars of meats, fruits, vegetables and pickles, and the deep iron kettles sunk in a counter in which she makes her preserves and "pudding," or "puddin' meat," a mixture of meat scraps from the butchered pigs that is similar to scrapple except that it contains no cornmeal or buckwheat-flour filler.

Eating is one of the pleasures the Amish consider legitimate, and they indulge themselves whenever an occasion arises—whether it be a wedding or a barn raising or a huge dinner after the Sunday services that the "House Amish," who worship in their homes, hold in turns throughout the year. Then the tables are weighed down with all the simple, good farm foods—pork and sauerkraut, chicken potpie, egg noodles, fried chicken and mashed potatoes, red beet eggs and pepper cabbage, apple butter and *schmierkäse* and vanilla pie.

I have heard, sadly, that even these sturdy eaters, like all the Pennsylvania Dutch, are starting to become calorie conscious and that instead of the full midday meal with "all the fixings" they are having soup-and-sandwich lunches. I hope this trend doesn't get too far, because what is going to happen to all these great regional cooks if there is no one to cook for, no *feinschmecker* to whom they can say, "Kum, esse"—come, eat?

61

CHAPTER **II** RECIPES

To serve 8 to 12

2 pounds chicken backs and necks
10 cups water
2 medium-sized celery stalks
  including the green leaves, cut
  into 3-inch lengths
1 teaspoon whole black peppercorns
3 teaspoons salt
A 2½-pound chicken, cut into 6
  or 8 pieces
½ cup finely chopped celery
¼ cup finely chopped fresh parsley
Freshly ground black pepper
½ pound egg noodles, ¼ inch
  wide, preferably homemade
  (Recipe Booklet), broken into
  3-inch pieces
2 cups fresh corn kernels, cut from
  about 4 large ears of corn, or
  substitute 2 cups thoroughly
  defrosted frozen corn
A pinch of crumbled saffron threads
  or ground saffron

Chicken-Corn Soup

Combine the chicken backs and necks and the water in a 6- to 8-quart casserole and bring to a boil over high heat, meanwhile skimming off the foam and scum as they rise to the surface. Add the cut-up celery, the peppercorns and 2 teaspoons of the salt, reduce the heat to low, and simmer partially covered for 45 minutes.

With a slotted spoon or kitchen tongs, remove and discard the chicken backs and necks and the celery. Add the cut-up chicken to the stock and bring to a boil over high heat, skimming the surface of foam and scum until it remains clear. Reduce the heat to low and simmer partially covered for about 30 minutes.

When the chicken is tender but still intact, transfer it to a plate. With a small sharp knife, remove the skin from the chicken and cut the meat from the bones. Discard the skin and bones; cut the chicken meat into ½-inch pieces and set aside.

Strain the stock through a fine sieve and return it to the pot. Add the finely chopped celery, the parsley, the remaining 1 teaspoon of salt and a few grindings of black pepper, and bring to a boil over high heat.

Stir in the noodles, corn and saffron, and cook uncovered over moderate heat for about 15 minutes, or until the noodles show only slight resistance to the bite. Add the reserved chicken and cook for a minute or so to heat it through.

Taste the chicken-corn soup for seasoning and serve at once from a heated tureen or in individual bowls.

To serve 6 to 8

A 5- to 6-pound roasting chicken,
  cut into 6 or 8 pieces
4 quarts water
2 medium-sized celery stalks,
  including the green leaves, cut
  into 3-inch pieces
¼ teaspoon crumbled dried saffron
  threads or ¼ teaspoon ground
  saffron
1 tablespoon plus ½ teaspoon salt
6 whole black peppercorns
1½ cups plus ¾ cup unsifted
  flour
6 tablespoons vegetable shortening,
  cut into ¼-inch bits
3 tablespoons butter, chilled and
  cut into ¼-inch bits, plus
  12 tablespoons butter
2 cups light cream
¼ cup finely chopped fresh parsley

Chicken Stoltzfus

Combine the chicken and water in a heavy 6- to 8-quart casserole and bring to a boil over high heat, skimming off the foam and scum as they rise to the surface. Add the celery, saffron, 1 tablespoon of the salt and the peppercorns, and reduce the heat to low. Cover the casserole partially and simmer for about 1 hour, or until the chicken shows no resistance when a thigh is pierced deeply with the point of a small sharp knife.

Meanwhile, place 1½ cups of flour and the remaining ½ teaspoon of salt in a deep bowl. Add the vegetable shortening and 3 tablespoons of butter bits and, with your fingers, rub the flour and fat together until they form a smooth dough that can be gathered into a compact ball. Wrap the ball in wax paper and refrigerate for about 1 hour.

When the chicken has cooked its allotted time, transfer the pieces to a plate with a slotted spoon. Strain the stock through a fine sieve, measure it and set aside 6 cups. (Reserve the remaining stock for another use.) With a small sharp knife, remove the skin from the chicken and cut the meat from the bones. Discard the skin and bones; slice the meat into 2- or 3-inch pieces and set aside.

About half an hour before serving, preheat the oven to 350°. Place the ball of dough on a lightly floured surface and roll it out into a rectangle about ⅛ inch thick.

With a pastry wheel or small sharp knife, cut the dough into 1-inch squares. Gather the scraps into a ball, roll out as before, and cut as many more squares as you can. Arrange the squares about ½ inch apart on ungreased baking sheets and bake in the middle of the oven for 12 to 15 minutes, or until they are golden brown.

While the pastry bakes, melt the remaining 12 tablespoons of butter over moderate heat in a heavy 5- to 6-quart casserole. When the foam begins to subside, add the remaining ¾ cup of flour and mix the flour and butter together thoroughly. Stirring the mixture constantly with a wire whisk, pour in the reserved 6 cups of chicken stock and the cream in a slow thin stream and cook over high heat until the sauce comes to a boil, thickens lightly and is smooth.

Reduce the heat to low and simmer for 2 or 3 minutes to remove any taste of raw flour. Then stir in the reserved chicken pieces and the chopped parsley and simmer for a few minutes longer to heat the chicken through. Taste for seasoning.

To serve, ladle the chicken mixture onto a heated platter and arrange the pastries attractively around it or on top.

Schnitz und Kneppe

To serve 6

Place the dried apples in a small bowl and pour in enough water to cover them by at least 1 inch. Set the apples aside at room temperature to soak for at least 8 hours, or overnight. Drain the apples in a sieve or colander and discard the soaking water.

Place the ham butt in a heavy 5- to 6-quart casserole at least 12 inches in diameter and pour in enough water to cover the ham by 2 inches. Bring to a boil over high heat, reduce the heat to low, and simmer partially covered for 1½ hours, or until the ham shows no resistance when pierced deeply with the point of a small skewer or sharp knife. Transfer the ham to a plate and discard the cooking liquid.

With a sharp knife, cut the ham into ¼-inch-thick slices and then into ¼-inch cubes. Return the ham to the casserole and add the apples, chicken stock and brown sugar.

Bring to a boil over high heat, stirring until the sugar dissolves. Reduce the heat to low and simmer partially covered for 15 minutes. Taste for seasoning.

While the stew is simmering, prepare the dumpling dough: Combine the flour, baking powder and salt, and sift them into a deep bowl. Add the butter bits and, with your fingers, rub the flour and fat together until they look like flakes of coarse meal. Add the milk and beat vigorously with a spoon until the dough is smooth.

Drop the dumplings on top of the simmering stew by the heaping tablespoon. Cover the casserole tightly, and simmer undisturbed for about 10 minutes longer. The dumplings are done when they are puffed and fluffy and a cake tester or toothpick inserted in the center of a dumpling comes out clean.

Remove the dumplings with a slotted spoon and pour the ham-and-apple mixture into a preheated bowl or deep platter. Arrange the dumplings on top and serve at once.

2 cups dried apples (½ pound)
3 pounds smoked ham butt
6 cups chicken stock, fresh or canned
2 tablespoons dark brown sugar

DUMPLINGS
2 cups unsifted flour
1 tablespoon double-acting baking powder
¼ teaspoon salt
2 tablespoons butter, cut into ¼-inch bits and softened
1½ cups milk

Apple Butter

To make about 3 pints

5 pounds tart cooking apples,
    peeled, quartered and cored
3 cups apple cider
4 cups sugar

Combine the apples and cider in a 4- to 5-quart enameled or stainless-steel pot and bring to a boil over high heat. Reduce the heat to low. Simmer partially covered for 20 to 25 minutes, or until an apple quarter can be easily mashed against the side of the pot with a fork.

Preheat the oven to 300°. Purée the apples through the finest blade of a food mill set over a deep bowl, or rub them through a fine sieve with the back of a spoon. Add the sugar and mix well.

Pour the apple purée into a shallow 14-by-8-inch baking dish, spreading it evenly and smoothing the top with a rubber spatula. Bake in the middle of the oven for about 2 hours, or until the apple butter is thick enough to hold its shape solidly in a spoon.

The traditional test for doneness is to dab a spoonful of the apple butter on a plate and turn the plate upside down. The apple butter should be thick enough to adhere to the inverted plate.

At once ladle the apple butter into hot sterilized jars, filling them to within ⅛ inch of the top. Seal the jars immediately, following the directions for home canning in the Recipe Booklet.

Spiced Cantaloupe

To make 1 quart

A 2-pound firm ripe cantaloupe
⅔ cup sugar
⅓ cup water
3 tablespoons distilled white
    vinegar
A 2-inch stick cinnamon
4 whole cloves

Cut the cantaloupe into quarters and, with a spoon, scoop out the seeds and stringy pulp. With a small sharp knife, remove the skin and the inner rind. Then cut the meat into 2-inch pieces, and pack the pieces into a 1-quart canning jar.

Combine the sugar, water, vinegar, cinnamon and cloves in a 2-quart enameled or stainless-steel saucepan and bring to a boil over high heat, stirring until the sugar dissolves. Cook briskly, uncovered, for 5 minutes.

With tongs, remove the cinnamon stick and tuck it down the side of the cantaloupe-filled jar. Then ladle the hot liquid over the cantaloupe, a few tablespoonfuls at a time, allowing the liquid to flow through to the bottom of the jar before adding more. Fill the jar to within ⅛ inch of the top. Following the directions for home canning in the Recipe Booklet, seal and process the jar for 12 minutes in a boiling-water bath.

Shoofly Pie

To make one 9-inch pie

1 cup unsifted flour
½ cup light brown sugar
¼ cup vegetable shortening, cut
    into ¼-inch bits
1 teaspoon baking soda
1 cup boiling water
⅔ cup light corn syrup
⅓ cup dark molasses
A 9-inch unbaked short-crust sweet
    pastry shell (Recipe Booklet)

Preheat the oven to 375°. To prepare the crumb topping, combine the flour, brown sugar and shortening in a bowl and rub them together with your fingertips until the mixture resembles coarse meal.

In a deep bowl, dissolve the soda in the boiling water. Then add the corn syrup and molasses, and stir to blend well. Pour the mixture into the unbaked pie shell and sprinkle the crumbs evenly over the top.

Bake the shoofly pie in the middle of the oven for 10 minutes. Reduce the oven temperature to 350° and continue baking for about 25 minutes longer, or until the filling is set and does not quiver when the pie pan is gently shaken from side to side. Do not overbake or the filling will become too dry. Cool the pie to room temperature before serving, and accompany it if you like with sweetened whipped cream or scoops of vanilla ice cream.

"Sweets and sours" is the Pennsylvania Dutch term for the famous extras that are served with lunch and dinner the year round. Favorites, clockwise from the top, include spiced cantaloupe, pepper cabbage, cole slaw, bread-and-butter pickles, crab-apple jelly, chowchow, pepper relish and apple butter. For recipes, see the Recipe Index.

To serve 6 to 8

A 5- to 6-pound roasting chicken,
    cut into 6 or 8 pieces
4 quarts water
2 medium-sized celery stalks,
    including the green leaves, cut
    into 3-inch pieces
¼ teaspoon crumbled dried saffron
    threads or ¼ teaspoon ground
    saffron
1 tablespoon plus 2 teaspoons salt
6 whole black peppercorns
½ cup coarsely chopped celery
2 medium-sized boiling potatoes,
    peeled and coarsely chopped
½ pound potpie squares *(see
    homemade egg noodles, Recipe
    Booklet)*
2 tablespoons finely chopped fresh
    parsley
Freshly ground black pepper

Chicken Potpie

In Pennsylvania Dutch cooking, potpies are pieces of noodle or baking-powder dough. They are boiled with meat and often potatoes to make rib-sticking potpie stews that are named for the kind of meat used. Thus, the following recipe made with chicken is called "chicken potpie" though it bears no resemblance to the pastry-encased potpies typical of other parts of the United States.

Combine the chicken and water in a heavy 6- to 8-quart casserole and bring to a boil over high heat, meanwhile skimming off the foam and scum as they rise to the surface. Add the pieces of celery, saffron, 1 tablespoon of salt and the peppercorns, and reduce the heat to low. Simmer partially covered for about 1 hour, or until the chicken shows no resistance when a thigh is pierced deeply with a small sharp knife.

With a slotted spoon, transfer the chicken to a plate. Strain the stock through a fine sieve and return 2 quarts to the casserole. (Reserve the remaining stock for another use.) With a small sharp knife, remove the skin from the chicken and cut the meat from the bones. Discard the skin and bones; slice the meat into 1-inch pieces and set aside.

Add the chopped celery, potatoes and the remaining 2 teaspoons of salt to the casserole and bring to a boil over high heat. Drop in the potpie squares and stir briefly, then cook briskly, uncovered, for about 15 minutes, until the noodles are tender. Stir in the reserved chicken and parsley and cook for a minute or so to heat them through. Taste and season with more salt if desired and a few grindings of pepper.

To serve, ladle the chicken potpie into heated individual bowls.

To make 3 or 4 cups

8 cups fresh crab apples (about
    2 pounds)
6 cups water
2 to 3 cups sugar

Crab-Apple Jelly

Pick over the crab apples carefully, removing the stems and discarding any badly blemished fruit. Wash the crab apples in a colander under cold running water and drop them into a 6- to 8-quart enameled pot. Add 6 cups of water and bring to a boil over high heat. Reduce the heat to low, cover the pot tightly, and simmer for 30 minutes, or until a crab apple can be mashed easily against the side of the pot with the back of a spoon.

Line a colander or sieve with four layers of damp cheesecloth and place it over a large enameled pot. The bottom of the colander or sieve should be suspended above the pot by at least 3 inches. Pour in the crab apples and, without disturbing them, allow the juice to drain through into the pot. (Do not squeeze the cloth or the jelly will be cloudy.)

When the juice has drained through completely, measure and return it to the first enameled pot. Discard the crab apples. Depending on the tartness of the juice, add from ¾ to 1 cup of sugar for each cup of juice. Bring to a boil over high heat, stirring until the sugar dissolves. Cook briskly, uncovered and undisturbed, until the jelly reaches a temperature of 220° (or 8° above the boiling point of water in your locality) on a jelly, candy or deep-frying thermometer.

Remove the pot from the heat and carefully skim off the surface foam with a large spoon. Ladle the jelly into hot sterilized jars or jelly glasses, following the directions for home canning in the Recipe Booklet.

Fastnachts

In a small heavy saucepan, bring the water to a boil over high heat. Drop in the potato quarters and boil briskly, uncovered, until a quarter can be easily mashed against the side of the pan with the back of a fork.

Drain the potatoes in a sieve set over a bowl, pat them dry with a kitchen towel and return them to the pan. (Measure and reserve 1½ cups of the potato water.) Then mash the potatoes to a smooth purée with the back of a fork (you will need about ½ cup of the potato purée). Beat the 4 tablespoons of butter bits into the potatoes, and cover the pan to keep the purée warm.

When the reserved potato water has cooled to lukewarm (110° to 115°), pour ¼ cup of it into a shallow bowl. Add the yeast and 1 teaspoon of sugar. Let the mixture stand for 2 or 3 minutes, then stir well. Set the bowl in a warm, draft-free place, such as an unlighted oven, for about 5 minutes, or until the yeast bubbles up and the mixture almost doubles in volume.

Combine 6 cups of the flour, ½ cup of the sugar and the salt in a deep mixing bowl, and make a well in the center. Drop in the potato purée, the yeast mixture, the eggs and the remaining 1¼ cups of potato water. With a large wooden spoon, mix the ingredients together and stir until the dough is smooth and can be gathered into a soft ball.

Place the ball on a lightly floured surface and knead, pushing the dough down with the heels of your hands, pressing it forward and folding it back on itself.

As you knead, sprinkle flour over the ball by the tablespoonful, adding up to ½ cup more flour if necessary to make a firm dough. Then continue to knead for about 10 minutes longer, or until the dough is smooth, shiny and elastic.

With a pastry brush, spread the 2 teaspoons of softened butter evenly over the inside of a large bowl. Set the dough in the bowl and turn it about to butter the entire surface. Drape the bowl with a kitchen towel and put it in the draft-free place for about 1½ hours, or until the dough doubles in bulk.

Line one or two large baking sheets with wax paper. Place the dough on a lightly floured surface and roll it out into a rough rectangle about ½ inch thick. With a small sharp knife or a pastry wheel, cut the dough into 2-inch squares, and make a 1-inch slash in the center of each. Arrange the squares about 1 inch apart on the paper-lined baking sheet and return them to the draft-free place to rise for 30 to 45 minutes, or until doubled in bulk.

Pour vegetable oil into a deep fryer or large heavy saucepan to a depth of 3 inches and heat it to a temperature of 375° on a deep-frying thermometer. At the same time, place about ½ cup of the remaining sugar in a paper bag and set it aside.

Deep-fry the dough squares 4 or 5 at a time, turning them with a slotted spoon, for 3 minutes, or until they are puffed and brown. Drain the fastnachts, or doughnuts, briefly on paper towels, then drop two at a time into the bag and shake to coat them with sugar. (Add more sugar to the bag as needed.) Place the fastnachts on a platter to cool while you fry and sugar the rest.

To make about 2 dozen doughnuts

2 cups water
1 medium-sized boiling potato, peeled and quartered
4 tablespoons butter, cut into ½-inch bits and softened, plus 2 teaspoons butter, softened
1 package active dry yeast
1 teaspoon plus 2½ cups sugar
6 to 6½ cups unsifted flour
1 teaspoon salt
2 eggs
Vegetable oil for deep frying

III

The Legacy of Quaker Elegance

In the dining room of their restored 18th Century Quaker house on Philadelphia's Society Hill, Harry and Lillian Prock treat their granddaughter, Terry Bisbee, to the kind of dining that has long been the pride of the city's gentry. The furnishings in the house are all in the style of the 18th Century and reflect the spirit of a less hurried time when gracious eating went hand in hand with polished luxury.

In the historical tapestry of American cooking, Philadelphia stands out like a glittering silver thread. Throughout the Eastern Heartland, from coast to Great Lakes, it is the only city that can claim to have originated a lavish style of eating all its own. It is a style that belongs mostly to the patrician, unhurried past—though a few elegant vestiges remain today—with food that was rich and refined, smooth and sumptuous, the kind on which dowagers dote. It encompassed the suavest of soups, luxurious dishes of capon and sweetbreads, squab and guinea hen, terrapin and oysters, the creamiest of desserts. It was compounded of dishes that harked back to British colonial days, an uninhibited use of ingredients imported from Europe and the Indies West and East, and an occasional sally into the simple earthy cooking of the Pennsylvania Dutch.

The dishes most often associated with Philadelphia today, perhaps, are the robust specialties with a strong Pennsylvania Dutch influence, such as scrapple, for example, and Philadelphia pepper pot *(Recipe Index),* a hearty gallimaufry of tripe, veal knuckle, vegetables, herbs and spices said to have been first tossed together by a Pennsylvania Dutch cook for Washington's troops at Valley Forge. In the 19th Century it was hawked on the city's streets, piping hot, in milk cans, and it is still to be found on many a dinner table.

But the earlier, more distinguished tradition of Philadelphia cooking had a distinctly English flavor, as befitted the city's Quaker heritage. The cooking of the mother country flourished here through the 18th and 19th Centuries, and it speaks for the city's conservatism that even today such typically English dishes as veal-and-ham pie, wine jelly and trifle, hot cross buns and apple dumplings, and the croquette and the cutlet—those dainty deceptions beloved of cooks of the Victorian era—can still be encountered in homes and clubs.

It was the Quakers who accounted for Philadelphia's cultural and culinary dominance of the middle Atlantic colonies, for unlike most settlements in America the city from the very beginning was planned and inhabited by people with the taste, wealth and ability to implement their vision. When William Penn was granted by Charles II, in payment of a debt of £16,000, the colony that was later called Pennsylvania (modestly, Penn himself proposed the name of New Wales), he sent ahead a surveyor from London to lay out the plan of the town in a neat gridiron design, choosing street names with the euphonious connotations of green trees—Chestnut and Walnut, Locust, Spruce and Pine. City development was spurred by Penn's offer to give any man who bought a 5,000-acre country estate for £100 a bonus of a lot in Philadelphia, an arrangement nicely conceived to promote the delicate balance between the temporal commerce of the city and spiritual contemplativeness of country life that suited an English Quaker gentleman.

Penn was a cultivated, open-minded man still under 40, with an abundance of initiative and energy. In the two years he was governor (1682-1684) the city grew at an amazing rate. By 1684 there were 600 "brave brick houses" and places of business; a year later the population had reached an impressive 9,000. Penn and his shrewd Quaker friends saw the importance of trade and commerce to the future of the colony. They organized whale fishing in Delaware Bay and set up trade with the other American colonies and the West Indies, exporting grain and lumber, meat, wool, tobacco and horses. They also established the kind of enterprises necessary to a civilized life—brick kilns, glassworks, tannery, paper mill, printing press and brewery. Penn, understandably proud of the success of his settlement, wrote home: "I have led the greatest colony into America that ever any man did upon a private credit, and the most prosperous beginnings that were ever in it are to be found among us. I will show a province in seven years equal to her neighbors of 40."

The Quakers of those days were not the sober types in drab homespun clothes that many of them were later to become. The more wealthy lived like lords. They wore powdered wigs and coats rich with gold lace, and ate and drank whatever they pleased—succulent turtle from the West Indies, the finest Madeiras, Burgundies and clarets. Penn himself had a taste for good living and lavish hospitality, and he set a style for Philadelphia entertaining that flourished long after his death in 1718.

To that proper Bostonian John Adams, arriving to attend the first Continental Congress in 1774, the Philadelphians' way of life seemed downright indulgent, and it shocked his frugal New England soul—although he does not seem to have resisted the temptations with much fervor. In his diary he describes a dinner at Cliveden, Chief Justice Chew's country seat in Germantown, on whose smooth green lawns the fateful Battle of Germantown was to be fought three years later, resulting in the British victory that forced Washington to camp at Valley Forge through

the winter. The dinner was at 4 o'clock, the fashionable hour to dine in those days, and it was, Adams notes, "a most sinful feast . . . everything that would delight the eye or allure the taste—meats, turtle and every other thing . . . flummery, jellies, sweetmeats of twenty sorts, trifles, whip'd syllabubs, fools etc. I drank Madeira at a great rate and found no inconvenience in it."

To another observer, Lord Adam Gordon, visiting from England, 18th Century Philadelphia was "a great noble city." The paved roads and brick sidewalks, well lighted with whale-oil lamps and well policed at night, were something to impress even a Londoner. Penn's "greene countrie towne" had come of age. It was successively the setting for the Continental Congresses, the Declaration of Independence and the Constitutional Convention and then became the capital of the United States, except for one year when the honor went to New York, until the government made the permanent move to Washington in 1800.

The presence of George and Martha Washington added an extra fillip to the already scintillating social life of Philadelphia. In the course of the four months that Washington spent there as President of the Constitutional Convention in 1787, he had 120 social engagements for tea and dinner, an average of one a day. When Philadelphia became the national

Arranged on a Sheraton-style sideboard, the Procks' dinner forms an elegant still life. In the antique tureen is the first course, consommé Bellevue, a mixture of chicken and clam broths served with dollops of whipped cream from the sauceboat at right. Breasts of chicken with ham slices in a sherried cream sauce follow, and a purée of broccoli flavored with ground nutmeg and garnished with chopped egg. Buttermilk soda biscuits and white wine accompany the main course. For recipes see the Recipe Index.

capital in 1790 he moved there as President of the United States, occupying a magnificent town house turned over to him by his friend Robert Morris, the banker who had provided much of the backing that kept the Continental Army alive. In Philadelphia, Washington found it necessary to entertain in a style and on a scale far beyond his own rather austere tastes. As part of his official social duties, for instance, he played host each Thursday at 4 to members of Congress at dinner parties that were considered to be in very handsome style. In the center of the dining table was a magnificent silver-rimmed *surtout de table,* an ornamental centerpiece six feet long and two feet wide brought by the financier Gouverneur Morris from Paris, on which were arranged china figurines and flowers. What these dinners lacked in gaiety—Washington never seems to have been at ease in company—they made up in good food.

Formal meals were served differently in those days: there were just two courses—although astonishingly generous ones—and all the dishes for each course came to the table at one time in a rather indiscriminate array. For the first course, a tureen of soup—perhaps a rich turtle soup or a light bouillon—was placed at each end of the table along with platters of fish; various other dishes of meat, poultry, vegetables and sauces filled the rest of the available space. The carving and serving were done by the host and hostess, with the attendant footmen merely changing the china and silver. The second course consisted of more main dishes including game, and the desserts—an opulent trifle (spongecake embellished with jam, custard and whipped cream), a frothy syllabub (cream beaten up with wine), floating island *(Recipe Index)* or a custardlike strawberry flummery *(Recipe Index).* When all this was consumed, the tablecloth was removed, decanters of the inevitable Madeira appeared with dishes of nuts and fruits, and the ladies, if there were any present, left the gentlemen to their drinking.

The size and scope of these dinners seem all the more formidable considering the conditions under which the cooks had to work. There were no stoves of any sort and all the cooking had to be done in and around the great fireplace in the kitchen, which must have been a taxing experience during the muggy Philadelphia summer. Heat under the pots could be adjusted only by hanging them, on their notched holders, nearer to or farther from the flames. Roasting had to be done on a spit in front of the fire, so meat was usually boiled or stewed, which was not only simpler but gave a more palatable and tender result.

Despite these difficulties, a great variety of foods was prepared for the Philadelphians' tables. Mutton, which has practically vanished from the American scene, was popular then and so was veal, but beef had not yet acquired the status it was to gain in the 19th Century. Turkeys and ducks were plentiful, as were chickens and pigeons and all manner of furred and feathered game. In a cookbook passed down to Martha Washington by her mother-in-law (and preserved by the Historical Society of Pennsylvania), there are directions for making a "frykecy" (fricassee) of chicken or hare as well as instructions that explain how to "dress a dish of mushrumps, make a lettice tart or a hartichoak pie." The language may seem strange and the spelling erratic, but many of the recipes stand

Opposite: Philadelphia pepper pot is a stick-to-the-ribs tripe soup enlivened with both red and black pepper. Legend has it that pepper pot was invented for George Washington and his troops during their winter at Valley Forge. In the version shown here *(Recipe Index)* the soup is fortified with cubes of potato, although some cooks prefer to add dumplings instead.

up pretty well today. "To make Red Deer of Beef" is basically a recipe for pot roast of beef in which the meat is rubbed with salt and spices, marinated in red wine and vinegar, and then slowly simmered in the marinade. "A Grand Leg of Lamb" is boned and stuffed with an intriguing filling of bread crumbs, thyme, marjoram, pepper, salt, lemon rind, capers and anchovies, then it is roasted, garnished with sweetbreads, kidneys and sausages, and served with an anchovy sauce *(Recipe Index)*.

In those days food was much more heavily flavored with spices, sugar, rose water and orange water, almonds and currants—a habit that had persisted from earlier times when the taste of tainted meat often had to be masked with strong seasonings. Along with the penchant for spices went a sweet tooth: 18th Century Philadelphians loved rich desserts and sweetmeats such as preserved fruits, quince marmalade and candied violets, rose petals and gooseberries. Fruits and flowers were turned into syrups and wines, and there were stronger beverages like mead, a drink of fermented honey, and shrub, for which brandy, wine, water, sugar and lemons were mellowed in a stone jar, strained and bottled.

It was in Washington's time that Philadelphia became noted for the excellence of its ice cream—a tradition that is still flourishing. Although Thomas Jefferson usually gets the credit for introducing this all-time favorite dessert to America in 1789 after encountering it in France, Philadelphians can claim to have known about it earlier. It first came to their public notice in July 1782, when it was served at a fete given by the French envoy at which Washington was present. Washington's own accounts for May 1784 list a sum of one pound thirteen shillings and fourpence expended for "a cream Machine for Ice," which probably turned out the "iced creams" served at his Thursday dinners. These probably were more like iced or chilled creams than the hard-frozen type of today. The first printed recipe for this treat, in a Philadelphia cookbook of 1792, directs that the mixture of cream, eggs and sugar be stirred at frequent intervals in a pewter bowl set in a larger bowl filled with ice, and that care be taken to prepare it "in a part of the house where as little of warm air comes as you can possibly contrive."

Undoubtedly the European influence helped to spread the image of ice cream as an elegant luxury. In 1800 an Italian confectioner named Bosio advertised the opening of a glorified ice-cream parlor where he would sell "all kinds of refreshments, as Ice Cream, Syrups, French Cordials, Cakes, Clarets of the best kinds, Jellies etc."

There was energetic promotion of ice cream during the great 1876 exposition in Philadelphia and the enthusiasm aroused there helped foster the tradition on a wider scale. And, being close to wonderful dairy country, the city has been able to cater to the increasing demands of ice-cream lovers ever since. By 1909 it boasted some 49 ice-cream manufacturing plants and 52 ice-cream "saloons."

Today there are still a considerable number of small independent ice-cream companies and stores that strive to preserve the old-fashioned, homemade texture and taste beloved by Philadelphians. Sauter's, a local confectioner, used to be the most famous, but it is now just a memory; today Bassett's seems to be the preferred place. Bassett's, in the Reading

Terminal Market, makes ice cream with a luxuriously high butterfat content and produces rich confections in all the usual flavors as well as such seasonal specialties as cassaba melon. They also feature color schemes and combinations for holidays like St. Patrick's Day, Valentine's Day, Washington's Birthday (what else but cherry?) and Christmas, when they make an eggnog ice cream and a festive red-and-green blend of mint and raspberry sherbet.

For private parties and the annual Philadelphia Assembly, the big social event of the year, which is not so much a ball as a prestigious, hallowed institution (when Washington danced there in the 1790s it was already almost 50 years old), ice cream has become over the generations a kind of art form in food. Using fruit and flower molds of pewter, caterers serve it up in a fantasia of shapes—bells, roses, melons, apples, peaches, bunches of grapes—and in imaginative combinations, such as raspberry ice and coffee ice cream and a twosome that seems to be particularly beloved of old ladies, orange sherbet and chocolate ice cream.

The pewter molds are rather expensive nowadays but quite often can be turned up in antique and gourmet cooking shops. I find they make ice cream a more attractive dessert than the usual scoop plopped on a plate. Pack the molds tightly and put them in a freezer for a few hours until the contents are good and hard, then rub the outside with a hot damp cloth to loosen the ice cream from the mold before turning it out. It looks even more appealing if you surround the individual servings with grape leaves or glossy lemon leaves.

There are other Philadelphia specialties that have managed to survive the transition to more contemporary eating patterns. Besides scrapple, there are the famous sticky or cinnamon buns on which many visitors love to breakfast, and a third is snapper soup *(Recipe Index)*. You will find it on the menus of the best restaurants such as Helen Sigel Wilson's and Bookbinder's or at the big hotels such as the Bellevue Stratford and the Barclay. And very good it is too, with juicy morsels of snapping-turtle meat wallowing in a thick liquid laced with sherry or Madeira.

One old delicacy that has not fared so well with the passing of time and tradition is terrapin. It is no longer easy to procure terrapin, a smaller species of turtle than the fresh-water snapper, though it once abounded in the coastal waters of the Delaware and Chesapeake Bays. Terrapin prepared in various styles was once a staple of old Philadelphia dinner parties but is now encountered only occasionally or if ordered by special arrangement. When Bookbinder's put it on their luncheon menu for a while several years ago they served only a few portions; and when the Bellevue Stratford served it at a recent Assembly supper it was not a success with many of the younger guests, whose preference was for fillet of beef. "It's an old dish and people don't even know what it is," I was told by Sam Bookbinder Jr., the fourth generation of the family that started the famous old seafood house in 1865. I can understand why, because the dish is expensive and tricky to make, even if you buy the terrapin meat already prepared instead of starting from scratch with live turtles. But it is a culinary link with America's past that I hate to see broken.

Recently I was lucky enough to taste terrapin prepared in the Phila-

Guests lunching on the Procks' veranda enjoy the sights and scents of a flower and herb garden, which Mrs. Prock tends herself, as well as a fine view of some Society Hill landmarks. The neighborhood name refers not to "high society" but to an early group of merchants, known as the Society of Free Traders, which owned property on the hill.

delphia style when some friends who knew that I was eager to sample the Philadelphia classics arranged a special luncheon at the Bellevue Stratford. This hotel, more than any other, is closely bound to the traditions and social life of the city, headquarters for coming-out parties and all sorts of civic functions. It dates back to 1902, when the old Hotel Bellevue merged with the Hotel Stratford and moved into palatial new premises on Walnut Street. It was considered so magnificent that the president of a Pittsburgh steel mill was advised by a friend that "to come to Philadelphia and not see the Bellevue Stratford is like going to Egypt without seeing the pyramids."

In January 1905 the hotel was the setting for the first time of the Assembly, an event described in the local press as "a scene the likes of which Philadelphia with all her generations of pomp and swelldom has never seen." The buffet menu for that glittering affair was luxurious and lavish. Before the dancing began at 2:30 a.m. the guests could first sip bouillon and nibble on salted almonds and then progress to terrapin, casserole of pheasant, and oysters in cream sauce or to a cold buffet of chicken salad, roast capon, Virginia ham, and fillet of beef in aspic. After this they could toy with ices, cakes and bonbons. Chilled champagne was the only wine served.

By the standards of that era, our own luncheon would have been considered comparatively modest, but it was still sumptuous enough to make me realize how paltry modern appetites are.

First we had the renowned consommé Bellevue *(Recipe Index)*, a delightful mingling of clam and chicken broths topped with a spoonful of whipped cream that melted in snowy swirls, marbling the pale gold soup and giving it a velvety consistency. Next came sweetbreads *en coquille (Recipe Index),* bordered with a piping of potatoes *duchesse.* With this we drank Pouilly-Fuissé, a white Burgundy with sufficient acidity to relieve the richness of the sauce.

Then, with a proud flourish, the captain presented a huge platter of terrapin à la Philadelphia with bread triangles fried to a golden brown. The light body meat and the dark leg meat had been lightly sautéed with shallots and then simmered in a white wine sauce, thickened before serving with an egg-yolk-and-cream liaison. The flavor of the meat was not at all gamy, as I had expected, but more delicate, reminiscent of turkey, and the flesh was meltingly tender.

This alone would have been a feast, but there was more to come: roast squab, stuffed with wild rice, chicken livers and truffles, served with *sauce périgourdine* and ringed by a garden of braised celery, asparagus spears,

For the floating-island dessert, three of the guests settle in Victorian wrought-iron chairs in a corner of the Procks' walled garden. The dessert consists of a smooth custard made with eggs, sugar, light cream and vanilla bean, and topped with islands of caramel-decorated meringue. Serving it is the Procks' daughter, Mrs. A. L. Bisbee Jr.

green beans, green grapes and artichoke bottoms stuffed with finely chopped mushrooms and hazelnuts and glazed with hollandaise. Dessert was vanilla ice cream laved with strawberry sauce. I would never have believed I could eat so much at one sitting but, after all, it's not every day that I get a chance to recapture the taste of a vanished age.

One element of the past that quietly survives in Philadelphia is the tradition of eating clubs. Most of them are strictly for men, and in many of them the members take over the kitchen and do their own cooking. Clubs were an English institution that flourished from the very beginning in Philadelphia—and today are just as entrenched and exclusive as they were a century or two ago.

There were all kinds of clubs then—eating, intellectual, sporting, agricultural and purely social. Benjamin Franklin founded a debating society called the Junto that argued serious questions of morals, politics and natural philosophy; by applying himself to one question that arose, "How may smoky chimneys best be cured?" he invented the Pennsylvania fireplace, better known as the Franklin stove.

Then there was the Farmer's Club, a dining club whose members were owners of country estates with supposedly working farms where they entertained one another once a month in the highest possible style. In 1884, one party rode to a Colonel Duffy's farm at Marietta, near Lancaster, in the private railroad car of the President of the Pennsylvania Railroad, who happened to be one of the members. On arrival they were led to a pond stocked with huge trout where, with baited rods handed to them by liveried servants, they fished for their dinner. This, served in the late afternoon, was not limited to the catch. There were also clams, turtle soup, capon, truffled chicken, lamb, turkey, deviled crab, ice cream with strawberries and lashings of wine.

Far and away the most venerable of all Philadelphia's eating clubs, and one even today surrounded by a veil of secrecy the CIA might envy (members say they are "not authorized" to discuss any of its activities), is the State in Schuylkill, or the Fish House as it is better known. Here originated the famous and lethal Fish House punch and also, reputedly, the technique of planking shad, a claim the Indians might contest. By a neat piece of semantics, the Fish House calls itself the oldest formally organized men's social club in the English-speaking world (London clubs of an earlier date were not, apparently, formally organized).

When the club was formed in 1732 it was with the intent that a small group of Quaker gentlemen, among them Penn's secretary, might spend an idyllic day every now and then dawdling on the banks of the Schuylkill River (pronounced "schoolkill" or, sometimes, "skook'l"), shooting game birds and fishing and cooking their catch for dinner, with no wives or servants present. It was this choice of locale that led to the club's original name, the Colony in Schuylkill (the name was changed to the State in Schuylkill after the Revolution). Since 1732 the club has moved its location and its ancient clubhouse (known as the Castle) four times, losing in the process not one smidgen of its elaborate rituals.

Today's members, called citizens, and 30 in number, meet on 13 "fishing days" from May to October, even though the present sad condition

Opposite: Holding a cauldron of his restaurant's celebrated snapper soup, chief chef Nathaniel Frison stands in front of Old Original Bookbinder's, a Philadelphia landmark since 1865. The place is not to be confused with Bookbinders Seafood House, a newer establishment run by a descendant of the Old Original's founder (who does not use the apostrophe). The older restaurant serves 125 quarts of snapper soup every day and, though the recipe for the specialty has not changed in a hundred years, it must now be made with frozen turtle meat because there are no longer enough snappers to satisfy the demand.

of the Schuylkill precludes fishing and the shad or salmon have to be bought in the market. On these occasions members wear special aprons with a perch, the club's symbol, embroidered on the bib and hang a towel at their waist. They clap on a strange straw hat modeled after Chinese mandarins' headgear, introduced by a clipper-ship captain who was a club member in the 19th Century, and proceed to the serious business of the day: cooking and eating. One of the club officers, as caterer, chalks on a blackboard the menu and the name of the citizen and apprentice responsible for preparing each course. The club's specialties are, naturally, seafood—planked shad and roe sauce in season, poached salmon with hollandaise or mayonnaise, crab gumbo, cream of clam soup and Boothbay fish chowder, to which little bits of crisp-fried sow belly are added before serving—but the *pièce de résistance* that opens and closes the "fishing season" is a whole suckling pig, roasted over an outdoor grill.

The drink served with all this is, of course, Fish House punch. The punch is "built"—never merely made—and quite a construction it is, consisting of a light rum, cognac, peach brandy, lime and sugar. It is left to steep for five hours before being served in a nine-gallon Lowestoft bowl donated by the same sea captain who introduced the club's headgear.

Apprentices, who may be in their fifties or sixties, have to wait for a member to die or resign before they may be elected, after passing a test that calls for tossing a mess of perch in a huge iron frying pan. Meanwhile they come in for most of the work and not much of the fun. Although an apprentice helps with the cooking and passes the punch with which the opening toast is drunk, he may not take a drink or sit down to eat until invited, and it is his job to set the table in a most particular and exacting way. According to the number of members and guests present, a certain distance, precisely marked on a numbered stick, must be maintained between the nose of George Washington's head on one plate and the nose on the next; and the Madeira glasses, butter plates and flatware all have just as rigidly prescribed positions.

There are more than a hundred other eating clubs in Philadelphia, as well as a host of less formal groups that meet regularly to eat good food, often in private homes. With all this interest and with such a background of fine food, one might expect Philadelphia's cooking to rise, like the cream in milk, to the very top level of American cuisine—yet it is almost unknown in other parts of the country. Tucked away in the private fortresses of the clubs and the sturdy stone mansions of the Main Line and Chestnut Hill, where the Old Philadelphians live, it has never left its own narrow boundaries.

Now, in the decade of the nation's bicentennial, might be the time to revive some of Philadelphia's fine eating traditions. Certainly the city itself is recapturing some of the gentle charm of Penn's "countrie towne." The colonial brick houses of Society Hill are being restored and spruced up, the face of the inner city is emerging cleaned and polished, and the green girdle of Fairmount Park, once a pleasance of country estates along the banks of the Schuylkill, stretches almost to the city's heart. In such a setting, it would be fitting to restore some of the gastronomic delights of a brilliant past.

*The Famous
Fish House Punch*

To make 1½ gallons of this historic potion, place 1½ cups superfine sugar and 1 quart fresh lime or lemon juice in a 2-gallon punch bowl and stir with a muddler or bar spoon to dissolve the sugar thoroughly. Stir in 2 quarts 80-proof light rum, 2 quarts cold water, 4 ounces peach brandy and 1 quart cognac. Allow the punch to "ripen" at room temperature for at least 2 hours, stirring occasionally. Place a solid block of ice in the bowl and garnish, if you like, with sliced peaches. Serve in punch cups.

Opposite: Rosy-ripe berries signal summertime in Philadelphia, where they have been favorites for more than a century: in the early 1800s the Quaker City's "strawberry gardens" were as much frequented by sweet-eaters as its ice-cream parlors. These three local berry-decked desserts *(Recipe Index)* are raspberry-and-whipped-cream roll *(left)*; strawberry-garnished flummery, a delicate custard of 17th Century English lineage; and *(at bottom)* a four-layered, cream-covered strawberry spongecake.

The Old Craft of Molding Ice Cream
Still Keeps Its Cool in Philadelphia

In front of the store, Mollie Zendler holds a raspberry-ice ring mold festooned with whipped cream. Her husband shows off a melon made of vanilla ice cream, raspberry ice and green whipped cream. The Christmas display below, photographed in a deep freezer, includes a strawberry Santa with a peach-ice-cream face.

Philadelphia may be the City of Brotherly Love and the cradle of American Independence, but many of its inhabitants are no less gratified to think of it as the ice-cream capital of the world. The ice-cream soda originated at a fair there in 1874, and the country's largest ice-cream factory, Breyers, is located there. But the city is especially proud of its numerous small ice-cream companies and stores that specialize in homemade ice cream and molded ice-cream fancies—a tradition that goes back to 1800, when an Italian confectioner opened the first "ice cream house." In 1948, Mollie and Fred Zendler, a German-born couple, arrived in town and soon began to cater to Philadelphians' fondness for custom-made ice-cream concoctions. They now boast an array of more than 300 molds, handmade of a mixture of tin and pewter, most of which are at least 50 years old. With this unique collection, using ice cream they make themselves, the Zendlers produce an entrancing gallery of figures, fruits and flowers that have been gracing the tables at Philadelphia's best parties, large and small, for almost a generation.

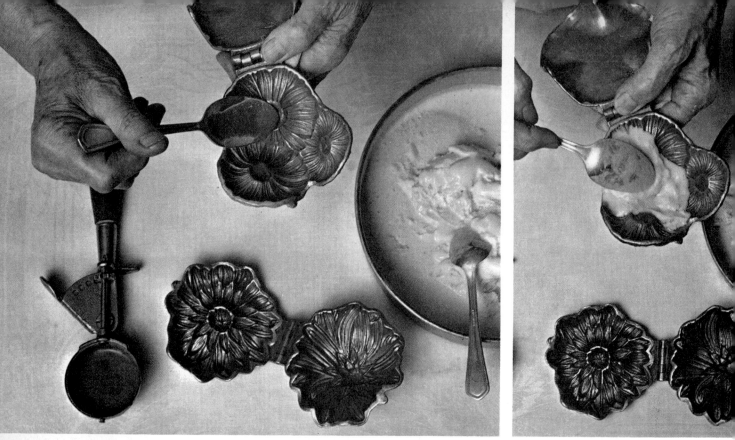

Mollie Zendler prepares a triple daisy in a mold that has been chilled for two hours at sub-zero temperature. Small scoops of chocolate ice cream form the centers. After a brief freezing, the center hardens and the rest of the mold is filled with bright, partly softened lemon ice cream *(above, right)*. The mold is then frozen for at least three hours.

This selection from the Zendlers' hundreds of hinged molds includes fruits and flowers and a frog atop a toadstool.

Mrs. Zendler unveils a dazzling sunflower, made in the mold seen in the foreground in the pictures opposite. The mold has been dipped in cold water for a few seconds and then gently pried open. The finished sunflower will be wrapped immediately in stiff tissue paper, stored in a freezer, and eventually delivered with dry ice.

Wielding an airbrush sprayer *(left),* the expert hand of Fred Zendler tints a cluster of grapes with red dye and then with blue to achieve a luscious purple.

Overleaf: The ice-cream fruits and flowers look almost as real as the eupatorium blossoms shading them. For a dinner at the Philadelphia Museum of Art the Zendlers supplied more than 400 of these fruits and flowers—an order that took several weeks to complete.

To serve 6

1 pound tripe, cut into ½-inch
    cubes
A meaty veal shank (about 1
    pound), sawed into 2 or 3 pieces
2 quarts water
4 to 6 whole black peppercorns
1 teaspoon salt
4 tablespoons butter
1 cup finely chopped onions
½ cup finely chopped celery
½ cup finely chopped green pepper
3 tablespoons flour
2 medium-sized boiling potatoes,
    peeled and cut into ¼-inch dice
Crushed dried hot red pepper
Freshly ground black pepper

Philadelphia Pepper Pot

Combine the tripe, veal shank and water in a heavy 4- to 5-quart casserole. The water should cover the meats by at least 2 inches; if necessary add more. Bring to a boil over high heat, meanwhile skimming off the foam and scum as they rise to the surface. Add the peppercorns and salt, reduce the heat to low, and simmer partially covered for 2 hours, or until the tripe is tender.

With a slotted spoon, transfer the tripe and pieces of veal shank to a platter or cutting board. Remove the veal from the shank, discard the bones and cut the meat into ½-inch pieces. Strain the cooking liquid through a fine sieve set over a bowl; measure and reserve 6 cups. If there is less, add enough water to make that amount.

In the same 4- to 5-quart casserole, melt the butter over moderate heat. When the foam subsides, add the onions, celery and green pepper and stir for about 5 minutes. When the vegetables are soft but not brown, add the flour and mix well. Stirring constantly, pour in the reserved cooking liquid in a slow, thin stream and cook over high heat until the soup thickens lightly, comes to a boil and is smooth. Add the potatoes, tripe and veal, reduce the heat to low, cover partially, and simmer for 1 hour.

Taste for seasoning. Add more salt if needed and enough crushed red pepper and freshly ground black pepper to give the soup a distinctly peppery flavor. Serve at once from the casserole or in individual soup plates.

To serve 6 to 8

2½ pounds snapping-turtle meat,
    thoroughly defrosted if frozen,
    cut into 2-inch pieces
1½ cups flour
1 teaspoon salt
½ teaspoon freshly ground black
    pepper
½ pound lean salt pork, trimmed
    of all rind, the pork cut into
    ¼-inch dice
1 cup finely chopped onions
½ cup finely chopped celery
½ cup finely chopped carrot
1 teaspoon finely chopped garlic
1 quart beef stock, fresh or canned
2 tablespoons tomato paste
1 medium-sized bay leaf, finely
    crumbled
½ teaspoon crumbled dried thyme
1 cup water (optional)
2 tablespoons dry Madeira

Philadelphia Snapper Soup

Pat the snapper meat completely dry with paper towels. Then combine the flour, salt and pepper in a paper bag, add the snapper pieces and shake vigorously to coat all sides evenly. Remove the meat from the bag and, one piece at a time, shake off the excess flour.

In a heavy 4- to 5-quart casserole, fry the pork dice over moderate heat until it is crisp and brown and has rendered all its fat. Transfer the dice to paper towels to drain. Brown the snapper 4 or 5 pieces at a time in the fat remaining in the pan. Turn the pieces frequently with a slotted spoon and regulate the heat so that they color richly and evenly without burning. As they brown, transfer them to a plate.

Pour off all but about 3 tablespoons of the fat from the pan and add the onions, celery, carrot and garlic. Stir over moderate heat until the vegetables are soft but not brown. Stir in the beef stock, tomato paste, bay leaf, thyme and reserved pork bits. Bring to a boil over high heat and add the snapper and the liquid that has accumulated around it.

Reduce the heat to low and simmer partially covered for 2 hours, or until the snapper is tender and shows no resistance when pierced with the point of a small sharp knife. Check the pan from time to time and regulate the heat to keep the soup at a gentle simmer. Add up to 1 cup of water if the liquid cooks away too rapidly.

Stir in the Madeira, taste for seasoning, and serve the snapper soup from a heated tureen.

Chicken Breasts and Ham with Sherried Cream Sauce

In a heavy 10- to 12-inch skillet, melt 2 tablespoons of the butter over moderate heat. When the foam begins to subside, add the shallots and, stirring frequently, cook for 2 or 3 minutes, until they are soft and translucent but not brown. Add the chicken breasts and stock, and bring to a boil over high heat, meanwhile skimming off the foam and scum as they rise to the surface. Reduce the heat to low and simmer partially covered for about 10 minutes, or until the chicken feels firm to the touch. With a slotted spoon, transfer the chicken to a plate and drape it with foil to keep it warm. Set the stock aside.

Melt 3 tablespoons of the remaining butter in a 1- to 2-quart saucepan over moderate heat. Add the flour and mix to a paste. Then, stirring the mixture constantly with a wire whisk, pour in the reserved chicken stock and shallots, and cook over high heat until the sauce comes to a boil, thickens heavily and is smooth.

Whisking constantly, add the cream, sherry, parsley, salt and white pepper. Reduce the heat to low and simmer uncovered for 3 minutes to remove any taste of raw flour. Taste for seasoning.

While the sauce is simmering, melt the remaining 4 tablespoons of butter in a heavy 12-inch skillet over high heat. Add the ham slices and, turning them over frequently with kitchen tongs, cook for a few minutes to heat the ham through.

To serve, place the ham slices on six heated individual serving plates and set a chicken breast half on each slice. Pour the sauce over the chicken and ham, dividing it evenly among the portions. Garnish the top with the strips of ham and serve at once.

To serve 6

9 tablespoons butter
2 tablespoons finely chopped shallots
3 one-pound chicken breasts, halved, skinned and boned
1½ cups chicken stock, fresh or canned
¼ cup flour
½ cup heavy cream
2 tablespoons pale dry sherry
1 tablespoon finely chopped parsley
½ teaspoon salt
A pinch of ground white pepper
6 thin slices cooked country ham, plus 1 thin slice country ham cut in matchlike strips

Strawberry Flummery

Combine ½ cup of the sugar, the cornstarch and salt in a heavy 2- to 3-quart saucepan and, stirring the mixture constantly with a wire whisk, pour in the milk in a slow, thin stream. Whisking constantly, cook over moderate heat until the mixture comes to a boil and thickens heavily. Reduce the heat to its lowest setting.

Ladle several tablespoonfuls of the liquid into the beaten egg yolk, mix well and, still whisking, gradually pour the yolk into the simmering liquid. Simmer for 3 or 4 minutes longer to cook the egg yolk through, but do not let the mixture come anywhere near a boil.

Remove the pan from the heat and stir in the vanilla. Cool to room temperature, then pour the flummery into a serving bowl. Cover with wax paper and refrigerate for at least 2 hours, or until the flummery is thoroughly chilled.

Just before serving, pick over the strawberries, removing the hulls and discarding any blemished berries. Wash the strawberries briefly in a sieve or colander set under cold running water. Spread the berries on paper towels and pat them completely dry with fresh towels. Cut each berry in half lengthwise. Place the halves in a bowl, add the remaining 2 tablespoons of sugar, and toss gently together with a wooden spoon to coat the berries evenly. Arrange the strawberries attractively on top of the flummery and serve at once.

To serve 4 to 6

½ cup plus 2 tablespoons sugar
⅓ cup cornstarch
¼ teaspoon salt
3 cups milk
1 egg yolk, lightly beaten
1 teaspoon vanilla extract
1 pint firm ripe strawberries

To serve 8

2 pairs calf's sweetbreads (about 1½ pounds)
A 7-pound leg of lamb, boned but not split, with shank meat cut off
1½ teaspoons salt
Freshly ground black pepper
4 tablespoons butter, melted, plus 4 tablespoons butter, cut into half-inch bits, plus 4 tablespoons butter, softened
1 tablespoon anchovy paste
4 tablespoons finely chopped fresh parsley
2 teaspoons capers, finely chopped
½ teaspoon crumbled dried thyme
¼ teaspoon finely grated fresh lemon peel
¼ teaspoon crumbled dried marjoram
1 cup soft fresh crumbs made from homemade-type white bread, pulverized in a blender or finely shredded with a fork
1 cup finely chopped onions
½ cup dry white wine
1½ to 2½ cups chicken stock, fresh or canned
12 breakfast-type pork sausages (about 1 pound)
¼ cup water
2 lamb kidneys, peeled and trimmed of fat
2 tablespoons strained fresh lemon juice
The yolks of 4 hard-cooked eggs
⅛ teaspoon ground white pepper
8 thin slices homemade-type white bread, cut into 3-inch rounds and fried in 4 tablespoons of butter
8 capers
16 flat anchovy fillets

Martha Washington's Grand Leg of Lamb

Starting 6 hours or more ahead, soak the sweetbreads in several changes of cold water for 3 hours. Place them in a 4-quart enameled or stainless-steel pan and pour in 2 quarts of fresh cold water. Bring to a simmer slowly over moderate heat and blanch the sweetbreads by simmering them for 3 minutes. With tongs or a slotted spoon, transfer the sweetbreads to a bowl of cold water to rest for 1 or 2 minutes. Pat them dry with paper towels, and gently pull off as much of the outside membrane as possible.

Cut the two lobes from the tube between each pair of sweetbreads with a small sharp knife. Discard the tubes. Put the sweetbreads on a large flat platter. Cover them with a towel and weight them with a casserole or skillet weighing about 5 pounds to flatten and remove excess moisture from the sweetbreads. Refrigerate the sweetbreads for at least 2 hours.

Preheat the oven to 450°. Season the lamb on all sides with ½ teaspoon of salt and a few grindings of pepper. To prepare the stuffing, combine the 4 tablespoons of melted butter and 1 tablespoon of anchovy paste in a bowl and mix well. Add 2 tablespoons of parsley, the chopped capers, thyme, lemon peel and marjoram. Then stir in the bread crumbs.

Close the opening at the shank end of the leg of lamb by sewing it with a large needle and heavy white thread. Then fill the pocket in the lamb with the stuffing, and sew up the opening securely. Tie the leg of lamb crosswise in 5 or 6 places and lengthwise 2 or 3 times to hold it in a neat cylindrical shape. For the most predictable results, insert the tip of a meat thermometer at least 2 inches into the roast.

Set the lamb on a rack in a shallow roasting pan and roast it in the middle of the oven for 20 minutes. Reduce the oven temperature to 350°. Sprinkle the chopped onions around the lamb, roast 15 minutes more, and pour the wine and 1½ cups of chicken stock over the onions. Continue roasting for about 1 hour longer, or until the lamb is cooked to your taste. A meat thermometer will register 130° to 140° when the lamb is rare, 140° to 150° when medium, and 150° to 160° when well done. Ideally the lamb should be medium rare.

Half an hour or so before the lamb is ready to be served, prepare the garnishes: Combine the pork sausages and ¼ cup of water in a heavy 10- to 12-inch skillet and bring to a boil over high heat. Reduce the heat to low, cover tightly and simmer for 5 minutes. Then uncover the pan and, turning the sausages occasionally with a spatula, cook over moderate heat for about 5 minutes to brown them on all sides. Drain the sausages on paper towels, transfer them to a heated plate and cover with foil.

With a sharp knife, cut the sweetbreads crosswise into ½-inch-thick slices. Cut the kidneys crosswise into ¼-inch-thick slices and then cut the slices into ¼-inch-wide strips. In a heavy 10- to 12-inch skillet, melt 4 tablespoons of butter bits over moderate heat. When the foam begins to subside, add the sweetbreads and kidneys and, stirring frequently, fry for 6 to 8 minutes, or until the pieces are lightly browned. Add 2 tablespoons of lemon juice, ½ teaspoon of the salt and a few grindings of black pepper, and taste for seasoning. Remove the skillet from the heat and cover to keep the sweetbreads and kidneys warm.

Force the hard-cooked egg yolks through a fine sieve with the back of a spoon, then beat in the 4 tablespoons of softened butter. Add the re-

90

Martha Washington's "grand leg of lamb" is served with sweetbreads, kidneys, sausages and richly garnished bread rounds.

maining ½ teaspoon of salt and ⅛ teaspoon of white pepper, and taste for seasoning. Spoon the mixture into a pastry bag fitted with a star tube and pipe an egg-yolk rosette onto the center of each bread round. Set a caper on each rosette and arrange 2 anchovy fillets around it. Set aside.

When the leg of lamb has roasted its allotted time, transfer it to a large heated platter, and let it rest while you prepare the anchovy sauce.

Strain the contents of the roasting pan through a fine sieve set over a 1-quart measuring cup, pressing down hard on the onions with the back of a spoon to extract all their juices. Pour the liquid into a small saucepan and add enough chicken stock to make 2 cups in all. Bring to a simmer over low heat. In a small bowl, beat the egg yolks, flour and 1 tablespoon of anchovy paste with a wire whisk until smooth. Ladle 2 or 3 tablespoons of simmering stock into the egg yolks and mix well. Whisking constantly, pour the yolks into the pan and cook over low heat until the sauce thickens lightly. Do not let the sauce come near a boil or the yolks will curdle. Taste and add 2 to 3 teaspoons of lemon juice.

To serve, mound the sweetbreads and kidneys at both the ends and sides of the leg of lamb and sprinkle them with the remaining 2 tablespoons of parsley. Arrange the sausages and bread rounds attractively on the platter, and present the anchovy sauce in a bowl or sauceboat.

ANCHOVY SAUCE
2 egg yolks
2 tablespoons flour
1 tablespoon anchovy paste
2 to 3 teaspoons strained fresh
　lemon juice

To make one 9-inch 4-layer cake

1 quart firm ripe strawberries
¾ cup plus 2 tablespoons sugar
2 tablespoons butter, softened
2 tablespoons plus 1 cup unsifted
    flour
A pinch of salt
6 egg whites
6 egg yolks
2 teaspoons vanilla extract
2 cups heavy cream, chilled

Strawberry Spongecake

Pick over the strawberries, removing the hulls and discarding any blemished berries. Wash the strawberries briefly in a large sieve or colander set under cold running water. Then spread them on paper towels to drain and pat them completely dry with fresh towels.

Select 2 cups of the most attractive berries and set them aside. Drop the remaining berries into a bowl, add ¼ cup of the sugar, and mash the berries to a thick purée by beating them against the sides of the bowl with the back of a spoon. Cover the bowl with foil or plastic wrap and let the puréed strawberries steep at room temperature until ready to serve.

Preheat the oven to 350°. With a pastry brush, spread the softened butter evenly over the bottom and sides of two 9-inch layer-cake pans. Add 1 tablespoon of the flour to each pan and tip it from side to side to spread the flour evenly. Invert the pans and rap their bottoms sharply to remove the excess flour.

Combine the remaining cup of flour and the salt and sift them together onto a plate or a sheet of wax paper. Set aside.

With a wire whisk or a rotary or electric beater, beat the egg whites until they are stiff enough to stand in unwavering peaks on the beater when it is lifted from the bowl. In another bowl and with the same beater, beat the egg yolks, ½ cup of the sugar, and 1 teaspoon of the vanilla together until they are thick and lemon-colored.

Sprinkle the sifted flour and salt over the egg whites, pour the egg-yolk mixture over them and, with a rubber spatula, fold together lightly but thoroughly, using an over-and-under cutting motion rather than a stirring motion.

Pour the batter into the buttered-and-floured pans, dividing it equally among them. Spread the batter and smooth the tops with the spatula. Bake in the middle of the oven for about 20 minutes, or until the cakes begin to shrink away from the sides of the pans and a cake tester or toothpick inserted in the centers comes out clean. Let the cakes cool in the pans for 4 or 5 minutes, then turn them out onto wire racks to cool completely to room temperature.

About half an hour before serving the cake, pour the cream into a large chilled bowl and whip it with a wire whisk or a rotary or electric beater. As soon as the cream becomes frothy, add the remaining 2 tablespoons of sugar and 1 teaspoon of vanilla. Continue to beat until the cream is stiff enough to stand in firm, unwavering peaks on the beater when it is lifted out of the bowl.

To assemble, slice each cake in half horizontally to make four thin layers. Place one of the layers, cut side up, on a serving plate and, with a metal spatula, spread it with about ½ cup of the puréed strawberries. Repeat two more times, spreading the third layer of the cake with all of the remaining puréed berries.

Carefully put the fourth layer on the top, cut side down. Then spread the whipped cream smoothly over the top and sides of the strawberry cake. Cut a dozen or so of the reserved 2 cups of whole strawberries in half lengthwise and set them on the plate, cut side up, in a ring around the cake. Arrange the remaining whole strawberries attractively on the top of the cake and serve at once.

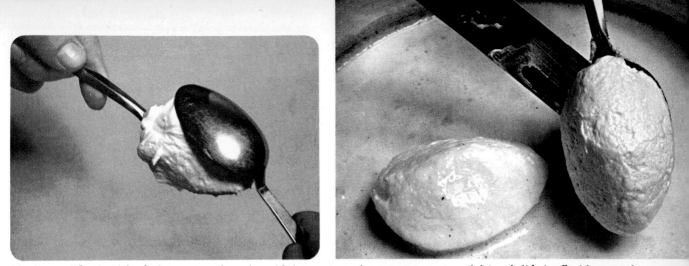

To shape a "floating island" into a smooth oval, mold the meringue between two spoons *(left)* and slide it off with a spatula.

Floating Island

With a wire whisk or a rotary or electric beater, beat the egg whites. As soon as they are frothy, add ½ cup of the sugar. Then continue to beat until the meringue is stiff enough to stand in unwavering peaks on the beater when it is lifted from the bowl.

In a heavy 8- to 10-inch skillet, heat 2 cups of cream and the vanilla bean over low heat. When small bubbles begin to form around the sides of the pan, reduce the heat to the lowest point.

To form each "island" scoop up the meringue in one dessert spoon and invert another dessert spoon over it to shape the meringue into an oval. Slide the meringue off the spoon onto the surface of the simmering cream. Make similar ovals of the remaining meringue. Simmer the meringues uncovered for 2 minutes, turn them over gently with a slotted spoon and cook for 1 or 2 minutes longer, or until they are just firm to the touch. Do not overcook the meringues, or they might disintegrate. Transfer the meringues to a kitchen towel to drain and let them cool to room temperature.

Strain the cream through a fine sieve, measure it and add enough more cream to make 2 cups. Return the vanilla bean and set the cream aside.

Combine the egg yolks and ⅔ cup of sugar in a heavy 2- to 3-quart saucepan and beat them together with a wire whisk. Whisking the mixture constantly, pour in the cream in a slow, thin stream. Add the vanilla bean and place the pan over low heat. Stir gently with a spoon until the custard coats the spoon heavily. Do not let the custard come anywhere near a boil or it will curdle. Strain the custard through a fine sieve into a bowl, discarding the vanilla bean. Cool to room temperature, then refrigerate the custard for 3 to 4 hours to chill it thoroughly.

About half an hour before serving, prepare the caramel. Combine ⅔ cup of sugar and ⅓ cup of water in a small heavy pan and bring to a boil over high heat, stirring until the sugar dissolves. Boil the syrup over moderate heat, gently tipping the pan back and forth until the syrup turns a tealike brown. This may take 10 minutes or more. Immediately remove the pan from the heat and pour the caramel into a bowl.

Arrange the meringues on top of the custard and, when the caramel is lukewarm, dribble it over them with a small spoon. To serve, ladle the meringues onto individual dessert plates and spoon custard around them.

To serve 8 to 10

MERINGUE AND CUSTARD
5 egg whites
½ cup plus ⅔ cup sugar
2 to 2¼ cups light cream
A 2-inch piece of vanilla bean
5 egg yolks

CARAMEL
⅔ cup sugar
⅓ cup water

IV

A Huge Natural Larder

On his boat in Long Island's Great South Bay, Arnold Van Popering harvests clams with the kind of tool used by generations of bay hand-clammers. The scissorslike tongs are thrust down into the mud, then opened and closed so the teeth can rake in the clams. Digging in water three to 10 feet deep, Arnold puts in a full day's work on the bay, summer and winter, collecting about five bushels of clams a day.

The Eastern Heartland is a huge natural larder. Its deep rivers and lakes, its rolling fields and placid ponds, its sheltering bays and shady woodlands—from Long Island's Montauk Point in New York to Keweenaw Point in Michigan—harbor an infinite variety of finny, furry, feathered and hard-shelled creatures for man to feast on the year round. Inevitably, much of the wildlife has suffered as man has multiplied and prospered, but an astonishing amount of game, fish and shellfish remains. In some places, because of the vegetation and protection provided by man, the wildlife population actually has increased: there are more deer now, for instance, than there were 50 years ago, and the numbers of quail increase every year.

Of all the areas where this natural bounty can be enjoyed, I have found two to be particularly rewarding—the waters along the Atlantic Coast and the region around Lake Michigan. I discovered the treasures of the former when I came to America and learned first about the shad that come from the ocean to spawn in Eastern rivers every spring, and later about the shellfish that grow in providential abundance in the waters around Long Island.

Of these delights—clams, lobsters, scallops and mussels among them —the greatest of all is the oyster, plump and succulent with a briny, unforgettable flavor as fresh as an ocean breeze. Long before the Dutch tilled their farms, or *bouweries,* on that finger of land that jabs east from New York City for 120 miles, Long Island's oysters were one of the chief foods of the 13 tribes of Delaware Indians who lived there.

95

The Oyster-Stand

Patrick Bryant's oyster stand was one of hundreds that dotted downtown Manhattan street corners in the latter half of the 19th Century. For shoppers and office workers, one of the more pleasant aspects of big-city life at the time was a 10-cent pause for an ample plate of Long Island blue points.

When the Dutch came, they were quick to take advantage of the water's riches. An entry in the journals of Jasper Danckaerts and Pieter Sluyter, two missionaries from the mother country, gives a vivid picture of a meal at the Long Island house of Simon de Hart. The travelers warmed themselves in front of a fire "halfway up the chimney, of clear oak and hickory, of which they made not the least scruple of burning profusely. There had already been thrown upon it, to be roasted, a pailful of Gowanes oysters, which are the best in the country. They are quite as good as those of England, and better than those we ate at Falmouth. We had to try some of them raw. They are long and full, some of them not less than a foot long. Everybody keeps the shells for the purpose of burning them into lime. They pickle the oysters in small casks, and send them to Barbadoes and the other islands. We had for supper a roasted haunch of venison which he had bought of the Indians. The meat was exceedingly tender and good, and also quite fat. It had a slightly spicy flavor. We were also served wild turkey, which was also fat and of good flavor; and a wild goose, but that was rather dry."

The name Gowanes probably referred to the Gowanus Canal that still runs through Brooklyn at Long Island's western end. (Today the canal is a conservationist's nightmare, but in those days it was fished for oysters.) If oysters a foot long sound incredible, it must be remembered that in the 17th Century they had spent peaceful decades undisturbed in their beds, waxing large and fat. At that time the harvesting of oysters was not yet big business, as it was to become in the mid-to-late 19th Century, when every town or city of any consequence had its oyster parlors, oyster cellars, oyster saloons and oyster bars. By then the oysters were not often so big, but they were so cheap and plentiful that for a dime oyster houses served as many as the customer could down. Anyone could afford oysters, and they were eaten at breakfast, dinner, supper and in-between hours. (Undoubtedly, one of the attractions was the strength of an old, persistent myth about oysters being "amatory" food—a conceit that the Shellfish Institute of America recently capitalized on with a tongue-in-cheek bumper sticker: "Eat fish, live longer. Eat oysters, love longer.")

The appetite for the mollusk spread westward and became so gargantuan that an oyster express service was started to carry Eastern oysters as far inland as Cincinnati. Wagons from Long Island drove furiously through the day and night, changing teams of horses, their precious cargoes swaddled in straw dampened with sea water to keep them alive until they could be transferred to tanks of salt water on river boats for the final stages of their odyssey.

The creature that caused all this commotion is known formally as *Crassostrea virginica,* the oyster native to the brackish bays and inlets of the Atlantic and Gulf Coasts. This is a different species of oyster from the West Coast varieties—the minuscule native Olympia and the giant Pacific Coast oyster introduced from Japan. While all Eastern oysters belong to the same family, they vary from north to south, even from bed to bed within the same locale. As with any other marine animal, their characteristics, flavor and growth are determined by their habitat, the food they take in and the temperature of the water they live in. Oysters grow faster in warm water. A southern oyster reaches marketable size in two years, a Chesapeake takes three, a Long Island four or five and a Cape Cod six.

Temperature also triggers the oyster's reproductive mechanism: an oyster will spawn only when the water reaches about 74°. This is what started the old wives' tale about oysters being inedible (some even said poisonous) in months lacking an "R," which is nonsense. Oysters wax fat in the winter but get thin and meager in the summer after they have spawned, a somewhat debilitating activity; at that time they are off the market because they are of such poor quality that they would hardly fetch a decent price. Furthermore, the months of June, July and August are the "setting" season, when the free-swimming larvae that have developed from the fertilized eggs seek a hard surface, such as old oyster or clam shells lying on the bottom, on which to attach themselves and grow. With the future harvest in mind, oystermen are understandably reluctant to disturb or dislodge these embryonic oysters, or spats, as they are called, by dredging or raking their beds.

Despite the purists who believe that the only decent way to serve an oyster is *au naturel,* swimming in its own salty liquor on the half shell, 19th and early 20th Century cookbooks reveal that considerable culinary ingenuity has been expended over the years on preparing oysters in every style imaginable. They have been broiled, roasted, pickled, stewed, fried, deviled, creamed and scalloped; they have been turned into pies, patties, croquettes, fritters, soups and chowders. One familiar recipe I found in a Brooklyn cookbook of 1911 was for angels on horseback, which consists of oysters wrapped in bacon and broiled until the bacon is crisp. It is an old English dish traditionally eaten at the end of a meal as a savory, but it also makes one of the best appetizers known to man.

Oysters are good broiled on the half shell too, with a sprinkling of lemon juice, seasoning and buttered bread crumbs on top—but be sure to drain them first and keep that lovely oyster liquor for an oyster bisque or stew. Then if you want to get really elegant, there are the classic dishes, such as oysters Rockefeller and several others, in which oysters on the half shell are arranged on beds of rock salt (which helps to keep them hot), topped with all manner of delicious spice and herb mixtures and broiled or baked in a very hot oven for a very short time. One such specialty that is particularly associated with New York is oysters casino *(Recipe Index),* for which the topping is chopped vegetables and bacon.

Much as I enjoy these extravagances, I am of the opinion that the best way to cook an oyster is as little as possible. I especially love them in a stew, the way it is served at the Oyster Bar in New York's Grand Central Station. The stew is simplicity itself: the oysters are just heated in a piping hot combination of cream, milk and oyster liquor until their edges curl, then the mixture is ladled into heated bowls in which pats of butter are melted *(for one version, see the Recipe Index).* This is a cold-weather New York favorite of mine. It is marvelous to plunge inside the terminal from the icy street and descend to the warm, cheerful clatter of the Oyster Bar. I like to sit at the worn pink-marble counter so that I can watch the countermen with their slim, rounded knives shucking the oysters in that casually competent way they have. The stew is served up

Overleaf: The clams and oysters of Long Island, New York, have been prized delicacies since the days of the Indians. Though some purists insist that they are best raw, inventive cooks of the area have learned to prepare them in an intriguing variety of ways. Steamer clams remoulade *(bottom left)* sets the mild-flavored mollusk off with a snappy mustardy mayonnaise. Manhattan clam chowder *(top left)* is a heady tomato brew, thickened with diced potatoes. Broiled clams *(top right)* are topped with herbed crumbs, while the broiled oysters casino *(bottom right)* plump up under a tangy cover of vegetables and bacon. All these dishes are listed in the Recipe Index.

Continued on page 100

steaming hot and looking almost indecently buttery and rich; the taste is ambrosial, the smoothness of the soup accented by the salty tang of the plump oysters hidden in its creamy depths. It is almost enough in itself to make the bitter winter months in the city bearable.

The name by which all Long Island oysters are now known is blue point. Originally this referred specifically to a superlative specimen that came from the waters around Blue Point on the Great South Bay, a long, narrow lagoon that stretches along the island's south shore, sheltered from the buffeting Atlantic by the barrier of Fire Island. These placid, shallow waters are not only the site of great oyster beds; they are also one of the world's richest sources of clams. Forty-four per cent of all the hard-shell clams consumed in the United States come from the Great South Bay. Most of them are still dug by hand, just as they have been for almost 200 years, by a sturdy breed known as baymen.

These men are a group apart, as much a part of Long Island as the storms that ravage its dunes or the gulls that skim its waters. Hardy, hard-working and fiercely independent, they go out in small boats in all weather and at all times of the year. With their primitive tools—tongs consisting of long wooden handles with sharp-toothed, curved rakes that mesh to form an iron basket at the end—they dig the bivalves from the bottom of the bay as their fathers, grandfathers and great-grandfathers did before them. Some are descended from the original Dutch and English settlers and they are and have always been the very sinews of the shellfish industry.

It is fascinating to watch a bayman at work. I went out one summer day with Jeff Zegal, a leading member of the Great South Bay Farmers Cooperative Association, which was formed to give the independent baymen greater leverage in the shellfish industry and enable them to compete with the big business concerns that use modern hydraulic dredges to suck the mollusks from the bottom.

Jeff Zegal, who dug his first clam at the age of nine, told me he had tried other jobs but came back to the business of his forebears because of the freedom it offered. As he put it, "You have no one to answer to but yourself." He goes out 12 months of the year, five days a week, cutting holes in the ice when the bay freezes over in winter.

We left the dock at West Sayville early in the morning, when the bay was still as glass and the summer heat only a threat. Jeff's clam boat is a flat-bottomed, puntlike craft with a small square cabin perched atop an open deck. Steering it out to a spot where he knew there was a clam bed below, Jeff anchored, then heaved a pair of 16-foot tongs from the cabin top and thrust them into the water. Vigorously he opened and closed the handles to dig the clams out of the mud, then brought up the tongs and dumped the contents into a metal basket on deck.

The tongs are heavy and it was a man's job to heft them this way hour after hour in the hot sun, especially when a rising breeze kicked up choppy waves that made the footing uncertain. But Jeff handled the tongs with that deceptive ease that is the mark of a craftsman. In three hours he had dug about two bushels of clams and we headed back; normally he would have stayed out for a seven-hour stretch and dug some five bushels, or 360 pounds, of clams. We took the catch to the cooperative, where a machine grades the clams into the five wholesale market sizes (from smallest to largest) : littlenecks, topnecks and cherrystones, the three sizes that are eaten raw on the half shell; and the medium and chowder clams, used mainly for chowder and soup. All are the same kind of hard-shell clam—they are just at different stages of growth.

There is another type that also comes out of the bay, the soft-shell clam, more generally known as the steamer. While the shell could hardly be called soft, it is thinner and more brittle than that of the hard-shell. Soft-shell clams have long necks that stick out beyond the shell, which provides a convenient handle to eat them with after you have steamed them —which is my preferred way of cooking them. Steaming opens their shells; then simply grasp one by the neck, swish it around in a cup of clam broth, dip it in melted butter and eat it neck and all, pulling the leathery black membrane away at the same time. In some Long Island restaurants, I have encountered another way to serve steamers that, while a bit lavish for such a simple delicacy, is an interesting variation. It is steamers remoulade *(Recipe Index)*, for which the clams are steamed and combined with a smooth sauce of mayonnaise, mustard, lemon juice and parsley. The distinctive flavor of the clams comes through the piquancy of the sauce, and the dish makes a refreshing summer appetizer.

There is a trick to getting hard-shell clams to relax and open up that is worth knowing about: freeze them. This kills the clams without affecting their flavor. When you take the clams from the freezer, rinse them in cool water for about three minutes, at which point the shells will begin to open and you can pry them apart and twist them off with your fingers. Some companies now market clams frozen in the shell, which is one of those simple but inspired ideas you wonder why no one thought of before. There are many advantages. No matter where you live, you can be pretty sure the clams are sea-fresh when you buy them and they can be kept in the freezer and taken out as needed. I find frozen clams indistinguishable from the fresh in flavor and texture.

Clams are even more versatile and adaptable than oysters. Clam chowder is one of the great native American soups, whether it comes New England style, with salt pork, onions, potatoes, clams, clam liquor and milk or cream, or Manhattan style *(Recipe Index)*, which has no milk but adds tomatoes, celery and thyme. Then there is a truly local dish, delightfully named Fire Island starve-to-death, that was a lifesaver during the Depression. The baymen would swap their clams for the farmers' potatoes and onions and everyone ate well despite the lack of money. This dish is made much the same way as a chowder, except that the only liquid is half a cup of water, which makes it a kind of clam stew. In those days, if anyone had the makings of piecrust around, the stew was covered with pastry and turned into clam pie.

A more sophisticated version of a clam pie is the clam quiche, or tart *(Recipe Index)*. Use clam liquor and light cream, mixed with beaten egg for the custard; then a little sautéed minced onion, crumbled crisp bacon and minced clams (the canned type are fine, if you can't get fresh) for the filling. This makes a delicious first course or hors d'oeuvre.

There is one other mollusk that I never seem to be able to get enough

These snowy ducks on a Long Island poultry farm are being fattened up before shipment to a cooperative processing plant —where as many as 20,000 ducks a day are frozen for sale throughout the United States and abroad.

of. This is the tiny delicate bay scallop, found mostly in the waters of eastern Long Island. Bay scallops have always been less plentiful than oysters and clams and therefore highly prized and correspondingly expensive. Like the clam and the oyster, the scallop has two shells, and it propels itself through the water by snapping them together, so it looks a little like a submarine flying saucer. The part that is eaten is the "eye," the muscle that holds the shells together. Pale pinkish white in color and only half an inch across, the eye is so exquisitely tender that it can be eaten raw, although in the uncooked state the flavor is rather strong.

However, if you marinate raw scallops in lime or lemon juice, as for a South American *seviche,* the action of the citric acid cooks the flesh slightly, turning it white, opaque and firm and toning down the fishy taste. The flavor of bay scallops is so subtle and sweet that the slightest overcooking will do mischief to them. I like them best broiled or sautéed very, very quickly with enough butter to keep them moist.

A less familiar variant of broiled scallops served to introduce one of the most satisfying meals I have ever had: a dinner one weekend at the Southampton home of a friend, a meal that was, in effect, a showcase of Long Island products. We began with scallops en brochette *(Recipe Index),* speared on skewers with bacon and brushed with butter, then seasoned and quickly broiled. Next came roast Long Island duckling stuffed with apricots and rice *(Recipe Index),* cooked in such a way that

the fat had drained out and the skin was beautifully crisp. This was served with Long Island new potatoes and cauliflower topped with browned buttered crumbs *(Recipe Index)*.

Everything we ate that evening came from the water or land within a 50-mile radius of where we sat. The ducklings, raised in huge numbers on farms dotting eastern Long Island, are descended from nine white Peking ducks brought from China by a sea captain in 1873, but they have become wholly a Long Island specialty, as domesticated as modern breeding techniques can make them. The plump birds are shipped all over the country, and with good reason. The tender flesh is richly flavored but not strong and is equally good served hot or cold.

That dinner at Southampton was but one of many memorable meals I have enjoyed on Long Island, always reveling in the marvelous freshness of the local food that most of my friends there take an inordinate pride in serving. Very often the main course is one of the species of fish with which the surrounding waters teem. Two of the best are bluefish and striped bass. The striped bass was one of the fish most admired by the early settlers, who lauded it as the "boldest, bravest, strongest and most active fish along the Atlantic seaboard." Nowadays, all summer long on the Island's beaches, you will see fishermen casting in the surf, patiently waiting (often in vain) for the exciting moment when the tough, aggressive striper strikes. Others prefer to bob in rowboats on Long Island Sound

The Big Duck, a 15-foot-high cement roadside stand in Riverhead, New York, is a whimsical testament to Long Island's $30 million-a-year duck industry. Half of the country's ducks are raised annually on the island's 30-odd duck farms.

Continued on page 106

103

Long Island fares well both on
native-born and naturalized bounty.
The brace of roast ducks at left,
stuffed with apricots and rice, are
descendants of a flock brought from
China nearly a century ago. Bay
scallops, here skewered and broiled
with bacon, are indigenous to Long
Island waters. Even cauliflower,
shown topped with bread crumbs,
is local; it has been grown on the
island since the 17th Century.
For recipes see the Recipe Index.

and in the bays, hoping for a run of the swift blues, when the waters boil with their thrashing bodies.

Long Islanders respect these fish and cook them simply but with great style. I remember lunching at Easthampton with *The New York Times* food editor, Craig Claiborne, one clear, cool September day. First we sipped homemade tomato soup, with all the rich ripeness of the local tomatoes and an ineffable accent of fresh thyme from his garden. Then we had a superb striped bass, poached and served cooled with tarragon mayonnaise and cucumber salad. The flesh of the bass is firm and white with a clean, fresh flavor. There could have been no simpler or more perfect meal. Another time, staying with friends on Fire Island, I feasted on bluefish caught right off the beach. Bluefish are a bit more oily than stripers and have a slightly stronger flavor; but these blues were little fellows and, when cleaned and sautéed whole, then served with lemon butter, they could not have been more delicate. They were followed by a pie made from tart little wild beach plums. Such uncomplicated, natural food, with the freshness of the outdoors in every mouthful, must be counted among the greatest of life's pleasures.

After the salt-water fish of Long Island, the fish I love the most are the fresh-water varieties of Michigan. In the state's 5,000 lakes and the rivers and streams that flow into them live fish too numerous to list completely. There are the tasty little pan fish, small and tender enough to be cooked simply in a skillet—yellow perch, bluegill, crappie, smallmouth bass and the tiny silvery smelt. A salt-water fish that took to fresh-water living, the smelt was introduced to Crystal Lake, Michigan, from Maine in 1906 as food for the salmon with which the lake had been stocked. The salmon died, but the smelt thrived, gradually making their way into nearby Lake Michigan and the other Great Lakes. When the ice breaks in the early spring, the smelt start running, leaving the lakes to spawn in the streams. The sudden onrush is the signal for people from nearby communities to get out with dip nets and buckets, scooping the little fish from the water by the hundreds all night long. Smelt have the sweetest of flesh, and bones so soft they can be pulled out in one piece with the head, either before or after they are cooked. I find they hold together better if you sauté them with the heads on and take out the bones later.

Michigan lakes and streams harbor many kinds of trout—the brown, brook, rainbow and the aristocrat of them all, the lake trout, technically known as *Salvelinus namaycush,* a droll blend of Latin and Algonquian Indian. Lake trout belong to the salmon family and while the average size is around four or five pounds, I saw some whopping specimens almost three feet long at a commercial fishery on Lake Superior. These trout have firm, pink flesh, rich and oily, rather like their salmon relatives; they are great favorites with sport fishermen and all the people of the Upper Peninsula—and have been at least since 1687, when a French traveler, Baron La Horton, wrote of "trout as big as one's thigh." Old-timers, I am told, turn up their noses at anything else and throw the little pan fish back in the water. Trout is all they fish for, and they know all the secrets of cooking it—not only pan frying and broiling it, but also, for example, steaming it on top of a kettle of potatoes, which not only economizes on pots, but keeps the flesh of the fish firm and fresh tasting.

Whitefish is another magnificent lake fish; La Horton marveled at the shoals of them "catched around the middle of the channel, between the continent and the isle of Missilimackinac [Mackinac Island]," and the whitefish is today very important to commercial fisheries. It is often smoked, like the lake sturgeon, the chub and the cisco, or lake herring; but I much prefer it broiled—the fine flavor of its firm, oily flesh is brought out best this way, especially when embellished with a simple lemon butter sauce. Strangely enough, although you can order broiled whitefish all over Michigan, you won't always taste it at its freshest and best. At one restaurant in Traverse City my order of whitefish had a suspicious brown cast and a dubious odor. When I told the waiter that I didn't think the fish was fresh, he replied blandly, "Of course not, it's frozen"—and this within sight of the waters in which it was caught!

For the many sport fishermen of Michigan and nearby states, the finest fish of Lake Michigan are coho and Chinook salmon. The Chinook and coho are much alike—although the Chinook grows to be bigger and its flesh is somewhat fattier—and both were originally salt-water fish of the West Coast. Now thoroughly at home in their fresh-water habitat, they are eagerly pursued by anglers not only for the sport but for the sumptuous eating they provide. The Lake Michigan coho's flesh is a paler pink than that of its West Coast cousin, and the flavor and texture are also more delicate. But it can be cooked in the same wonderfully varied ways as other salmon—poached, broiled, braised or, in a more complex dish I came across in Manistique, stuffed with a mixture of rice, scallions, parsley and lemon peel *(Recipe Index)*.

Fish and shellfish are, of course, only part of the Eastern Heartland's wildlife larder. It wasn't so long ago, no more than 60 or 70 years, that game was as common a sight in American markets and on American tables as beef or chicken is today. Our grandparents ate wild duck and doves, venison and quail as a matter of course.

Even now, despite suburban encroachments on the land, there are unspoiled areas in all these states that teem with deer, bear, waterfowl, upland birds such as pheasant, partridge, grouse and quail, and with small game—rabbits and hares, raccoons and woodchucks, squirrels and opossum. Many people in these areas regard game as part of the seasonal food cycle, like corn on the cob and pumpkin pie, and some even count on their marksmanship to keep the family food budget balanced.

In the green wilderness of Michigan's Upper Peninsula, hunting is a way of life. Since the days of the French fur trappers and the settlers who sold the pelts of fur-bearing animals but ate the meat, Michigan has been noted for the excellence of its game cookery. Even the unprepossessing muskrat, rechristened marsh rabbit in many recipes for obvious reasons, is considered good eating, as are the beaver, the raccoon, the rabbit, the opossum and the woodchuck; all these are prepared simply—usually braised or stewed but sometimes roasted. Venison, though, is the favorite game. It was the meat most often served in 19th Century logging camps and still retains its popularity throughout the state. Venison stew *(Recipe Index)* is a staple. Venison jerky is made with lean strips of tender meat

Continued on page 111

A Superior Way to Cook Lake Superior Trout

On the shore of Lake Superior near his summer home on Michigan's Upper Peninsula, Wilmer Savela beams over a catch of trout *(left)*. In the photographs on this page he demonstrates a useful technique for cooking the fish, learned from oldtime fishermen. Two long sticks, each whittled to a flat-edged point, are pushed from mouth to tail through trout that have been scored with a sharp knife to break the skin. The sticks are then thrust into the ground at an angle so that one side of each fish is exposed to the fire *(right)*. After half an hour or so before the fire, the sticks are switched so the other sides can cook. Just before the fish are done, Mr. Savela bastes them *(below)* with a strong salt-and-water solution. Then the trout are carefully eased off the sticks, the heads are removed and the fish served whole or in steaks with a squirt of lemon juice.

cut from the loin, round or flank, pickled in a strong brine, and then cold-smoked until completely dry, when it may be used in the same way as dried beef. Venison chops may be served with a spicy barbecue sauce (*Recipe Index*). Cubed venison round goes into Cornish pasties, and cooked chopped venison into the Christmas mincemeat. The Germans who live in the copper country of the Upper Peninsula make their traditional *Sauerbraten* with venison, and the Italians and Swedes grind it up and mix it with ground pork for sausage. The Italian sausage is pungent with garlic and spices, the Swedish has ground onions and potatoes mixed in. Everyone, of whatever origin, makes deerburgers from the tougher cuts, which are ground and mixed with suet to give the dry meat moisture.

Venison or any other meat from the kill—rabbit, squirrel, duck or woodchuck—is the basic ingredient in a famous stew tossed together by hunters in the Michigan woods; called booyaw or boolyaw (probably a corruption of the French *bouillon*), the dish is composed of cut-up game, salt pork to make up for the dryness of the meat, onions and chunks of carrot and potato. Moreover, booyaw is a highly personalized dish: you are expected, when making the stew, to add your own special touch to it with a dash of whatever is at hand for flavoring. There is no set formula—it is one of those things that test the mettle of the cook. When you are out in the woods with an appetite honed by fresh air, a poor booyaw will be tolerated; a good one can be gastronomic bliss.

Farther south, in the more settled areas of the Eastern Heartland, game is less plentiful, but there is still much to be savored, thanks to strict game laws that have protected and preserved many species. Even the wild turkey, once in danger of extinction, is now on the increase. This large, beautiful bronze native bird, which Benjamin Franklin thought should have been adopted as the nation's symbol rather than the marauding bald eagle (he described the latter as "a Bird of poor moral character, like those among men who live by sharpening and robbing"), can be shot in limited quantity in certain states—Indiana, Ohio, Pennsylvania and New York all have a short turkey-hunting season. The wild turkey, being extremely wary and fast-moving, is a challenge to the hunter, but if you do bag one, you will find that it is totally unlike the domesticated turkey of which it is the ancestor. While the flesh is not really gamy, due to the turkey's mild diet of nuts, berries, leaves and grasses, it is definitely wild. One of the best wild turkeys I ever tasted was roasted not in the oven but on a spit over a charcoal fire with liberal bastings of butter, a method that retains all the natural juices and flavor. I had it prepared this way at the home of friends in Pennsylvania, a state that still boasts a good supply and has two turkey-hunting seasons, one in November and one in May. The bird was served with creamy whipped potatoes, the dried corn of the region, cooked and well buttered, and thin, thin slices of huge ripe beefsteak tomatoes—a simple but wholly gratifying feast.

Certain native birds have not fared as well as the turkey. The passenger pigeon, slaughtered by the hundreds of thousands, is long since extinct, and the pinnated grouse, or prairie chicken, is now seldom found in the Eastern Heartland. You still find a fair to good amount of ruffed grouse, though, and plenty of the native bobwhite, a delicious little quail

Opposite: This tempting broiled stuffed coho salmon was caught in nearby Lake Michigan. The coho, a native of the Pacific Northwest, was introduced into the Great Lakes in 1966 and is a protected sport fish, barred to commercial fishermen. Most mature cohos weigh 6 to 12 pounds but some reach a hefty 30 pounds. The 8-pounder shown here is stuffed with herb-flavored rice (*Recipe Index*), nested in wedges of sweet and red peppers, and garnished with lemon and onion slices. It was eaten with stuffed squash, roasted corn, white wine and old-fashioned Michigan applesauce cake (*Recipe Index*).

that is at its best simply broiled, sautéed or roasted and served on toast that has been spread with the quail's own chopped sautéed giblets. It takes minimum cooking and should be lavishly basted with butter or, for roasting, wrapped with salt pork to prevent the delicate flesh from drying out; for like most upland game birds it has little natural fat. (Quail was the "hot bird" that went with a "cold bottle" of champagne in the Gay Nineties—a favorite of Chicago's expensive belles and their well-heeled beaux, which may explain why the ladies the French call *poules* were known there as quail.)

Two of the favorite upland game birds of the Eastern Heartland, pheasant and partridge, are not native species but exotic migrants. The gray, or Hungarian, partridge was first introduced in the 18th Century, while the ring-necked pheasant came here in the 1880s, when the American consul in Shanghai sent a shipment of Chinese pheasant to his farm in Oregon. Both pheasant and partridge, unlike migratory waterfowl, are easily domesticated and raised on game farms or preserves, which has led to their greater availability and wider acceptance. They like to feed on cultivated grain; this gives their flesh a milder flavor than that of waterfowl, whose diet consists mainly of aquatic plants and insects, nuts and tree seeds.

Pheasant often live surprisingly close to populated areas. I have seen them strutting across a lawn in the Hamptons on Long Island, breaking cover from a cornfield in Illinois and pecking about in a roadside peach orchard in the fruit belt of southwest Michigan. They are so gorgeous to look at, with their coppery, speckled plumage, long graceful tails and

Nearly half a million hunters stalk Michigan's white-tailed deer every fall, shooting up to 120,000 during the short season. Below, hunters prepare a feast at a lodge in Toivola, on the Upper Peninsula, where the heavy concentration of deer provides excellent hunting. While Chester Guidotti fries potatoes and onions, Philip Houle cooks venison steaks and chops.

iridescent green heads that I don't think I could ever bring myself to shoot one—though I have no scruples about tackling one at the table.

More than any other game bird, pheasant seems to lend itself to a great range of methods of preparation. I like it roasted with some kind of stuffing—chestnut, sage and onion, or apple (apples and pheasant might have been made for each other)—or just with a sour-cream sauce. It's also marvelous braised with sauerkraut, the way the Pennsylvania Dutch and other German groups prefer it *(Recipe Index)*. In Illinois I had a delicious dish of pioneer-style pheasant for which the bird was quartered, dredged in seasoned flour, browned in bacon fat and then simmered in the covered pan until tender; it was served with a sauce made from the thickened juices and heavy cream. And in a farmhouse near Vincennes, Indiana, I was served a roasted pheasant with a wonderfully nutty stuffing made of onion, celery and filberts and accompanied by a currant-jelly sauce *(Recipe Index)*. A really young and tender pheasant can even be sautéed like chicken. But no matter how young the pheasant, its meat is lean and can be ruined by being overcooked or by not being provided with the fat it lacks, a point to remember when you roast, broil or spit-roast the bird.

More challenging to the hunter's skill are the wild ducks that come winging in over the marshes and ponds in the path of their migratory flyways—the Atlantic Coast and the Mississippi Valley. Every fall when the season opens, thousands of Eastern Heartland hunters huddle against the morning cold in blinds and boats waiting for the blood-quickening call of mallard, teal and widgeon on the wing. I have never sat in one of those chilly blinds, but I have tasted the fruits of the hunters' patience, and very good eating it is. Wild duck is a far cry from the Long Island duckling and just as good in its own way. Leaner, with darker meat and a stronger, untamed taste, it requires quick cooking so the meat will not dry out. My favorite way is that advocated by James Beard, a consultant for this book, who roasts it just to the point where it is still bloody and really rare. At Jim's house once I had a mallard—shot by one of the students in his cooking class—roasted this way and finished off with a coat of crushed black peppercorns. The contrast between the hot peppery crisp outside and the red, rare meat was absolutely superb.

The delights of game are unending. I happen to be a devotee of the lowly rabbit, for instance; those who scorn it should try it done German style, cooked in beer or with cider vinegar and gingersnaps. And I would hate to overlook one small aspect of nature's bounty that has graced Michigan menus ever since French missionaries first discovered this native food. That is the frog, or, more precisely, the legs of the frog. Whether you classify this as fish or flesh, it certainly is wild. I have never eaten better frogs' legs than those I had at the London Chop House in Detroit, prepared roadhouse style, so called because of the way they used to be served in roadhouses, dipped in batter and deep-fried. The frogs' legs I am accustomed to in the East are big and fleshy, but these were tiny and crunchy and could be eaten in two or three bites, bones and all. Now that the Michigan bogs are no more, most of the frogs' legs have to be brought in from Wisconsin and Minnesota, but that's beside the point. They are as much a part of the culinary history of the state as pasties or cherry pie.

Three German short-hair pointers keep Marvin Maier company on his 640-acre pheasant preserve near South Bend, Indiana. Each spring Maier receives 10,000 ringneck chicks from an Iowa pheasant hatchery. Kept in pens at first to fatten on a ton of feed a day, the birds are released a month before the opening of the hunting season so they will become accustomed to living in the wild. The season opens on September 1, but the best hunting is in December when snow makes the birds more visible and they have become larger and wilier.

Four hunters pose with their morning's bag of pheasants in a field on the Maier preserve *(right)*. No game bird imported into the United States has bred as successfully as the Chinese ringneck, which has spread to 34 states in just 100 years. In most hunting regions only cocks can be taken, but on a licensed preserve like this hens may be shot as well. Although pheasants cannot fly very high or far, it takes a good shot to bring one down because of its fast, erratic flight; many are still around for the next season.

Feminine liberation has had no effect on this species: the cock pheasant is brilliantly feathered and the hen is drab.

To serve 4

9 tablespoons butter, plus
    6 tablespoons butter, softened
4 to 5 slices homemade-type white
    bread, trimmed of all crusts and
    cut into ¼-inch cubes (about
    2 cups)
½ cup finely chopped celery
1 cup finely chopped onions
½ cup filberts, pulverized in a
    blender or with a nut grinder
¼ teaspoon ground sage
1 teaspoon salt
Freshly ground black pepper
A 3- to 3½-pound oven-ready
    pheasant
2 tablespoons thin strips orange
    peel, each cut about ⅛ inch wide and
    1 inch long
1 tablespoon thin strips lemon peel,
    each cut about ⅛ inch wide and
    1 inch long
1¼ cups chicken stock, fresh or
    canned
2 tablespoons currant jelly
2 tablespoons port
1 tablespoon cornstarch

Roast Pheasant with Filbert Stuffing and Currant Sauce

Preheat the oven to 400°. To make the stuffing, melt 8 tablespoons of the butter over moderate heat in a heavy 8- to 10-inch skillet. When the foam begins to subside, add the bread cubes and stir until they are crisp and brown. With a slotted spoon, transfer the cubes to a deep bowl.

Add 1 tablespoon of butter to that remaining in the skillet and drop in the celery and ½ cup of the onions. Stirring frequently, cook over moderate heat for about 5 minutes, or until the vegetables are soft but not brown. With a rubber spatula, scrape the entire contents of the skillet over the bread cubes. Add the filberts, sage, salt and a few grindings of pepper, and toss together gently but thoroughly.

Wash the pheasant quickly under cold running water and pat it dry inside and out with paper towels. Fill the cavity loosely with the stuffing and close the opening by lacing it with small skewers and cord or sewing it with heavy white thread. Fasten the neck skin to the back of the pheasant with a skewer and truss the bird neatly. With a pastry brush, spread 4 tablespoons of the softened butter evenly over the surface of the bird.

Lay the bird on its side on a rack set in a shallow roasting pan. Roast the pheasant in the middle of the oven for 10 minutes. Turn it over, brush it with the remaining 2 tablespoons of softened butter, and roast it for 10 minutes longer. Then turn the bird breast side up and baste it with the fat that has accumulated in the pan. Continue roasting for 20 to 30 minutes, or until it is golden brown, basting the bird with its pan juices every 10 minutes. To test for doneness, pierce a thigh with the point of a small skewer or with a sharp knife; the juices that trickle out should be clear yellow. If they are still tinged with pink, roast the pheasant for about 5 minutes longer.

Meanwhile drop the strips of the orange and lemon peel into enough boiling water to immerse them completely and cook briskly, uncovered, for 5 minutes. Drain in a sieve and run cold water over the peel to set the color. Reserve the peel.

When the pheasant has roasted for its allotted time, transfer it to a heated platter. Remove the trussing string and drape the platter loosely with foil to keep the bird warm while you prepare the sauce.

With a large spoon, skim as much fat as possible from the surface of the liquid remaining in the roasting pan. Add 1 cup of the chicken stock, the remaining ½ cup of onions, the currant jelly and port. Bring to a boil over high heat, stirring constantly and scraping in the brown particles that cling to the bottom and sides of the pan. Reduce the heat to low and simmer uncovered for about 5 minutes.

Dissolve the cornstarch in the remaining ¼ cup of chicken stock and stir it into the simmering sauce. Cook, still stirring, until the sauce comes to a boil, thickens and clears. Strain the sauce through a fine sieve into a sauceboat or gravy bowl and stir in the reserved orange and lemon peel. Taste for seasoning.

Serve the pheasant at once, garnished, if you like, with additional slices of orange peel and accompanied by the sauce.

Roast pheasant is more than fair game when laden with filbert stuffing, moistened by currant-and-fruit-peel sauce and served with Brussels sprouts.

To serve 6

4 large firm ripe tomatoes, or
    substitute 4 cups chopped drained
    canned tomatoes
2 dozen large hard-shell clams,
    shucked and drained, and their
    liquor
3 tablespoons butter
1 cup finely chopped onions
¼ cup finely chopped carrots
¼ cup finely chopped celery
3 cups water
1 medium-sized bay leaf
½ teaspoon crumbled dried thyme
Freshly ground black pepper
3 medium-sized boiling potatoes,
    peeled and cut into ¼-inch dice
    (about 2 cups)

To serve 4

2 cups water
2 teaspoons salt
1 cup long-grain white rice, not the
    converted variety
24 dried apricots (about 1½ cups),
    quartered
Freshly ground black pepper
A 5- to 6-pound duck
2 cups chicken stock, fresh or
    canned
½ cup finely chopped onions
½ teaspoon finely chopped garlic
⅛ teaspoon crumbled dried thyme
2 tablespoons apricot preserves
2 tablespoons cornstarch combined
    with 2 tablespoons cold water

Manhattan Clam Chowder

If you are using fresh tomatoes, drop them into boiling water for 15 seconds, then peel off the skins with a small sharp knife. Cut out the stems and cut the tomatoes in half crosswise. Squeeze the halves to remove the juice and seeds, then coarsely chop the pulp. Canned tomatoes need only to be drained thoroughly and chopped.

Chop the clams fine and reserve them. Strain the clam liquor through a fine sieve lined with a double thickness of dampened cheesecloth; measure and save 3 cups of the liquor. (If there is less than 3 cups of liquor, add enough water to make that amount.)

In a heavy 3- to 4-quart saucepan, melt the butter over moderate heat. When the foam begins to subside, add the onions, carrots and celery and, stirring frequently, cook for about 5 minutes, or until the vegetables are soft but not brown. Add the chopped tomatoes, clam liquor, 3 cups of water, bay leaf, thyme and a few grindings of pepper, and bring to a boil over high heat. Reduce the heat to low, cover the pan partially and simmer for 45 minutes.

Stir in the potatoes and continue to simmer partially covered for about 12 minutes longer. Then add the chopped clams and cook the chowder for 2 to 3 minutes more. Pick out and discard the bay leaf.

Taste the chowder for seasoning and serve at once from a heated tureen or in individual soup plates.

Roast Duck with Apricot-Rice Stuffing

Preheat the oven to 425°. To prepare the stuffing, bring the 2 cups of water and 1 teaspoon of the salt to a boil over high heat in a small saucepan. Pour in the rice, stir once or twice, and reduce the heat to low. Cover the pan tightly and simmer for 10 minutes. Drain the rice in a sieve and transfer it to a bowl. Add the apricots and a liberal grinding of black pepper and mix well.

Wash the duck quickly under cold running water and pat it dry inside and out with paper towels. Rub the inside of the duck with the remaining teaspoon of salt and a few grindings of black pepper. For a crisper skin, prick the surface around the thighs, the back and the lower part of the breast with the tip of a sharp knife.

Fill the cavity of the duck loosely with the stuffing and close the opening by lacing it with small skewers and cord or sewing it with heavy white thread. Fasten the neck skin to the back of the duck with a skewer and truss the bird neatly.

Place the duck breast side up on a rack set in a large shallow pan and roast it in the middle of the oven for 20 minutes. Pour off the fat from the roasting pan or draw it off with a bulb baster. Then reduce the heat to 350° and roast for about 1 hour longer.

To test for doneness pierce the thigh of the bird deeply with the point of a small skewer or a sharp knife. The juice that trickles out should be a clear yellow; if it is still slightly tinged with pink, roast the duck for another 5 to 10 minutes. Transfer the bird to a heated serving platter and discard the string and skewers. Let the roast duck rest for about 10 minutes for easier carving.

Meanwhile, prepare the sauce in the following way: Pour off all but about 3 tablespoons of the fat remaining in the roasting pan and add the chicken stock, onions, garlic and thyme. Bring to a boil over high heat, stirring constantly and scraping in the brown particles that cling to the bottom and sides of the pan. Reduce the heat to low and simmer uncovered for about 5 minutes.

Add the apricot preserve and the cornstarch-water mixture and, still stirring, cook over low heat until the sauce comes to a boil and thickens lightly. Strain the sauce through a fine sieve into a sauceboat or gravy bowl, pressing down hard on the onions with the back of a spoon to extract all their juices before discarding the pulp. Taste for seasoning.

Serve the duck at once, accompanied by the sauce. If you like, you may garnish the duck with dried apricots that have been simmered in water to cover for 30 minutes, or until tender, and thoroughly drained.

Barbecued Stuffed Coho Salmon

First prepare the marinade in the following manner: Combine the wine, lemon juice, ½ cup of the oil, the onion, garlic, parsley sprigs, ginger, thyme, Tabasco, salt and pepper in a small enameled saucepan and, stirring occasionally, bring to a boil over high heat. Pour the marinade into an enameled casserole or roasting pan large enough to hold the salmon comfortably, and set it aside to cool to room temperature.

Wash the salmon inside and out under cold running water and pat it dry with paper towels. With a sharp knife, score both sides of the fish by making four or five evenly spaced diagonal slits about 4 inches long and ¼ inch deep. Place the salmon in the cooled marinade and turn it over to moisten it evenly.

Cover the pan tightly with foil or plastic wrap and marinate at room temperature for about 3 hours, or in the refrigerator for about 6 hours, turning the fish occasionally.

Light a layer of briquettes in a charcoal broiler and let them burn until a white ash appears on the surface, or preheat the broiler of your stove to its highest setting.

Transfer the salmon to paper towels and pat it completely dry with more paper towels. Strain the marinade through a fine sieve set over a bowl. To prepare the stuffing, combine the rice, scallions, chopped parsley and lemon strips in a small bowl. Pour in ¼ cup of the strained marinade and mix well. Set the remaining marinade aside.

Loosely fill the salmon with the stuffing, then close the opening with small skewers and kitchen cord. With a pastry brush, spread the remaining tablespoon of oil over the hot grill or the broiler rack. Place the salmon on top and brush it with a few spoonfuls of the reserved marinade. Broil 3 or 4 inches from the heat, basting the salmon frequently with the remaining marinade. The salmon should be broiled for about 15 minutes on each side, or until it is evenly and delicately browned and feels firm when prodded gently with a finger.

Serve the salmon at once from a heated platter, with the lemon slices arranged attractively in a row along the top of the fish. Garnish it further, if you like, with red and green pepper strips and onion rings.

To serve 6 to 8

1½ cups dry white wine
½ cup strained fresh lemon juice
½ cup plus 1 tablespoon vegetable oil
1 medium-sized onion, peeled and thinly sliced
3 medium-sized garlic cloves, crushed with the side of a cleaver or a large heavy knife
3 sprigs fresh parsley
1 teaspoon ground ginger
½ teaspoon crumbled dried thyme
¼ teaspoon Tabasco sauce
1 teaspoon salt
¼ teaspoon freshly ground black pepper
A 5- to 5½-pound coho or other salmon, cleaned and with head and tail removed
1 cup freshly cooked rice, made from ½ cup long-grain white rice, not the converted variety
¼ cup finely chopped scallions, including 2 inches of the green tops
¼ cup finely chopped fresh parsley
The peel of ½ lemon, cut into matchlike strips
1 lemon, cut crosswise into ¼-inch-thick rounds

½ pound butter, cut into ½-inch
    bits and softened
1 tablespoon finely chopped fresh
    parsley
1 teaspoon finely chopped garlic
1 teaspoon Worcestershire sauce
½ teaspoon crumbled dried
    oregano
½ teaspoon salt
¼ teaspoon freshly ground black
    pepper
Rock salt
3 dozen small hard-shell clams,
    shucked, with the deeper half
    shell of each reserved
¾ cup soft fresh crumbs made
    from homemade-type white
    bread, pulverized in a blender or
    finely shredded with a fork

John Clancy's Broiled Clams

Cream the butter by beating and mashing it against the sides of a bowl with the back of a spoon until it is light and fluffy. Beat in the parsley, garlic, Worcestershire, oregano, salt and pepper. With your hands, pat and shape the butter mixture into a cylinder 9 to 10 inches long and 1 inch in diameter. Wrap in wax paper and refrigerate the cylinder for at least 2 hours, or until it is firm.

Preheat the broiler to its highest setting. Spread the rock salt to a depth of about ½ inch in six individual shallow baking pans—each large enough to hold half a dozen clams comfortably. (Or spread a ½-inch layer of salt in the bottom of one or two shallow baking-serving dishes large enough to hold all the clams.) Arrange the pans on one or two large baking sheets and set them in the oven to heat the salt while you prepare the clams.

Scrub the reserved clam shells thoroughly under cold running water, then pat them dry and place a clam in each shell. With a small sharp knife, cut the cylinder of butter into ¼-inch-thick slices. Sprinkle each clam with 1 teaspoon of the bread crumbs and set a slice of seasoned butter on top. Then arrange the clams in one layer in the salt-lined pans.

Broil the clams about 4 inches from the heat for 3 minutes, or until the crumb topping is brown. Serve at once, directly from the baking dishes.

NOTE: The bed of salt is not indispensable to the success of this dish, but it will help keep the shells from tipping and, if heated beforehand, will keep the clams hot. You may, if you like, bake the clams in any shallow pan or pans large enough to hold the shells snugly in one layer, and serve them from a heated platter.

To serve 4 to 6

¼ pound salt pork, trimmed of all
    rind and cut into ¼-inch dice
2 pounds boneless venison,
    preferably loin, trimmed of all
    fat and cut into 2-inch cubes
½ cup flour
1 cup finely chopped onions
½ teaspoon finely chopped garlic
2 cups chicken stock, fresh or
    canned
1 medium-sized bay leaf, crumbled
½ teaspoon crumbled dried thyme
1 teaspoon salt
¼ teaspoon freshly ground black
    pepper
4 medium-sized boiling potatoes,
    peeled and quartered
2 medium-sized carrots, scraped and
    cut into 2-inch lengths
2 tablespoons distilled white
    vinegar

Venison Stew

In a heavy 4- to 5-quart casserole, fry the salt pork over moderate heat, stirring the dice about with a slotted spoon until they are crisp and brown and have rendered all their fat. Transfer them to paper towels to drain, and pour off all but about 4 tablespoons of the fat from the pan.

Roll the cubes of venison in the flour to coat them evenly, then shake off the excess flour. Over high heat brown the venison in the fat remaining in the casserole, 4 or 5 pieces at a time. Turn the venison cubes about occasionally and regulate the heat so that they color richly and evenly without burning. As they brown, transfer the cubes to a plate.

When all the venison has been browned, add the onions and garlic to the casserole. Stirring occasionally, cook for 5 minutes, or until they are soft and translucent but not brown. Pour in the stock and bring to a boil over high heat. Add the bay leaf, thyme, salt and pepper and return the venison to the casserole together with the liquid that has accumulated around it. Reduce the heat to low, cover tightly and simmer for 1 hour.

Drop the potatoes and carrots into the casserole and turn them with a spoon to moisten them evenly. Continue to simmer covered for 20 to 30 minutes longer, or until the vegetables are tender and the venison shows no resistance when pierced deeply with the point of a small sharp knife. Stir in the vinegar and taste for seasoning. Then sprinkle the reserved pork bits on top and serve at once, directly from the casserole.

Broiled Skewered Scallops

Light a layer of briquettes in a charcoal broiler and let them burn until a white ash begins to appear on the surface, or preheat your kitchen broiler to its highest setting.

Wash the scallops under cold running water, spread them on paper towels, and pat them completely dry with fresh towels. Combine the lemon juice, salt and pepper in a small bowl and mix well. Drop in the scallops and turn them about with a spoon to coat them evenly.

Thread the scallops and bacon onto four long skewers, looping the bacon slices up and down to weave them over and under alternate scallops. Push the scallops compactly together. With a pastry brush, thoroughly coat the scallops with a few spoonfuls of the melted butter.

Broil about 4 inches from the heat, turning the skewers from time to time and basting the scallops frequently with the remaining melted butter. They should broil for about 4 to 5 minutes. The scallops are done when they are opaque and firm to the touch, and the bacon is brown.

With the side of a knife, slide the scallops and bacon off the skewers onto a heated platter or individual plates. Serve at once, accompanied by the lemon quarters.

To serve 4

1 pound (1 pint) fresh or defrosted frozen bay scallops
2 tablespoons strained fresh lemon juice
1 teaspoon salt
¼ teaspoon freshly ground black pepper
8 slices lean bacon
8 tablespoons butter, melted and cooled
1 lemon, cut lengthwise into quarters

Oysters Casino

Preheat the broiler to its highest setting. Spread the rock salt to a depth of about ½ inch in 6 individual shallow baking pans—each large enough to hold half a dozen oysters comfortably. (Or spread a ½-inch layer of salt in the bottom of one or two shallow baking-serving dishes that are large enough to hold all of the oysters.) Arrange the pans on one or two large baking sheets and set them in the oven to heat the salt while you prepare the oysters.

In a heavy 6- to 8-inch skillet, fry the bacon over moderate heat until it is crisp and brown and has rendered all its fat. With a slotted spoon, transfer the bacon to paper towels to drain. Crumble the bacon and set aside.

Add the shallots, celery and green pepper to the fat remaining in the skillet and, stirring frequently, cook for about 5 minutes, or until the vegetables are soft but not brown. Drain the vegetables in a small sieve and drop them into a bowl. Add the reserved bacon, the lemon juice, Worcestershire and Tabasco, and toss together gently but thoroughly.

Scrub the oyster shells thoroughly under cold running water, then pat them dry. Arrange them in a single layer in the salt-lined pans and place an oyster in each shell.

Spoon the vegetable-and-bacon mixture on top of the oysters, dividing it evenly among them.

Broil about 3 inches from the heat for 4 to 5 minutes, or until the oysters plump up and their edges begin to curl slightly. Serve at once, directly from the baking dishes, and garnish the oysters with lemon wedges.

NOTE: While the bed of salt helps to keep the shells from tipping and, if heated beforehand, will keep the oysters hot, it is not indispensable to the success of this dish. You may, if you like, bake the oysters in any shallow baking pan or pans large enough to hold the shells snugly in one layer, and serve them from a heated platter.

To serve 4

Rock salt
2 slices lean bacon
½ cup finely chopped shallots
¼ cup finely chopped celery
2 tablespoons finely chopped green pepper
2 teaspoons strained fresh lemon juice
1 teaspoon Worcestershire sauce
3 drops Tabasco sauce
2 dozen large oysters, shucked, and the deeper half shell of each reserved
1 lemon, cut lengthwise into quarters

V

Orchards and Farm Lands

The seasons I like best in America are spring, when the rush of blossoms and new leaves hints at the prodigality of the land, and fall, when the countryside is ablaze with the fulfilled promise of the year's harvests. In late October I love to drive in the soft golden sunlight through New York's Hudson River Valley, where gnarled apple trees crosshatch the hills and roadside stands are piled with their fruitful offerings—Baldwin, Cortland, Northern Spy, Monroe, Rome Beauty, Winesap, McIntosh, Jonathan and Delicious. If I have a favorite eating apple, it is the Golden Delicious with its yellow skin and crisp sweet flesh, which lives up to its name when eaten either alone or with a piece of cheese. For cooking, I find that the Rome Beauty and Greening are best for the many baked-apple dishes in which American country cooking abounds—pies, dumplings, cobblers, pandowdy.

Altogether, the Eastern Heartland grows almost half the country's apple crop. This rich harvest—more than a million tons a year—is the legacy of the colonists and pioneer homesteaders who planted the region's first apple trees—and of that strange, half-legendary folk hero, Johnny Appleseed. As every schoolchild learns, this gentle eccentric, born John Chapman in Massachusetts in 1774, wandered thousands of miles, often barefoot, from his home state to Indiana, carrying his kitchen (an inverted saucepan) on his head and preaching among other things that "fruit is next to religion."

Chapman's mission in life was growing and selling apple trees. Just before 1800 he arrived in western Pennsylvania with a bag of apple seeds.

Young Robert Smith uses a 19th Century cast-iron nutcracker to get his fill of some of the nuts harvested from a nut orchard in Fremont, Ohio. Nuts are one of the most unusual of the many cultivated tree crops that make the Eastern Heartland famous for its orchards.

For the next 40 years he traveled the frontier, planting seeds, tending the saplings and selling them throughout the newly settled states of Ohio and Indiana. No fruit was more important to pioneer life than the apple. It was an invaluable addition to the limited diet of hog and hominy, for it could be used in so many ways—eaten fresh, or cooked, dried and preserved, or fermented for cider, applejack and vinegar. Once brought from seed to sapling, apple trees needed little attention and could be counted on to bear fruit after five years or so.

Johnny Appleseed died near Fort Wayne, Indiana, in 1845, but not long ago I saw piles of his favorite apple, the Rambo, in the Indianapolis Farmers' Market, and I am sure that here and there in fields across Pennsylvania, Ohio and Indiana, trees are still growing that are directly descended from his seeds.

Apples are but one of the prime orchard crops of the Eastern Heartland. New Jersey prides itself on its peaches and Michigan calls itself the cherry capital of the world—with good reason, for more cherries are grown there than in any other state. Almost all of Michigan's cherry trees grow within a few miles of Lake Michigan. The beneficent lake waters temper the icy winter cold and, in spring, keep the air cool long enough to retard the budding of the trees until the danger of frost is past.

The densest concentration of cherry trees in the world, 22,600 to every square mile, is found on the lake's eastern shore, in the area around Traverse City—a fact that no one around Traverse City lets a visitor forget during the seven-day National Cherry Festival, held in July at the height of the tourist season. Between parades and competitions, cherries may be served in every possible guise: in puddings and pies, crumbly sweet shortcake, rolls and breads, dumplings and cream puffs, even a light and refreshing cherry fruit cup made with port and flavored with cinnamon and orange peel. I must say, though, that more memorable for me was the beautiful sight of the orchards in full bloom in May—an exquisite curtain of white petals with the blue waters of the lake glinting through like the sky through a gauzy cloud.

Orchards are only one clue to the Eastern Heartland's incredible fertility. The broad farms of Indiana and Illinois yield almost a quarter of the country's corn and a fifth of its pork. New York is outranked only by Wisconsin as a dairy producer. New Jersey, the most densely populated state in the country, exceeds all others in gross income per farm acre. Since most roads seem to lead through its smoggy industrial heart, this may be hard to believe, yet tucked away all over New Jersey, and especially in its southern half, are dairy and poultry farms and the truck farms that grow produce for the megalopolis that surrounds and is gradually but inexorably encroaching on them.

It is a curious and saddening paradox that despite all this productiveness, fresh local foods are in fact disappearing from retail markets and restaurant menus throughout the Eastern Heartland. Fewer and fewer of New Jersey's vegetables go directly to the markets of the nearby cities, more and more to canning and frozen-food factories. Most of Michigan's cherries vanish into the maw of processing plants, its grapes into vats of juice. Much of the milk from the great dairy herds of New

York, Pennsylvania and Ohio is sold to processors who turn it into bland cheese or low-calorie skimmed-milk products. In its place, you are quite likely to be given an ersatz substitute. (I well remember encountering, in a motel in the heart of Pennsylvania's dairy country, a packet of so-called nondairy creamer on the breakfast table!)

I would be the first to admit that mass-production methods are the only practicable way to meet the mass demands of America, and there are many all-American processed foods that I would not fault. For example, whenever anyone asserts that this country has never produced a fine cheese of its own I retort, "Liederkranz." When I first wandered into a New York supermarket, my nose led me straight to this ripe, soft, strongly odorous cheese nested in its chaste cardboard box. Liederkranz is a great and gutsy cheese and I would far rather have it than those overrefrigerated, underripe imported Bries and Camemberts you find in stores today at extortionate prices. A cheese with the forthright democratic qualities of America itself, Liederkranz tastes as good with red wine as with beer and it costs far less than most imported cheeses.

It is an Ohio product that has been made in the town of Van Wert in the western part of the state ever since 1926, when the Monroe Cheese Company moved there from Monroe, New York, in search of a dependable supply of rich, fresh milk. Three years later, the business was taken over by the Borden Company, which is now the sole manufacturer and distributor of the cheese.

As with so many good things in the world of food, the origin of Liederkranz was purely serendipitous. In the 1880s a young Swiss cheese maker named Emil Frey, who worked for the Monroe Cheese Company, spent two years trying to duplicate for New York City's German delicatessens an imported cheese called Bismarck Schlosskaese, which was too delicate to travel well. He never succeeded, but stumbled instead on a golden-crusted, pungent, spreadable cheese that he sent to a delicatessen owner, Adolph Tode, to try out on his fellow members of the Liederkranz Singing Society in Manhattan. They tasted, they approved and Tode dispatched a telegram: "It's better than Bismarck. Send more." And so Liederkranz was christened.

Although Liederkranz is mass produced, it is carefully prepared and ripened under special temperature and humidity control. The making of good cheese can never be a hurried, scamped procedure. Patience, knowledge and dedication are as important as the quality of the milk or the temperature of the curing room. All great soft ripened cheeses, of which Liederkranz is one, are as chancy and idiosyncratic as wine, for their texture and flavor depend on minute organisms or bacteria that transform mild milk into powerful cheese. Some of America's best cheeses are produced by long-established family businesses like the Kolb-Lena Cheese Company of Lena, Illinois, which counts among its products a sharp Cheddar, a blue and a Swiss, as well as two soft ripened cheeses that are considered by many food authorities to be on a par with the Brie and Camembert of France.

Commercially or individually, the pursuit of excellence in food is an experience that is more often talked about than undertaken. It is, for many

Continued on page 129

125

The Old-fashioned Harvest of a Gentleman Nut Farmer

The Oaks Tree Farm, owned by Harvey Oaks of Fremont, Ohio, is something of an arboreal museum. It contains 150 kinds of shade and ornamental trees, along with most of the nut-bearing varieties cultivated by the pioneers who settled Ohio late in the 18th Century. A custom jeweler by profession, Oaks bought the 12-acre farm as a hobby in 1965, and since then has acquired an awesome amount of tree-and-nut lore. He treats his orchards with tender care, adding new trees to the grove by grafting such varieties as English walnut onto black walnut rootstock. The payoff for his labors is gastronomic rather than financial. Though he sells some of each autumn's 100-bushel harvest to local markets, Oaks's chief pleasure is in regaling his family and neighbors with the raw materials for chestnut dressing, pecan pies, pickled walnuts and after-dinner splurges of cracking and munching.

A ripened chestnut is ready to fall from its prickly bur.

A hickory sheds its husk when ripe.

At right, neighborhood children help gather the farm's 500-pound chestnut crop. Of the 16 varieties of nuts grown by Oaks, eight are displayed in the foreground and identified by number below.
1 Hickory
2 Black walnut
3 English walnut
4 Butternut
5 Almond
6 Filbert
7 Heartnut
8 Chestnut

Black walnuts ripen in rough green husks, which turn black after the nut falls.

126

people, just too much trouble. Happily, there are others who still care enough about good food to invest time and energy and loving care in producing and preparing it, and thanks to them my memory summons up many never-to-be-forgotten tastes and culinary delights encountered in the region of this book.

It is simple food that I recall most vividly, for simple food can be sublime. The plainer and more artless the dish, the more skill and time are required to make it consummately good. There was the pot of old-fashioned sunshine strawberry jam my friend, cookbook author Elaine Ross of Hartsdale, New York, gave me one Christmas, the product of a blazing hot summer turned to good account. I am surprised at how few people seem to know about the sunshine jams, which are based on one of the oldest pioneer tricks—letting nature do the cooking. In one old recipe you are instructed to put the cleaned berries on a smooth, sun-warmed stone with a surface that will hold rain water—or lacking such a stone, a shiny skillet. You crush a few of the berries and, as the sun's heat extracts the juice, sprinkle them with sugar or honey, adding more berries as each layer juices up.

Elaine's method is more up to date and reliable. After briefly boiling three quarts of strawberries with six pounds of sugar and the juice of a lemon, she skims the mixture, pours the berries and juices into shallow pans in a single layer, and covers each pan with a pane of glass propped up at one corner to let air circulate. Then she leaves them out in the sun for three days, stirring twice a day, until the liquid thickens. (If you don't get three consecutive days of strong sun, she says, you have to leave them out longer.)

It is amazing what a difference the sun-cooking makes. Sunshine strawberry jam is like no other, for the strawberries remain whole, suspended in their thick red syrup, and the flavor is delicate and hauntingly sweet, the very essence of the berry. It is even better, I have found, if you can make it with tiny wild strawberries.

It often seems that wild fruits and berries, with their intense, pure flavor, survive cooking in a way that the large, bland, cultivated types cannot. Wild blueberries make a better pie than the plump big ones, and while I love to eat the luscious cultivated Japanese persimmon—large and orange with soft jellylike pulp that tastes as exotic as a mango or guava—I would never dream of cooking it. The wild American persimmon is completely different. Bite into one in midsummer and its astringency will pucker your mouth like alum, but by late fall the autumn sun and nippy nights will have tempered it to a honeyed sweetness. Indiana's persimmon pudding, a country dessert, can be cooked for hours without losing one whit of the fruit's special flavor, which indeed seems to become even more concentrated.

I had been tantalized for years, hearing about this pudding *(Recipe Index)*, but never had a chance to taste it until one September when I spent a few days on Carl Betz's farm in Martinsville, about 30 miles from Indianapolis. Friends in Indianapolis had been rather vague about how persimmon pudding is made. There are many versions, it seems, some baked, some steamed, although the basic ingredients are eggs, sug-

Opposite: The proof of the nuts is in the nibbling, and a little embellishment turns nuts into a super nibble. At far left are spiced mixed nuts—almonds, black walnuts and filberts that have been dipped in a sugar-and-spice paste and baked to a crisp. The ladle holds crunchy salted oven-toasted pecans. The mixed-nut brittle below the glass of cider is chock-full of filberts, almonds and black walnuts. The basket at the bottom brims with sherried walnuts—walnut halves enveloped in a sherry-and-spice syrup. All are in the Recipe Index.

129

A postage stamp issued in 1966 commemorates the lifework of John Chapman, better known as Johnny Appleseed, the gentle eccentric who left a trail of orchards through Ohio and Indiana. Carrying little more than a spade and a bag of apple seeds, Chapman began around 1800, at the age of 27, to plant and prune apple trees throughout the Ohio Valley. For the rest of his life Johnny traveled alone, and denied himself the companionship of a wife— but in recompense for his celibacy on earth he fully expected to have two wives in heaven.

ar, flour, milk, persimmon pulp, baking soda and butter. According to how you make it, or how long you bake it, the pudding can be moist or dry, cakelike or chewy, gelatinous or grainy, and it can range in color from purplish brown to deep brown. The longer the pudding bakes, the better it keeps. In the old days it was baked in a slow oven in a crock and then sealed, but now most people freeze it if they want to keep it from one year to the next.

Carl Betz's sister-in-law, Betty BreedLove, is a dab hand with persimmon pudding. The recipe was given to her by her mother-in-law (who got it from *her* mother) but Betty has her own way of making it.

"I use an old beat-up enamel colander and I rub the persimmons through with my hands to get the pulp because I found it didn't work with a spoon," she told me. "Then I mix it all up with a wooden spoon in my great big old bread bowl I've had for years. It's cracked and the outside is taped, but there are some things you just love to cook in; you get so you thoroughly enjoy them and you can't do it in anything else." She never uses any aluminum container, which would discolor the pulp, until other ingredients are mixed in; then the batter is poured into a big shallow aluminum pan, for at this point it will not discolor. The pudding is baked for three hours, stirred every 15 minutes for the first two hours, until it starts to reduce and thicken and take on a waxy look.

I had not expected to see persimmon pudding made, because it seemed too early in the autumn for the fruit to be ripe, but after breakfast Carl and I drove over the roads that wind through his 165-acre farm to the part of the woods where the persimmon trees grow. There, miraculously, the grass was covered with ripe, squashy little persimmons, even though there had been no frost, no cold nights.

Slipping down the muddy hillside, we filled brown-paper sacks and plastic bags with a great haul—a good four quarts. Since only the soft, broken fruits are good for pulp (the firm type won't do), my hands were soon coated with a sweet stickiness. Back home, the persimmons had to be picked over—washing would have disintegrated them, they were so ripe—and then rubbed through the colander by hand until we had accumulated exactly three cups of pulp. The rest were put in plastic bags and frozen for future use.

Dinner was going to be quite a production, so Carl and I went out for lunch, driving from Martinsville in Morgan County to Nashville in neighboring Brown County, a trip that totally revised my mental picture of Indiana as a flat plains state with cornfields stretching to the horizon. This part of Indiana, south of Indianapolis, is hilly and heavily forested with hardwood trees, maples and sycamores. Little towns ride the ridges of the hills, and tucked back in the woods are simple rustic houses.

After passing through a town named Bean Blossom we came to Nashville, an artists' colony full of gift shops and antique shops in wonderful old gingerbready Victorian houses. We lunched at the Nashville House, a combination restaurant and country store where you can buy all kinds of local products—sassafras bark for tea, hickory-nut cookies and candies, sorghum syrup and fudge, sugar-cured hickory-smoked hams and smoked pork sausage.

The Nashville House is famous for its fried biscuits *(Recipe Index)*, another Indiana specialty. These are made from a yeast dough that has risen only once, and which is cut out in rounds like biscuits and dropped into deep hot fat. The biscuits puff up into roly-poly spheres, turning brown and rolling themselves over. They are brought to the table piping hot in a basket, and you split them and eat them with quantities of butter and apple butter. The outside is crispy brown, the inside light and delicate, and you just can't stop eating them.

I could have lunched on these fried biscuits alone, but I can never resist good country ham, so I ordered the Hoosier ham steak with red gravy, cottage-fried potatoes and bread-and-butter pickles, while Carl had the smoked pork ring sausage, which was solidly meaty and a little like a Polish *kielbasa* in flavor. For dessert we had hickory-nut pie, made like pecan pie, from locally gathered wild nuts.

When we got back to the farm after lunch, we found that Betty's sister and brother-in-law, Dorothy and Lewis Kelly, had arrived from Chicago to stay the weekend, and the clock warned us that it was high time to start work on dinner.

Carl Betz is more gourmet than country cook. He retired from business some years ago to his farm, where he raises beef cattle and every year taps his sugar maples for syrup. He is a member of the Chaine des Rôtisseurs (an international organization of professional chefs and skilled amateur chefs originally devoted to the art of roasting) and has one of the finest wine cellars I have ever seen. Good cooking is his main interest and, knowing that I was more interested in Indiana recipes than in classic French cuisine, he had devised a special menu. Betty would make the persimmon pudding while he prepared batter-fried chicken *(Recipe Index)*, fried biscuits and apple Jonathan *(Recipe Index)*.

In the Indianapolis Farmers' Market the day before, I had seen a basket of beautiful huge orange tomatoes for $1.49 and, city dweller that I am, could not resist the bargain. The orange and yellow tomatoes have a much sweeter, rounder flavor than the more acid red type you get along the East Coast, and when they are ripe their toughish skins peel off easily, without having to be dipped into boiling water first. Peeled, sliced and dressed with oil, vinegar, salt, pepper and chopped fresh herbs, they make one of the finest, simplest salads I know, and this was to be my contribution to dinner.

By the time the meal was ready, all those tempting smells drifting out from the kitchen had made everyone ravenous. Betty BreedLove, her daughter Betsy-Jane, the Kellys, Carl and I ate at a big table on a screened porch overlooking a valley thicketed with trees. On the sloping hillside, the dogwood was just beginning to turn rust red.

First we polished off two or three batches of hot fried biscuits, spreading them with apple butter and Carl's own maple syrup. Then came the batter-fried chicken, with a crispy, golden crust that did not crumble away from the chicken as it so often does, but adhered properly to the still-moist meat inside. Our two desserts tasted as good as they smelled. The apple Jonathan was a rich cake made of fresh apple slices drenched in maple syrup, covered with batter and baked; it was served with heavy

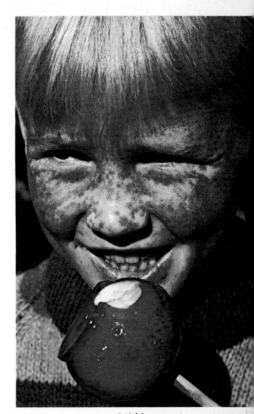

Happiness, as every child knows, is a crunchy candied apple, a treat that can easily be prepared at home:

CANDIED APPLES
Remove the stems of 8 firm ripe apples and, from the top, spear the core of each apple with a candy-apple or frozen-dessert stick or a small wooden skewer. Combine 4 cups of sugar, ½ cup of light corn syrup and 1½ cups of water in a small saucepan and bring to a boil over high heat, stirring until the sugar dissolves. Cook briskly, uncovered, until the syrup reaches a temperature of 285° on a candy thermometer or until a drop spooned into ice water separates into firm threads. Remove from the heat and stir in ¼ teaspoon of red food coloring. Then twirl the apples in the hot syrup, one at a time, and stand them on wax paper to cool.

cream. The persimmon pudding, cooled to room temperature and served with whipped cream on top, was dark, dense and sweet, more like a candy than a pudding.

As we ate, we talked about food—what else?—and I welcomed the opportunity to learn about some of the specialties that Carl and the Kellys agreed are basic to the country cooking of Indiana and Illinois. As both states are prime producers of corn and hogs, those mainstays of the pioneer kitchen are still very much in evidence, though there have been some innovations. Barbecued pork has become popular, and for special parties and festivals a whole pig will be roasted. Mostly, though, the regional favorites are roasts of pork, pork chops, ham and sausage—what they call in Indiana "whole-hog" sausage, made not from the fatty cuts but from the lean loin and shoulder. There is even a pork cake *(Recipe Index)*, customarily made at Christmas, a moist kind of spice cake in which sausage meat or finely chopped salt pork is mixed with brown sugar, molasses, flour, soda, raisins, citron and spices.

In the fall, pork is teamed with apples: for instance, spicy Indiana farm sausage patties *(Recipe Index)* may be served with pancakes and fried apple slices for breakfast, baked pork chops topped with sliced apples for dinner. Abe Lincoln, whose favorite breakfasts were fried apples with salt pork, and ham with cream gravy and biscuits, would find little difference in Illinois eating today.

Seasonal produce also inspires other local recipes, like pumpkin bread *(Recipe Index)*, spicy as gingerbread; stuffed mangoes (not the Caribbean fruit, but the old-fashioned word for bell peppers); green-tomato pie, and corncob jelly, a country specialty in which red corncobs are boiled in water with sugar, after which the delicately flavored liquid is thickened with pectin.

Meals in the hard-working farm districts of Indiana and Illinois have to be hearty. This is the meat-and-potatoes belt where calories don't count. When church groups give "pitch-in" suppers, long trestle tables are set up, outdoors under the trees in summer, in the church basement in winter, and covered with checkered cloths. Everyone brings a dish or two and loads the tables with pots of bean soup or pork and beans, Swiss steak with brown gravy and mashed potatoes, stewed chicken and dumplings, and perhaps a stuffed fresh ham *(Recipe Index)*. Or there may be roast chicken with sage stuffing, scalloped potatoes and fried pork chops with pan gravy *(Recipe Index)*. A rather more frivolous type of social evening is the basket supper or basket social, where an element of uncertainty adds a piquant overtone to the food. Each woman prepares a basket of good things, and these baskets are then auctioned off to the men. The bidders have no idea what is inside until they get their purchase—and each buyer must share the contents of his basket with the person who brought it. Chances are that whatever else is in it there will be some kind of pie and home-baked bread.

Another favorite summer feast popular throughout Illinois and Indiana is the corn roast. Carl Betz told me of a special way of roasting corn that he prefers to the usual method of putting the ears directly into the fire or ashes. He soaks the fresh roasting ears, still in their husks, in water

Opposite: In a Michigan orchard a fresh-from-the-oven apple pie, made with chunk-cut apples and no bottom crust, rests in the shade of the tree that bore its fruit. Orchards like this one make up a richly productive fruit belt that runs some 215 miles along Lake Michigan, roughly from Benton Harbor to Traverse City. In one recent year, Michigan sent nearly 600 million pounds of apples to market.

and then stacks them at the back of his covered barbecue grill to cook along with the meat.

In Carl's part of Indiana, he told me, there is always plenty of local corn, a profusion of tomatoes and a few other common vegetables such as beets, carrots and peppers. But the old-fashioned truck gardens, with greenhouses that produced a wider variety of vegetables and herbs, have gradually gone as the land has been swallowed up by housing. "A few friends and I formed a gourmet group a while ago," Carl said, "and we meet twice a year for specially planned dinners. I'd love to be able to serve really fine young vegetables like those you find in France, but the only way I could do it would be to grow them myself."

After all, why not? His words recalled to me one of the most delightful discoveries I made in all my Eastern Heartland travels. Just a year before, I had stopped overnight at the Perry Davis Hotel in Petoskey, Michigan, not far from Traverse City. On the table at dinner was a platter of raw vegetables—not the usual celery and carrot sticks one is presented with in most eating places, but a selection of the kind of tiny, perfect vegetables usually to be found only in France and Belgium where they are known as *primeurs* because they are picked in their infancy.

Naturally I had to find out and see for myself just where these miniature marvels were grown, so next morning I drove out to Bluff Gardens in nearby Harbor Springs, to the farm from which they came. There at a roadside stand were little bunches and piles arranged like a glowing still life—sunbursts of carrots with leafy tops, wine-dark clusters of baby beets, heaps of purple eggplant no more than three inches long, pale-green pattypan squash the size of silver dollars, diminutive peppers in the most gorgeous colors of chocolate brown and creamy yellow, and tight, brilliant green little heads of lettuce.

I learned that the owners of the farm, Mr. and Mrs. Leonard Carpenter, had started by peddling their produce via horse and buggy to local residents and hotels and in 1951 first began to pick their vegetables in the *primeur* stage. As the demand grew, they abandoned the horse and buggy for a roadside stand and increased their acreage. They now have about 60 acres planted with carrots, peppers, potatoes, eggplant, zucchini, beets, string beans, Brussels sprouts, snow peas, pattypan squash, lemon cucumbers, cherry tomatoes, corn and lettuce. Only the cherry tomatoes, the corn and one type of lettuce, the Tom Thumb, are true miniature varieties. The rest of the vegetables are planted every two weeks and picked when the carrots, beans and zucchini are no longer than a finger, the potatoes, beets and Brussels sprouts merely pebble-sized.

The Carpenters and their helpers pick the vegetables by hand in the early morning and take them from the fields to racks where they are sorted, washed twice and bunched for selling. The vegetables on sale when I was there were not inexpensive—a tiny ear of corn was 10 cents, the carrots were 65 cents a bunch, the potatoes 95 cents a pint and the baby beans $1.10 a pound—and the prices may have risen by now. But who would put a price on such excellence? Anything so rare, so beautiful, so lovingly raised is worth every penny you pay for it. It represents a concern for quality that is the very soul of good food, anywhere.

Corn Plus Pigs
Equals Big Business

In Illinois and Indiana, prosperous years begin with a bumper corn crop, and the commercial hog raisers of these states have a practical rule of thumb to explain why: to put one pound of pork into a butcher's window, you must first put four pounds of corn into a pig. On their 48 million acres of rich, flat farm land, using highly mechanized procedures, the farmers of the two states raise one quarter of the nation's corn and nearly one fifth of its pigs. Because pigs are big business, Illinois and Indiana corn growers plan for pigs rather than people. They usually keep half of their huge crop (upward of one billion bushels in a normal year) as fodder for their own animals, and most of the rest is sold to commercial livestock feeders. Only 8 per cent of the corn is consumed by human beings—and most of that in the form of oils, syrups, starches, breakfast cereals and liquor. In the end, less than 1 per cent of the huge crop reaches people as kernels in the can or corn on the cob.

A sow and her piglets root for insects in an Indiana field. The main business of pig feeding, however, is done under much more controlled conditions, as pig farmers work to remodel the animal to provide more high-protein meat and less high-calorie fat for diet-conscious American consumers. Many hogs feed upon scientifically blended foods, and in one experiment hogs have to get up on their haunches to eat at an elevated trough. The exercise this involves has increased the weight of the hogs' hams by as much as 5 per cent.

135

Lush cornfields like this make Illinois one of the two (with Iowa) biggest contributors to America's most valuable cash crop.

At the Covered Bridge Festival, a truck farmer shows dried fruits, flowers, vegetables and a collection of huge dipper gourds.

A young cook presents a favorite old dessert: fried apple pies.

Every October the people of Parke County, Indiana, hold a 10-day fair, the Covered Bridge Festival, which celebrates and briefly re-creates the rural life of 19th Century America. In the colorful stalls of the 1970 fair, women in period costume displayed time-tried ways of stewing chickens, barbecuing beef, frying "riz" crullers and baking pastry. Not to be outdone, the Rosedale branch of the American Legion grilled halved broilers, 200 at a time, and Boy Scouts cranked out wild-persimmon ice cream by the freezerful. No one left the festival hungry, but many fairgoers paused at the booth of Mrs. Jennie Paddock *(right),* to pick up a jar or two of an Indiana specialty, corncob jelly, to take home and spread on slices of their own home-baked bread.

138

To make about 16 muffins

6 tablespoons butter, softened
2 cups unsifted flour
4 teaspoons double-acting baking
    powder
¼ teaspoon baking soda
½ teaspoon ground mace
½ teaspoon salt
¼ cup sugar
2 eggs
1 cup sour cream
3 medium-sized firm ripe cooking
    apples, 2 apples peeled, cored
    and finely chopped (about 1 cup)
    and 1 apple cored and cut
    lengthwise into ⅛-inch-thick
    slices

To serve 10 to 12

9 tablespoons butter, softened, plus
    8 tablespoons butter, chilled and
    cut into ¼-inch bits
2 tablespoons plus 3¼ cups
    unsifted flour
2 cups sugar
1 teaspoon ground cinnamon
3 cups firm ripe blueberries
1 tablespoon double-acting baking
    powder
½ teaspoon ground nutmeg
¼ teaspoon ground cloves
1 teaspoon salt
3 eggs
¾ cup milk
2 cups heavy cream

Apple Muffins

Preheat the oven to 425°. With a pastry brush, spread 2 tablespoons of softened butter evenly inside 16 muffin cups (each cup should be about 2½ inches across at the top). Combine the flour, baking powder, baking soda, mace and salt, and sift them together into a bowl. Set aside.

In a deep bowl, cream the remaining 4 tablespoons of butter and the sugar, beating and mashing them against the sides of the bowl with the back of a large spoon until the mixture is light and fluffy. Beat in the eggs, one at a time. Then add about 1 cup of the flour mixture and, when it is well incorporated, beat in ½ cup of the sour cream. Repeat, beating in the remaining flour and then the rest of the cream and stir until the batter is smooth. Stir in the chopped apples and spoon the batter into the muffin cups, filling each cup about halfway to the top. Insert a slice of apple, peel side up, partway into the top of each muffin.

Bake in the middle of the oven for 15 to 20 minutes, or until the muffins are brown and a cake tester or toothpick inserted in the centers comes out clean. Turn the muffins out of the tins and serve at once.

Blueberry Crumb Cake

Preheat the oven to 375°. With a pastry brush, spread 1 tablespoon of softened butter over the bottom and sides of a 13-by-9-by-3-inch baking dish. Add 2 tablespoons of the flour and tip the dish to spread it evenly. Invert the dish and rap the bottom sharply to remove excess flour.

Prepare the crumb topping by combining the 8 tablespoons of butter bits, ¾ cup of the flour, 1 cup of the sugar and the cinnamon in a deep bowl. Working quickly, rub the flour and fat together with your fingertips until the mixture resembles flakes of coarse meal. Set aside.

Wash the blueberries in a colander under cold running water. Remove the stems and discard any berries that are badly bruised. Spread the berries on paper towels and pat them completely dry with fresh towels.

Combine the remaining 2½ cups of flour, the baking powder, nutmeg, cloves and salt, and sift them together into a bowl.

In a deep bowl, cream the remaining 8 tablespoons of softened butter and 1 cup of sugar by beating and mashing them against the sides of the bowl with the back of a spoon until they are light and fluffy. Beat in the eggs, one at a time. Add about 1 cup of the sifted flour mixture and, when it is well incorporated, stir in ¼ cup of the milk. Repeat twice more, alternating 1 cup of the flour with ¼ cup of milk and beating well after each addition. Gently stir in the blueberries.

Pour the blueberry batter into the buttered-and-floured baking dish, spreading it evenly and smoothing the top with a rubber spatula. Then sprinkle the reserved crumb topping evenly over the cake.

Bake in the middle of the oven for 40 to 50 minutes, or until the top is crusty and a toothpick or cake tester inserted in the center of the cake comes out clean. Serve the blueberry crumb cake warm or at room temperature, and present the cream separately in a pitcher.

Batter-fried Chicken

To serve 4

In a deep bowl, beat the egg and milk lightly together with a wire whisk. Combine the flour, baking powder and ½ teaspoon of the salt, and add them to the egg mixture a few tablespoonfuls at a time, stirring gently after each addition. Stir until the batter is smooth, but do not beat or over-mix. Set the batter aside at room temperature for about 30 minutes.

Preheat the oven to its lowest setting. Then line a large shallow baking dish with a double thickness of paper towels and place it in the middle of the oven.

Pour vegetable oil into a deep fryer or large heavy saucepan to a depth of 2 to 3 inches and heat the oil until it reaches a temperature of 360° on a deep-frying thermometer.

Meanwhile, pat the pieces of chicken completely dry with paper towels and season them evenly on both sides with the paprika and the remaining teaspoon of salt.

Dip the chicken drumsticks and thighs into the batter, one at a time, and when they are thoroughly coated place them in a deep-frying basket. Lower the basket into the hot oil and deep-fry the chicken for 12 to 15 minutes, turning the drumsticks and thighs frequently with kitchen tongs so that they color richly and evenly.

To test for doneness, after 12 minutes lift a thigh out of the oil and pierce it deeply with the point of a small skewer or sharp knife. The juice that trickles out should be pale yellow; if it is still tinged with pink, deep-fry the chicken for 1 or 2 minutes longer. Transfer the drumsticks and thighs to the paper-lined dish to drain, and keep them warm in the oven.

Then dip the wings and breasts into the batter, place them in the deep-frying basket, and lower it into the oil. Fry the white-meat pieces for about 7 or 8 minutes, then drain them on the paper-lined dish.

Arrange the chicken attractively on a heated platter and serve at once.

1 egg
½ cup milk
1 cup unsifted flour
1 teaspoon double-acting baking powder
1½ teaspoons salt
Vegetable oil for deep frying
A 3- to 3½-pound chicken, cut into 8 serving pieces
2 teaspoons paprika

Apple Jonathan

To serve 6 to 8

Preheat the oven to 400°. With a pastry brush, spread 1 tablespoon of the softened butter evenly over the bottom and sides of a shallow 3-quart baking dish. Combine the flour, baking powder and salt, and sift them together onto a plate or a sheet of wax paper.

In a deep bowl, cream the remaining 4 tablespoons of butter and the sugar, beating and mashing the mixture against the sides of the bowl with the back of a spoon until it is light and fluffy. Beat in the egg. Add about ½ cup of the flour mixture and, when it is well incorporated, stir in 2 tablespoons of the milk. Then beat in the remaining ½ cup of flour and the remaining 2 tablespoons of milk and stir until the batter is smooth.

Drop the apple slices into a bowl, pour in the maple syrup, and stir until the slices are coated on all sides. Spread the apple slices evenly in the bottom of the buttered baking dish and pour in the batter, smoothing the top with a rubber spatula.

Bake in the middle of the oven for 30 to 35 minutes, or until a cake tester or toothpick inserted in the topping comes out clean. Serve the apple Jonathan hot or at room temperature, spooning it out of the baking dish into individual dessert bowls. Present the cream separately in a pitcher.

5 tablespoons butter, softened
1 cup flour
2 teaspoons double-acting baking powder
½ teaspoon salt
½ cup sugar
1 egg
¼ cup milk
6 medium-sized tart cooking apples (about 2 pounds), peeled, cored and cut lengthwise into ⅛-inch-thick slices
½ cup pure maple syrup
1 cup heavy cream

Pear Upside-down Cake

Preheat the oven to 350°. With a pastry brush, spread the tablespoon of softened butter evenly on the sides of a 9-inch springform cake pan. Then stir 6 tablespoons of the melted butter and the brown sugar together and pat the mixture smoothly over the bottom of the pan.

Peel the pears with a small sharp knife and cut them in half lengthwise. Scoop out the cores with a small spoon. Then arrange the pear halves in one layer in a heavy 10- to 12-inch skillet and add enough water to cover them by 1 inch. Bring to a boil over high heat, reduce the heat to low, and simmer uncovered for 5 to 10 minutes, until the pears show only slight resistance when pierced with the point of a sharp knife.

With a slotted spoon arrange the pears, cored side down, on a wire rack to drain. To flatten each pear, cut a round slice about ¼ inch thick off the curved side of each half. Place one of the round slices, cut side down, in the center of the sugar-coated pan. Arrange the trimmed halves, core side up, around the round slice so that their stem ends face the center and the pears radiate from it like the spokes of a wheel. Chop the remaining round slices of pear coarsely and set them aside.

Combine the flour, baking soda, cinnamon, ginger, cloves and salt, and sift them together into a bowl. Combine the molasses, honey and hot water in a small bowl and mix together thoroughly.

In a deep bowl, beat the egg and sugar with a large spoon or a wire whisk. Stir in the remaining 8 tablespoons of melted butter. Add about 1 cup of the flour mixture and, when it is thoroughly incorporated, beat in about ½ cup of the molasses-and-honey mixture. Repeat twice, alternating 1 cup of the flour mixture with ½ cup of the molasses-and-honey mixture, and beating well after each addition. Gently stir in the reserved chopped pears and dribble the batter slowly into the pear-lined pan.

Bake in the middle of the oven for about 1½ hours, or until the topping is golden and a toothpick or cake tester inserted in the center comes out clean. Let the cake cool in the pan for about 5 minutes.

To unmold and serve the cake, place an inverted serving plate over the top of the pan. Grasping plate and pan together firmly, turn them over. Rap the plate on a table and the cake should slide out easily. Remove the sides of the pan and serve the cake warm or at room temperature.

Spiced Mixed Nuts

Preheat the oven to 275°. With a pastry brush, spread the tablespoon of softened butter over a large baking sheet. Combine the sugar, cinnamon, cloves, nutmeg, ginger, allspice and salt in a small bowl and mix well. Add the egg white and water and stir until the mixture is a smooth paste. With a table fork, stir in about ½ cup of the nuts and, when they are evenly coated, transfer one at a time to the baking sheet. Coat the remaining nuts by the half cupful and arrange on the sheet in one layer.

Bake the nuts in the middle of the oven for 45 minutes, or until the spice coating is crisp and golden brown. Cool to room temperature and store the spiced mixed nuts in a tightly covered jar until ready to serve.

To make one 9-inch cake

1 tablespoon butter, softened, plus 14 tablespoons butter, melted
1 cup light brown sugar
3 medium-sized firm ripe pears
2½ cups unsifted flour
1½ teaspoons baking soda
1 teaspoon ground cinnamon
1 teaspoon ground ginger
¼ teaspoon ground cloves
1 teaspoon salt
½ cup dark molasses
½ cup honey
¾ cup hot water
1 egg
½ cup sugar

To make about 1 pound

1 tablespoon butter, softened
¾ cup sugar
1 teaspoon ground cinnamon
½ teaspoon ground cloves
¼ teaspoon ground nutmeg
¼ teaspoon ground ginger
¼ teaspoon ground allspice
½ teaspoon salt
1 egg white, lightly beaten
2 tablespoons cold water
1 cup whole blanched unsalted almonds
1 cup unsalted broken black walnuts
½ cup whole unsalted filberts

Orchard-fresh fruits are essential to the tempting trio shown opposite. From the left: peach custard, pear upside-down cake and apple muffins.

To serve 6

3 medium-sized firm ripe peaches
1 cup heavy cream
1 cup milk
3 eggs plus 2 egg yolks
¼ cup sugar
1 teaspoon vanilla extract
¼ teaspoon ground nutmeg,
    preferably freshly grated

To make about ½ pound

1 tablespoon butter, softened
1½ cups sugar
½ cup dry sherry
½ teaspoon ground cinnamon
⅛ teaspoon ground nutmeg
2 cups unsalted walnut halves

To make about 2 pounds

1 cup whole unsalted blanched
    almonds
1 cup unsalted broken black walnuts
½ cup whole unsalted filberts
1 teaspoon salt
1 tablespoon butter, softened, plus
    2 tablespoons butter, cut into bits
1½ cups sugar
1 cup light corn syrup
⅓ cup water
1 teaspoon vanilla extract

Peach Custard

Preheat the oven to 325°. Drop the peaches into enough boiling water to immerse them completely and boil briskly, uncovered, for 2 or 3 minutes. With a slotted spoon, transfer the peaches to a sieve or colander and run cold water over them. Peel the peaches with a small sharp knife, halve them and remove the pits. Place each peach half, cut side down, in a 6-ounce custard cup and set aside.

In a small heavy saucepan, warm the cream and milk over moderate heat until small bubbles appear around the sides of the pan. Remove the pan from the heat and cover to keep warm.

With a wire whisk or a rotary or electric beater, beat the eggs and additional egg yolks together in a bowl for 2 or 3 minutes. When they begin to thicken and cling to the beater, beat in the sugar. Then, beating the mixture constantly, pour in the warm cream-and-milk mixture in a slow, thin stream. Add the vanilla and pour the custard mixture over the peaches. Sprinkle the tops with the nutmeg.

Arrange the custard cups in a large shallow baking pan set in the middle of the oven. Pour enough boiling water into the pan to come about 1 inch up the sides of the cups. Bake for 30 to 40 minutes, or until a knife inserted in the custard comes out clean. Remove the cups from the baking pan, cool to room temperature, and serve at once. Or refrigerate and serve the peach custard chilled.

Sherried Walnuts

With a pastry brush, spread the tablespoon of softened butter over a large baking sheet and set it aside.

Combine the sugar and sherry in a heavy 1-quart enameled saucepan and bring to a boil over high heat, stirring until the sugar dissolves. Then cook briskly, uncovered and undisturbed, until the syrup reaches a temperature of 240° on a candy thermometer or until about ⅛ teaspoon of the syrup dropped into ice water instantly forms a soft ball.

At once remove the pan from the heat and add the cinnamon, nutmeg and walnut halves. Stir gently for a few minutes, until the syrup becomes opaque and creamy. While the mixture is still soft, spread it on the buttered baking sheet and, with two table forks, carefully separate the candy-coated walnut halves. Set the sherried walnuts aside to cool to room temperature, then store in a tightly covered jar until ready to serve.

Mixed-Nut Brittle

Preheat the oven to 350°. Mix the almonds, black walnuts, filberts and salt in a large shallow baking dish. Toast the nuts in the middle of the oven for about 5 minutes, stirring them from time to time. Then turn off the heat, but leave the nuts in the oven to keep them warm.

With a pastry brush, spread the tablespoon of softened butter over a large baking sheet and set it aside. Combine the sugar, corn syrup and water in a heavy 2- to 3-quart saucepan and bring to a boil over high heat, stirring until the sugar dissolves. Then cook briskly, uncovered and undisturbed, until the syrup reaches a temperature of 290° on a candy thermometer or until about ⅛ teaspoon of the syrup dropped into ice water immediately separates into hard but not brittle threads.

Remove the pan from the heat and immediately beat in the 2 tablespoons of butter bits, the vanilla and the warm nuts. Pour the candy onto the buttered baking sheet and set it aside to cool to room temperature. Break the mixed-nut brittle into pieces with a kitchen mallet or your hands, and store in a tightly covered jar until ready to serve.

Indiana Persimmon Pudding

Preheat the oven to 350°. With a pastry brush, spread the tablespoon of softened butter evenly over the bottom and sides of a 1-quart soufflé dish.

Combine the flour, soda, cinnamon, ginger and nutmeg, and sift them together onto a plate or a sheet of wax paper. Set aside.

Wash the persimmons gently under cold running water and pat them dry with paper towels. With a small sharp knife, cut the persimmons into quarters and pick out the seeds. Purée the fruit through a food mill set over a deep bowl, or rub through a coarse sieve with the back of a spoon. You will need about 1 cup of puréed persimmons.

Add the sugar to the purée and mix well with a wooden spoon. Stir in about ½ cup of the flour mixture and, when it is thoroughly incorporated add ¼ cup of the milk. Stir in the remaining ½ cup of flour mixture and then the rest of the milk, beating well after each addition. Add the 2 tablespoons of melted, cooled butter, the vanilla and raisins.

Pour the batter into the buttered soufflé dish, spreading it evenly with a rubber spatula. Bake in the middle of the oven for 50 to 60 minutes, or until the pudding begins to shrink away from the sides of the dish and a cake tester or toothpick inserted in the center comes out clean.

Serve the persimmon pudding at once, directly from the baking dish. Spoon the whipped cream into a serving bowl and present it separately.

Indiana Farm Sausage

In a deep bowl, combine the pork, onions, sage, parsley, thyme, basil, marjoram, chili powder, pepper flakes and ground red pepper, garlic, salt and black pepper. Knead vigorously with both hands, then beat with a wooden spoon until the mixture is light and fluffy.

Divide the mixture into halves and, on wax paper, shape and roll each half into a cylinder about 6 inches long and 2 inches in diameter. Wrap the sausages in fresh wax paper and refrigerate for at least 2 hours, or until firm to the touch.

Just before cooking, slice the sausages into rounds about ½ inch thick. In a heavy 10- to 12-inch skillet, melt the butter with the oil over moderate heat. When the foam begins to subside, add 5 or 6 sausage rounds and fry them for 3 or 4 minutes on each side. To test for doneness, pierce the sausages with the point of a knife. The juice that trickles out should be clear yellow; if it is tinged with pink, fry the sausages for a minute or so longer. Drain briefly on paper towels, then arrange the sausages on a heated platter and drape with foil to keep them warm while you fry the rest. Serve at once.

To serve 4 to 6

1 tablespoon butter, softened, plus 2 tablespoons butter, melted and cooled
1 cup unsifted flour
1 teaspoon baking soda
½ teaspoon ground cinnamon
½ teaspoon ground ginger
¼ teaspoon ground nutmeg, preferably freshly grated
1 pound (about 2 dozen) fully ripe wild persimmons
1 cup sugar
½ cup milk
1 teaspoon vanilla extract
½ cup seedless raisins
½ cup heavy cream, chilled and whipped

To make 2 pounds

2 pounds lean ground pork
⅓ cup finely chopped onions
2 tablespoons crumbled dried sage leaves
1 tablespoon finely chopped fresh parsley
1 teaspoon crumbled dried thyme
1 teaspoon crumbled dried basil
1 teaspoon ground marjoram
1 teaspoon chili powder
1 teaspoon dried sweet pepper flakes
1 teaspoon ground hot red pepper (cayenne)
½ teaspoon finely chopped garlic
2 teaspoons salt
1 teaspoon freshly ground black pepper
2 tablespoons butter
2 tablespoons vegetable oil

VI

Folk Wines and Other Potables

That grand old man of gastronomy and oenology, André Simon, once wrote that man since the beginning has been distinguished from the beasts and other forms of earthly life by his quest for something stronger to drink than water. In this endeavor he has spent considerable time, ingenuity and hard cash.

The most primitive peoples have their fermented brews, some of them both unspeakable and, to our palates, undrinkable. The more sophisticated societies would seem to agree with Somerset Maugham's contention that the human race was born two drinks below par, for they go to considerable lengths to correct this imbalance. And nowhere in America has this been done with more gusto and inventiveness than by the various peoples who settled and built up the Eastern Heartland.

The American taste for beer, cider, wines and spirits is as old as our earliest colonies. The very first arrivals brought the taste with them from Europe, and they saw no reason to change their habits just because they had changed continents. The Pilgrims carried a supply of beer aboard the Mayflower; in fact, it may have been an imminent shortage that caused them to put in at Plymouth Rock rather than venturing farther south. An entry in a diary kept by one of the party, dated December 19, 1620, explains: "For we could not now take time for further search or consideration; our victuals being much spent, especially our beere. . . ." On such everyday wants and needs does history hinge.

Had the Pilgrims only known, a brewery already existed in America, established eight years earlier in a log house at the tip of Manhattan Island

Apple cider, served here with sugar doughnuts, is just one of many native beverages with which people of the Eastern Heartland slake their thirst. Other drinks of the area include pear and peach ciders, beer, and folk wines made with flowers, vegetables, herbs and berries.

by two Dutch settlers. It was in this house, in 1619, that the colony's first white child, Jean Vigne, was born. He, perhaps inevitably, grew up to be a brewer, learning his trade in the employ of the Dutch West India Company and then starting his own brewery in a street so chock full of them it was called Brouwer Street. By 1676 the island had four beer taverns and six that sold wine.

Beer in those days was made not only from malted grain—barley, wheat, corn, oats—but from all sorts of other ingredients as well, such as spruce bark and persimmons, pumpkins and Jerusalem artichokes. Malt beer was the basis for many other drinks. Mostly it was spiked with rum, the cheapest and most easily procurable spirit, and sweetened with sugar or molasses. These were potent tipples. The original recipe for flip, a pre-Revolutionary drink, combined in a two- or three-quart tankard two thirds strong beer, a gill of rum, some molasses and a pinch of dried pumpkin. Into this was plunged a red-hot flip iron, also known as a loggerhead, which made the liquid seethe and bubble and gave it a slightly scorched taste. The expression "to be at loggerheads" arose from the common spectacle of two men in a tavern, inflamed with drink, brandishing flip irons at each other as they argued.

The restless 19th Century Americans who moved west into what is now Ohio and beyond seized on whatever they could find to make home brews that would relieve the monotony and rigors of frontier life. Almost everything that blossoms or fruits can be brewed or fermented or distilled, and the pioneers concocted a wide (though not always tasty) assortment of wines and cordials from the astonishing variety of wild plants that grew so profusely in their westward path.

The legacy of those inventive imbibers persists. In a scattering of kitchens, cellars and backyards, particularly in farm country, native fruits, berries and weeds are still being converted lovingly into home-style drinks. Not beer, though. With the influx of German immigrants after 1840 came a great burgeoning of breweries in cities where the newcomers settled in force—New York, Philadelphia, Cincinnati, Chicago—and the start of the great American beer industry. If any home brewing goes on now, the law takes a dim view of it. Wine and cider are the only alcoholic drinks that may legally be made by private citizens.

Cider has as venerable a history in this country as beer, for it was a staple beverage of the farmers, produced from the apples grown in the orchards that were and still are the pride of the Eastern Heartland states. Of these, New Jersey can claim special honors. Apple seeds imported from England were planted there as early as 1632, and the colonials became so adept at cider making that a century or so later the visiting Swedish botanist Peter Kalm pronounced their version the best he had ever tasted anywhere. This judgment, recorded in Kalm's *Travels in North America* along with his perceptive observations on the New World's natural history and farming methods, may well have been the first published testimonial ever given an American food product.

Nor were New Jerseyites content with simple cider. As early as 1698 a Scottish settler named William Laird began to distill it for himself and his neighbors, producing apple brandy, now better known as applejack

or, to those familiar with the power of this potion, as "Jersey lightning." In 1780 one of Laird's descendants began commercial production of the tawny spirit; and Laird & Co. still flourishes in Scobeyville, New Jersey, nearly 200 years later, turning out 95 per cent of the applejack distilled in the United States.

Applejack (the American cousin of the Calvados of Normandy) is the final step in the transformation of the sweet and innocent apple to an ardent spirit. The mid-point in that transformation is fermented, or hard, cider. Fresh apple juice contains its own sugar and yeast and, if left to itself, will ferment until the sugar turns to alcohol and the cider becomes hard. Most of the cider drunk in the colonies was this type; it is dry rather than sweet and the alcohol content can be 8 per cent or more, according to how long it has been left to ferment. It is a completely different thing from the sweet cider we buy in the markets, in which the fermentation has been stopped by pasteurization or the addition of preservatives. For applejack, the cider is fermented until it is about 12 proof, or 6 per cent alcohol by volume, and then it is distilled into an 80- to 100-proof brandy.

You don't find anyone making hard cider in this country any more, except in rural districts where a farmer by mistake or on purpose lets his apple juice stand too long before bottling it. The English consume a great deal of it, and I must say that its clean, dry bite makes sweet cider, good as it is, seem pallid by comparison. Until the middle of the 19th Century hard cider was an everyday drink in America, too, and not considered harmful by anybody, despite an old proverb that warned: "Cider smiles

Cider Making on Long Island, painted in 1871 by William M. Davis, depicts a preindustrial process step by step. Ripe apples were shoveled into a circular trough *(left),* and crushed with a horse-drawn roller; the juice-laden pulp was carried by the bucketful to a hand-operated press *(center)* that squeezed the cider into barrels. Customarily prized as a drink, cider was also sometimes used for barter; one early-19th Century diarist meticulously recorded in his journal that he had traded "one-half barrel of cider for Mary's schooling."

149

in your face and then cuts your throat." President John Adams, who drank a tankard of it every morning, lived to be 91, as sound and ripe as the apples themselves. Unfortunately there came a time when cider began to be regarded as the first step on the ruinous road to alcoholism. The temperance movement that sprang up in the 1830s included hard cider in its list of proscribed beverages, and in time whole orchards fell before the axes of the crusaders. A pamphlet published by the Women's Christian Temperance Union called cider "the Devil's kindling wood," citing the case of a hapless young man who, having drunk cider in the harvest fields as a boy, progressed through ale, beer and wine to brandy.

Today the only hard cider you are likely to see in stores is imported from Europe and it is rather expensive—a great pity, as the dryness of hard cider is excellent in cooking. One has only to think of that great dish of Normandy, *tripe à la mode de Caen* (don't ever try to make it with sweet cider or it will be utterly inedible). Sweet cider, hard cider and applejack can all play definite culinary roles, not only in desserts but in alliance with pork, which has a decided affinity for the apple. Ham takes on a luscious flavor when marinated in or basted with cider, and so does loin of pork, roasted and then flambéed with applejack.

As cider was one of the cheapest and most plentiful liquids in pioneer homes, it appears in many old recipes—for cider pie *(Recipe Index)*, for instance, or cider cake or cider pudding, which was often served with a hot cider sauce. One of the simplest was cider toast: toasted bread in a bowl, sprinkled with ginger and sugar and soaked with hot cider.

There were two other types of cider made in the old days, rarer than that made from apples. One was perry, from pears; the other, from peaches, was called peachy, a word that passed into the colloquial language as a synonym for something excellent, or "peachy."

Peaches, pears and many other fruits were also used by the settlers to make cordials, shrubs and ratafias, homespun relatives of liqueurs. They are very easy to make. For a simple cordial, immerse crushed or cut fruit with sugar to sweeten it in spirits—rum, brandy, whiskey or vodka—until the liquor is well infused with the flavor of the fruit, a process that may take perhaps two or three months. Shrub is a combination of spirits with small fruits like cherries or raspberries, or the juice and rind of oranges or lemons; while ratafia (pronounced ra-ta-fee'-a) is a cordial with crushed fruit pits added, which lend it a distinctive, slightly bitter, almondy flavor. These are rather fun to make and have around, and are cheaper than liqueurs because all you pay for is the spirits and the fruit.

The most varied and interesting of the native Eastern Heartland drinks are the wines—which range from primitive folk, or "weed," wines to the table wines *(pages 156-157)* produced commercially from the grapes grown in certain parts of the region. There is a very old country tradition of making wine from fruits, nuts, grains, berries, vegetables and leaves, which are converted to alcohol through the insidious action of yeast and sugar. These folk wines are much easier and cheaper to make than wine from grapes: the ingredients are always at hand, there for the picking, and the process is much more straightforward. If your lawn is yellow with dandelions in spring, or your meadow covered with clover, all you need are a few other simple ingredients and plenty of patience and you can convert them into a cellarful of wine.

I remember as a child being taken at Christmastime to the house of an elderly lady who proudly brought out, along with her rich fruitcake, a decanter of her own elderberry wine. It was dark, flavorful and pretty high in alcohol, a bit like port or Madeira (I didn't recognize the taste at the time; to my childish palate it was just jolly good). Although I was allowed only a tiny cordial glass, it brought on a pleasant muzzy warmth.

Many years later, when my taste buds were more experienced, I traveled the Eastern Heartland and realized just how many kinds of folk wines there are. In fact, the list of growing things from which wine can be made is endless—dandelions, marigolds, carnations, daisies, elder blossoms, pansies and roses are just some of the flowers that can be used. There are barley wine and rice wine (the Japanese *sake*), wines made from beets, carrots, celery, parsnips, spinach, tomatoes, potatoes and even onions. Herbs like mint, sage, parsley and balm, the scented leaves of the rose geranium and the tender young leaves of the wild grape can be made into wine, and so can just about every berry you can pick—blackberries, blueberries, gooseberries, mulberries, raspberries, fresh currants.

Some of the most successful wines are made from berries of the *Rubus* genus, or family, to which the familiar raspberry and blackberry and the less prevalent thimbleberry and cloudberry belong. In Pennsylvania I tasted a wine made from the appropriately named wineberry, a type of raspberry that emigrated from Asia. The drink had a beautiful rose color and a dry round flavor that tasted better the more I sipped it. The dewberry, or trailing blackberry, is another good candidate for wine making. When combined with rhubarb, it makes an extremely good drink, with a Madeira-like quality.

The characteristics of wines made from flowers seem to be completely different. Frequently they have a smooth, haunting sweetness that reminds me of a white dessert wine such as a muscatel. A friend in Indiana invited me to try a most unusual wine she makes from the sweet-scented blossoms of the locust tree. If it had been presented to me in a decanter as a new discovery in imported dessert wines, I would have been completely fooled. It was a revelation, totally unlike any other folk wine I had ever tasted. Golden, headily perfumed and honey-sweet, it was second cousin to the exotic, intensely fragrant rose water and orange-flower water of the Middle East, which are distilled from rose petals and the blossoms of the bitter-orange tree and are used to scent and flavor sherbets, ice creams, cakes, rice puddings and pastries. Locust-blossom wine is wonderful in a fruit compote, or to sip with a rich dessert. It would be worth planting a locust tree just to be able to make this superlative wine.

Folk wines do not require complicated equipment and many of the things you need may be already in your kitchen *(page 153)*. But one essential item you probably don't have at hand is a permit from the federal Alcohol and Tobacco Tax office in your state. The law allows you to make up to 200 gallons of wine without paying any tax, but you must get a federal permit first. It is also advisable to ask the state tax bureau about any local regulations. I have a suspicion that some people tend to over-

Continued on page 156

Home-bottled Wines:
An Old Yet New Folk Art

Over 200,000 American families stock their cellars
with wines they make themselves from such
unpretentious raw materials as the common dandelion.
One 17th Century journal described the dandelion as
being "effectual for the hypochondrical passion," but
curative or not, its golden petals *(right)* produce
a delightful, faintly sweet tipple. Throughout the
Eastern Heartland during May, fields of dandelions
like this one in Mount Joy, Pennsylvania, spring up,
begging to be picked. But since almost any plant can
be fermented, the possibilities are really endless. And
half the fun of a folk wine lies in bottling it yourself.

152

Home wine making requires little special equipment: some outsized bottles, like those at right; special stoppers called fermentation locks, in the tops of the bottles; and a siphon, shown here wrapped around the middle bottle. The fermentation locks, partly filled with water to seal out air, are ingeniously designed to indicate by the water levels in their tubes the moment when the wine is fully fermented. The fermenting process takes about one month for the peach wine in the two left-hand bottles, and three months for dandelion wine, in the right-hand bottle. The siphon is used to draw the wine out of the bottles, leaving the sediment at the bottom. In the final step the wine is bottled and left to mature *(next pages)*.

A Sampler of Folk Wines

Mrs. William Penn's gooseberry wine recipe, given below, and the glowing glasses and carafe on the opposite page are both part of a tradition of folk-wine making that has thrived for centuries in many lands. Although generally considered a country pursuit, folk wine can be made wherever there is room to store a few large jugs or containers. The ingredients can be anything from onions to rhubarb, from bananas to cantaloupe, from daisies to dill. You may choose whatever fruits, vegetables, flowers or herbs are in season; the process varies accordingly but is surprisingly simple. You may already have much of the equipment you need: crocks, enameled pots, spoons (but nothing of metal for it affects both the color and taste of the wine), and a piece of plastic or rubber tubing for siphoning. Some items you probably do not have are glass jugs of 2-, 4-, or 5- gallon capacity, fermentation locks, a cork plunger, corks and wine bottles.

The first step is to prepare the juice that is to be fermented. If you are using fruit, crush it with a fruit crusher or potato masher to release the juices. Flowers, herbs and vegetables must be steeped in boiling water and then strained. Citrus is often added to provide the necessary acidity. Fermentation of the juice— known as "must" in the language of wine makers—occurs when yeast cells act on the sugar in the must and transform it into alcohol. Some fruits, especially grapes, contain enough yeast and sugar naturally to start fermenting by themselves. With most ingredients, however —and always with flowers, herbs and vegetables—it is safer and faster to give

nature a helping hand by adding an extra dose of yeast and sugar. Baking yeast, either in cake form or in envelopes as active dry yeast, is generally available at grocery stores.

During active fermentation, which may last three days or three weeks or even longer, the must will hiss and bubble visibly. A fermentation lock *(page 153)* is useful at this point to keep bacteria in the air away from the fermenting wine. When fermentation stops, the wine is ready for clearing. Sometimes the wine will clear after sitting for days or weeks in a cool place, but often it must be strained or siphoned off into fresh containers so that the sediment can be discarded. This process, known as racking, may have to be done more than once, but the wine should be allowed to rest a few days between rackings. Eventually, it should become clear enough so that a candle flame can be seen through it without distortion.

Before the wine becomes really palatable, it must age and mellow for a period of time, specified in the particular recipe. During the maturing process the wine again must be protected from bacteria in the air, which would turn it into vinegar or otherwise spoil it. Sometimes it can age right in its jug, stoppered with a fermentation lock; or you can bottle it for longer aging, and seal it with new, nontapered wine corks, inserted with a cork plunger to ensure a tight fit.

Three basic wine recipes are presented here, and two more are given on page 201, along with a list of books on the finer points of folk wines and a list of stores selling wine-making equipment.

Flower   DANDELION

To 5 quarts of freshly picked dandelion blossoms add 8 quarts of boiling water and let stand overnight. Drain through cheesecloth. Add 6 sliced oranges, 6 sliced lemons, 2 pounds of seedless raisins, 7 pounds of white cane sugar and one yeast cake. Let stand 15 days, stirring every day. Strain and put into fermenting jugs of 2- to 5-gallon capacity with small necks. Stopper with fermentation locks or a wad of sterile cotton. Leave three or four months. Siphon out the wine to within 1 inch of the bottom and let stand 2 months more. When clear, bottle in sterile wine bottles and seal with new, straight corks using a cork plunger. Will yield 8 to 10 bottles.

An old Pennsylvania Dutch recipe from Betty Groff, Mount Joy, Pennsylvania

Vegetable   CARROT

Scrub 6 pounds of carrots clean—don't peel them—and mash them. Put them in one gallon water, bring to the boil and simmer gently until tender. Then strain off the liquid (you can use the carrots for food—most dogs love them). Into the fermenting vessel put four pounds of sugar, 2 sliced lemons and 2 sliced oranges and pour the hot liquid over them. Stir until the sugar is dissolved and stand until lukewarm. Then add 1 tablespoonful of chopped raisins and 1 pound of whole wheat (optional) and sprinkle 1 ounce of yeast on top. Leave to ferment for fifteen days, then skim, strain and bottle.

To get the fullest flavour, keep it for nearly a year—if you can.

From *Successful Wine Making at Home,* by H. E. Bravery

Fruit   ELDERBERRY

Combine in a crock 5 pounds of elderberries, 2½ quarts of water, 2½ pounds of sugar and 1 yeast cake. After 15 days, strain, add another 2 pounds of sugar and pour into fermenting jugs. Fit with fermentation lock and let stand until fermentation has ceased (about 3 months). It is then ready to drink but since it makes such a beautiful deep red wine, try to save a bottle for next Christmas—it will be even better!

An old Pennsylvania Dutch recipe from Betty Groff, Mount Joy, Pennsylvania

---

Too make gosbery wine or of any other fruit

Take to every gallan of gousberys
A gallan of watter,
bruse the gosberys and pore the water one them,
Lett it stand a weeke straining it often.
[add] as many pounds of sugar as gallans of [gosberys]
then Lett it Run through a gelly bagg:
tunn it up
you may boyle it in a furnis.
in a fortnight or 3 weeks you may drinke it—

From *Penn Family Recipes,* 1702

STRAWBERRY

WINEBERRY

LOCUST BLOSSOM

DANDELION

CHERRY APPLE

WILD GRAPE

APRICOT

Seven folk wines stand ready
for drinking. Most are sweet,
and of heavier consistency
than conventional wine.

Trends in Eastern Vineyards

Some of America's best and most popular champagnes and other sparkling wines come from New York State vineyards, as do a good many red and white table wines, sherry and port. In the main, the grapes from which all these wines are made are American varieties of the species Vitis labrusca. These are native to various parts of the Eastern Heartland where the winter cold is tempered by the presence of large bodies of water —the Finger Lakes region of central New York, sections of the Hudson River Valley and of the Lake Erie shoreline. The most important varieties of grape are Concord, Delaware, Catawba, Isabella, Dutchess and Elvira. The hardiness of the Eastern vines enables them not only to withstand the winter but to resist the diseases that have from time to time ravaged the vinifera species of Europe and California. But the wines themselves often have a strong wild taste, sometimes referred to as "foxy," so called, presumably, from "fox grapes," the early American term for native wild grapes. Some wine drinkers favor the foxy taste, but most prefer wines from the vinifera grapes. So a number of Eastern vintners, following the lead of Dr. Konstantin Frank, have experimented with French hybrid and European vines like Pinot Chardonnay, Pinot Noir and Johannisberg Riesling, grafting them onto American rootstocks. Such vineyards as High Tor, Gold Seal, Boordy, Dr. Frank's Vinifera and those of the Great Western and Taylor companies have succeeded in producing dry white and red table wines that are attracting new attention from connoisseurs (opposite page).

look the formality. Driving once through a rather desolate part of Michigan, which I had been told was full of game poachers and old ladies who made weed wines, I tried to track down a Polish woman known for her skill. It was a weird experience; there were no names on the mailboxes or on the streets and a kind of watchful, wary silence hung over the place. It was like the opening of a Western when the stranger rides into town and finds the street suddenly deserted. I could feel invisible eyes raking me over. The storekeeper at the only store in town was vague—she allowed as how there *might* be someone of that name in town, but she didn't know where. There was no listing in the local telephone book.

Finally, on the way out of town I stopped at a rundown house that showed some signs of habitation and asked the girl who came to the door if she knew the lady who made weed wines. By chance, I'd hit on the house of her son, and the daughter-in-law was just about to give me some information when her husband slouched up behind her, surly, unshaven, a poacher if I ever saw one. He looked at me coldly, denied all knowledge of any such activities and said in a menacing way, "Lady, you're wasting your time." Discretion urged flight. I don't think I look like a "Revenooer," but maybe the government does use women these days.

Making weed wines is a homely sort of enterprise, but making wine from grapes requires considerably more skill and effort. I have always felt that one of the most rewarding and fascinating professions is that of a wine maker. To grow your own grapes, make your own wine and nurse it to maturity must be as absorbing and totally involving as bringing up a child —and in these days probably much less traumatic.

Some of my friends own vineyards and make wine on a commercial scale, but there are others, like Ed Giobbi, who buy the grapes and make their wine at home because it is an integral and important part of their background and tradition. As Ed says, "The poorest Italian has bread and he has wine, even when he may not have anything else. If you take wine away from an Italian, you might as well bury him."

Ed is a second-generation Italian-American who in his own way is a latter-day Renaissance man. He's an artist, a fabulous cook, and on the 15-acre property in New York State where he lives with his pretty, soft-voiced Southern wife Ellie and their three young children, he raises chickens, grows all his vegetables and makes about 150 gallons of wine a year. "If I had a couple of people working for me," he said one day when I was there for lunch, "I'd raise my own beef and pork, but there's just so much I can do. I grow things because even though it takes a lot of my time, if you're interested in what you eat, you make the effort. If you're not, you accept what they give you and take your chances."

A meal at the Giobbis' is always an excitement, because in the huge living room and kitchen where the family spend most of their time you feel a part of everything that's going on. I hung over the kitchen counter talking to Ellie and Ed as she peeled shrimp and he cleaned squid for a special recipe his mother had sent from Italy where she now lives. He rolled the seafood in a mixture of lemon juice, seasonings and bread crumbs, wrapped the squid around the shrimp, skewered them, brushed them with oil and broiled them. This was our lunch, with bread Ellie had baked and tomatoes picked when they were not quite ripe, still yellow, firm and tart the way Italians like to eat them. (They use fully ripened ones for cooking.)

With this we had Ed's white wine, drawn from the barrel and still a trifle sweet because it needed more fermentation, but deliciously soft and fragrant, like a German Moselle. We sliced peaches from trees grown from pits Ed's father had planted, dropped them into the glasses to soak in the wine and ate them for dessert. The wine, which is 14 per cent alcohol, left me feeling relaxed and a little dreamy. It was a perfect summer meal.

After lunch Ed showed me his winery, a small stone building, dim and cool, with a dirt floor under which are buried bottles of a wine he made six years ago and is saving for his daughter Gina's wedding. "I'm going to save some from each batch I make," he said.

Every year, in late September or early October, he and a friend drive down to New York City, go to the railroad yards in the Bronx and buy boxes of zinfandel, alicante and muscatel grapes right off the cars. Like most Italians he likes to use the California varieties; many other home wine makers use grapes of the Eastern region. Ed's father, who taught him wine making, also taught him how to select grapes that produce good wine. For red wine, the grapes must be small and tight, not big, juicy and watery. For white, he looks for those that are yellow, almost brown, full of concentrated sweetness; the closer they are to raisins, the better the wine will be. It takes eighteen 42-pound boxes of grapes to make a 50-gallon barrel of wine, and Ed makes three barrels a year at an approximate cost of $2.50 a gallon.

It takes him, altogether, about four days' work. First the grapes are crushed by hand over an open 50-gallon barrel and the juice is left to ferment, which takes anywhere from a week to a fortnight. You can hear it fizzing and fermenting in the barrel, and eventually the solid matter, or bulk, floats up to the top and the liquid stays below. When this happens, Ed drains the wine from the barrel and presses the bulk in the wine press until all the wine in it pours out of the sides and into a keg. "I get the bulk so dry you could put a match to it," he told me. The wine goes into a closed barrel with a small opening into which a glass fermentation lock is inserted; the gases in the still-fermenting wine escape through water-filled chambers in the lock, which also prevents air from entering. When the water stops bubbling, all the gas has escaped. The barrel then can be sealed and the wine aged. After about six months it is drawn off so that the sediment can be removed and the barrel cleaned; the wine is replaced and aged for another few months. Then the young wine is ready to be drawn off and drunk, or put into bottles to age further.

Ed taps a barrel and transfers his wine to gallon jugs only when the moon is on the wane. "If you do it when the moon is on the rise," he said, "it clouds up and won't clear. People say this is an old wives' tale, but I know wine makers who swear by it—my father did. Everyone makes wine his own way and this is the way I learned from him. I like *my* wine, but then all wine makers think their wine is the greatest. They are like fathers. You can have the ugliest child in the world and you tell everyone she's beautiful."

Some of New York's Finest

Listed below are some of New York State's best wines, selected with the help of Sam Aaron, consultant for the Wines and Spirits volume of this series.

WHITE TABLE WINES

RIESLING, PINOT CHARDONNAY *and* GEWURTZTRAMINER, *Vinifera Vineyards; wines from pure European transplanted vines; expensive, but hold their own with European counterparts.*
BOORDY WHITE, *Boordy Vineyards; from hybrid vines, and similar to the light, fragrant wines of France's Loire Valley.*
ROCKLAND WHITE, *High Tor Vineyard; bright, lively hybrid.*
BULLY HILL WHITE, *Bully Hill Vineyards; excellent estate-bottled wine from French hybrid vines.*
CHARLES FOURNIER NATURE, *Gold Seal Vineyard; excellent hybrid.*
CHARLES FOURNIER PINOT CHARDONNAY, *Gold Seal Vineyard; a fine wine from pure European transplanted vines.*
DIAMOND, ELVIRA AND VERGENNES, *Widmer Vineyards; three of the best wines from native grapes.*

RED TABLE WINES

BOORDY RED, *Boordy Vineyards; similar to Beaujolais and pleasantly fruity.*
BACO NOIR, *Great Western; a hybrid of solid character.*
BULLY HILL RED, *Bully Hill Vineyards; full-bodied hybrid, longer-lived than most.*

CHAMPAGNES

BLANC DE BLANCS, CHARLES FOURNIER, *Gold Seal Vineyard; made from France's finest white grape, the Pinot Chardonnay.*
TAYLOR BRUT, *the most popular seller in the United States.*
GREAT WESTERN BRUT
GOLD SEAL BRUT

A Small-Scale Vineyard
Builds a Big Reputation

Compared to most New York State wineries, Everett Crosby's High Tor is minuscule, but no wine maker could cherish his product more. Crosby began by dabbling in grape growing on the terrace of his Manhattan penthouse. In 1950 he gave up his amateur status to buy a 78-acre farm on the side of High Tor, a mountain near New City. With his wife and one or two paid assistants, Crosby now cultivates 12 acres of vines. The grapes he grows are French hybrids: a variety of Seibel for red wine, one of Seyve-Villard for white wine. Every year Crosby sells about 2,500 gallons of his wine to perceptive oenophiles who have discovered his "estate bottled" High Tor brand.

High Tor's grapes are carefully tied up, as they grow, to keep them off the ground *(above)*; in autumn, assistant Eric Greaves *(right)* picks the fully ripened grapes.

In the making of red wine, crushed grapes are fermented in open vats for a week *(above)*; aging is done in casks.

The Society of the Friendly Sons of St. Patrick in the City of New York

126th Anniversary Dinner

March 17th, 1910.

Delmonico's

VII

When Eating Out Became "In"

An ornate menu cover from an age of elaborate dining out welcomes an Irish fraternal organization to its 1910 St. Patrick's Day feast. Given at Delmonico's, New York's premier restaurant of the time, the meal featured guinea hen and saddle of lamb, cooked—of course—in the French style. Only one dish on the menu paid tribute to the Auld Sod: Limerick bacon on a bed of kale.

The fluid, flexible, footloose American way of life we know today is not, as most of us would suppose, a phenomenon strictly of the 20th Century. It was a product of the Industrial Revolution, which during the 19th Century changed beyond recognition the face of the country and the living and eating habits of Americans. An expanding network of highways, canals and railroads moved people and goods from the East into the Middle West and beyond. Traveling came to be commonplace, hotels sprang up in cities to which the new means of transport brought prosperity —Cincinnati, Pittsburgh, Chicago—and eating out became not only customary but fashionable. In New York a glittering culinary tradition arose that persists to this day—the tradition of the luxurious, expensive restaurant where social lions prowled and preened, and big spenders got every cent of their money's worth.

One of the events that marked the start of the age of mobility was the opening of the Erie Canal, symbolized in November 1825 when Governor De Witt Clinton poured a keg of Lake Erie water into New York Bay. The canal was the waterway that linked the Hudson River to Lake Erie, 350 miles to the west, providing a vital artery between the eastern cities and those of the Great Lakes states of Ohio, Michigan, Indiana and Illinois. New York became the portal through which freight and immigrants from Europe flowed into the interior and the produce of the Eastern Heartland flowed out.

Travel on the canalboats, towed by horses plodding on the canal banks, was slow, but it was cheaper and in most instances more comfortable and well-provisioned than the bone-shaking stagecoach. Charles Dickens, who toured the United States in the early 1840s, describes in *American Notes* the kind of meal he had on a canalboat. Dickens was a caustic critic of much that he saw here, but in this case he seems to have been impressed at least by the size of the meal and the friendly spirit in which it was eaten: "At about six o'clock, all the small tables [on which passengers otherwise slept] were put together to form one long table, and everyone sat down to tea, coffee, bread, butter, salmon, shad, liver, steaks, potatoes, pickles, ham, chops, black-puddings, and sausages. 'Will you try,' said my opposite neighbour, handing me a dish of potatoes, broken up in milk and butter, 'will you try some of these fixings?' "

The heyday of "canawling" was brief, for the railroad era put an end to it. Railroads were swifter, more convenient and covered more territory. By 1875 there was hardly an American town or village beyond earshot of the whistle of the steam engine, the wonderful iron horse.

In the wake of the railroads came another phenomenon, the American hotel, home to hundreds of thousands of people who were transient and rootless, some of them poor but all of them full of hope and optimism. This was the new breed of Americans who shaped the new America. Without the means or the occupational security to build homes of their own, they settled like chattering flocks of migratory birds in hotels—and boardinghouses as well—that were designed not so much for the bona fide traveler as for the workers in the new towns and industries that sprang up along the routes of the railroads.

It was an outsider, English novelist Anthony Trollope, who with a social commentator's eye saw the pattern of the emerging America; in 1861 he recorded his observations in his book *North America:* ". . . in this young world the cities have come first . . . have begun by the erection of first-class hotels and the fabrication of railroads. . . . The first sign of an incipient settlement is an hotel five stories high . . . with two hundred bedrooms. . . . When the new hotel rises up in the wilderness, it is presumed that people will come there with the express object of inhabiting it. The hotel itself will create a population—as the railways do. . . ."

It is easy to understand why even young married couples preferred to live in hotels—proudly referred to as "palaces of the people." They were cheap: for not much more than a dollar a day the boarder got a bedroom, the use of the public rooms and bar—where a shot of hard liquor sold for a dime—and as much food as could be packed away. Trollope recalls hearing one ravenous young woman order "boiled mutton and caper sauce, roast duck, hashed venison, mashed potatoes, poached eggs and spinach, stewed tomatoes . . . and . . . squash," all of which arrived at once on individual dishes, a mode of dining he considered barbarous.

Wherever he went, Trollope found travelers eating. On the riverboats and ferries they sat down to suppers of "beefsteaks, and tea, and apple jam, and hot cakes, and light fixings, to all which luxuries an American deems himself entitled. . . ." Tots of four lisped their requests for "beef-steak, . . . and stewed potato, and buttered toast, and corn cake, and coffee—and . . . mother, mind you get me the pickles."

For young and old alike, steak, manifestly, had become the national pas-

The dining car, which first appeared to much acclaim in the late 1860s, was a reflection of the lavish restaurant culture that had begun to develop in New York City. Vying with one another for excellence of food and service, many railroads featured dishes for which the regions they traversed were famous: the Reading served scrapple, the Baltimore & Ohio was renowned for its terrapin stew, many Western trains offered elk, antelope and buffalo meat, and the Northern Pacific advertised itself as "The Line of the Great Big Baked Potato."

sion—steak from the steers raised on the vast open grazing lands of the Great Plains. Some of the meat, Trollope noted with a shudder, came to table awash in "palpable, undisguised grease, floating in rivers," but on the other hand he was impressed by the quantity of beef consumed—about double the amount his own countrymen ate—and after a visit to the farm lands of Middle America he sang a positive paean to its fertility: "I began then to know what it was for a country to overflow with milk and honey, to burst with its own fruits, and be smothered by its own riches."

Trollope concluded that the food served to Americans on the go could not compare with that served in private homes, and at the time he was right, of course. Yet his judgment proved premature. Seven years after his book was published, a new culinary wonder emerged on the American scene, the railroad dining car. In 1868 the first regularly scheduled dining car went into service, on the Chicago & Alton line, and it was not long before almost every long-distance train followed suit.

Dinner generally cost from 75 cents to a dollar, and the passenger could have just about anything he wanted (the railroad's goal in this case was not profit but prestige). In 1877 the Chicago & North Western line, for instance, was offering 35 main courses and 25 desserts. There was beefsteak prepared in half a dozen ways, veal, ham, venison, lamb, mutton and chicken; also on the menu were woodcock, snipe, pheasant, golden plover, duck and prairie chicken. There were seven different oyster dishes and eight different kinds of bread.

The food on most of the trains was as good as it was varied. Fresh-killed game, often picked up at stops along the way, was prepared by chefs who knew their business. Matching the meals was the service, which was faultless, with snowy white linens, solicitous attention from stewards, and an excellent choice of wines. There was intense rivalry among the railroads as to which could provide the most delicious, elegant eating.

In 1882 the Pennsylvania Company's New York-Chicago run was enhanced by the addition of a dining car that a Chicago publication described as being "the most beautiful, comfortable and well-arranged of all the many dining cars . . . entering or leaving the city at present." It boasted four double silver chandeliers, a carved mahogany sideboard, thick carpets, plush chairs and a wine rack that held 125 bottles.

This era of opulent eating on wheels, which reached its zenith around the turn of the century, may have begun with the dining car of the Chicago & Alton, but its real inspiration lay a thousand miles east in New York City—and the proof of this gastronomic debt was evident in the name proudly given to that first car: *Delmonico*. By the late 1860s New York had grown incomparably rich and cosmopolitan; it had become the playground of moguls and merchant princes who liked the finer things of life and could afford them. The establishment that more than any other expressed the city's affluence and taste was Delmonico's Restaurant.

The rise of Delmonico's, and of the restaurant culture it apotheosized, happened, like so much else in 19th Century America, with amazing rapidity. When the Erie Canal opened in 1825 there were no restaurants, as we know them today, in New York or anywhere else in the country. The nearest approximation was the "ordinary," as taverns and inns were

Delmonico's Restaurant added luster to its already brilliant reputation when, in 1897, it moved uptown into lavish new quarters at Fifth Avenue and 44th Street in Manhattan. Behind its awninged façade were richly decorated public dining rooms and even glossier private rooms, like the one shown opposite, where the wealthy and well born gave opulent dinner parties. On these elegant premises no one worried about expense, and often food was the least of it: at one yachtsman's party each place was graced with a 20-inch cut-glass bowl in which floated a replica of the host's yacht, furnished with pine spars, silk rigging and satin sails; his bill came to $400 a head.

called, or hotel dining rooms where a table d'hôte meal was served for a fixed price at set hours, where quantity definitely took precedence over quality, and the service was crude at best.

Giovanni Del-Monico, an immigrant Swiss wine merchant, changed all that. With his brother Pietro, who had run a pastry shop in Bern, Giovanni in 1827 opened a café and pastry shop in Manhattan where they sold Pietro's pastries along with coffee, chocolate, bonbons, ices and spirits. New Yorkers were charmed. The coffee was strong and fragrant, the chocolate was rich and thick, the pastries light and flaky, made with the finest ingredients and an artist's touch. Many customers had never tasted anything like this and they came back again and again. In 1831 the brothers—now John and Peter Delmonico—opened New York's first restaurant: "Delmonico and Brother, Confectioners and Restaurant Français, 23 and 25 William Street."

The food, prepared by expert French chefs, was delicious and continental, entrancing the palates of New Yorkers, whose customary fare was plain and uninspired. For the first time, unfamiliar vegetables like eggplant and endive appeared on a menu, and such delights as *petits gâteaux*. But most of all it was the atmosphere of the restaurant and the solicitude of the owners that the first clients, unused to European niceties, found remarkable.

Bon vivant Sam Ward, as an old man, recalled the impression the place had made on him as a youth of 16: "I remember entering the café with something of awe. . . . The dim religious light soothed the eye, its tranquil atmosphere the ear. . . . I was struck by the prompt and def-

Rector's, a restaurant near New York's Times Square, was in great vogue at the turn of the century. Prices *(opposite)* were not low for the era, but the owner, Charles Rector, went to great lengths to please his customers. The story is told that when Diamond Jim Brady waxed ecstatic over *filets de sole Marguery,* a dish made only by the Café Marguery in Paris, Rector withdrew his son George from Cornell Law School and sent him to infiltrate the Marguery's kitchen and ferret out the sacred recipe. It took the young man several months to do so, but he was rewarded, the story goes, when Diamond Jim, in one heroic sitting at Rector's, downed nine portions of the dish.

erential attendance, unlike the democratic nonchalance of Holt's Ordinary, in Fulton Street, or at Clark & Brown's in Maiden Lane. . . ."

From such modest beginnings grew the legendary Delmonico's, the most luxurious eating establishment New York was to boast for many decades. Under the aegis of Lorenzo Delmonico, nephew of John and *restaurateur extraordinaire,* the restaurant shifted location several times as society moved uptown, and the ever-more-resplendent premises were the setting for New York's most scintillating balls, assemblies and private parties until well into the 20th Century.

While direction of the enterprise was in the hands of Lorenzo the Great, as he was affectionately known, the kitchens were for 34 years the domain of a complementary genius, Charles Ranhofer, a Frenchman who had been *chef de cuisine* for an Alsatian prince before coming to work for the Russian consul in New York in 1856 at the age of 20. In 1861 he became chef of Delmonico's only rival, the Maison Dorée on Union Square, but soon the wily Lorenzo persuaded him to switch his allegiance to the splendid new Delmonico's that had just moved to Fifth Avenue and 14th Street. There Ranhofer's towering talent was given full rein. How well he did was aptly summed up by New York's social arbiter, Ward McAllister, coiner of the phrase "Four Hundred" and the power behind the queen of New York society, Mrs. William B. Astor. "Tell Ranhofer the number of your guests and nothing more," McAllister advised, "and you will have perfection."

"Dinner at Del's" became the smart thing, and at least two of the restaurant's habitués had dishes christened in their honor. A creamed chicken concoction named after Foxhall Keene, son of a Wall Street potentate, has come down to us, slightly garbled, as chicken à la king. A certain lobster dish was originally called à la Wenberg for a sea captain, Ben Wenberg, who had discovered this exotic new way of preparing lobster in a wine-spiked cream sauce on one of his voyages. Then Captain Ben had a falling out with Charles Delmonico, Lorenzo's nephew and successor, and the dish, which had become a favorite for after-theater suppers, was rechristened Newberg; it is as lobster à la Newberg or Delmonico that it is listed in Ranhofer's book, *The Epicurean,* a tome of almost 1,200 pages containing 4,000 recipes.

Like all great chefs, Ranhofer was no rigid classicist indissolubly wedded to the *grande cuisine,* but a creative artist who in constructing his menus drew on his American experience and the full array of native foods. He served gumbo with hard crabs, Creole style; strawberry shortcake; canvasback ducks with hominy; terrapin in every style—Philadelphia, Baltimore, Maryland, Trenton; and even such simple American dishes as succotash and clam chowder.

When it was necessary—and the price was right—Delmonico's could put on a really dazzling show for the elite of New York, for Presidents, and for visiting royalty and less exalted celebrities. In 1868, when Charles Dickens was visiting America for the second time, the New York Press Club honored him at a special banquet at Delmonico's. Ranhofer's menu was a culinary and literary masterpiece—*crème d'asperges à la Dumas, timbales à la Dickens* and *côtelettes de grouse à la Fenimore Cooper* were a few of the dishes. At the end of the banquet Dickens rose and publicly made amends for his earlier censure of American manners and mores. He not only praised the food he had just relished but added that everywhere he had been "received with unsurpassable politeness, delicacy, sweet temper, hospitality [and] consideration."

An even more sumptuous banquet was underwritten in 1873 by importer Edward Luckmeyer. Luckmeyer had received an unexpected windfall from the government—a $10,000 refund for customs duties—and he decided to blow it all on a dinner to end all dinners. Naturally, he felt that only Lorenzo Delmonico and Charles Ranhofer could be trusted to plan this gala. According to Leopold Rimmer, then Delmonico's headwaiter, it was "the greatest affair that ever could be got up in any land. The table was eighteen feet wide and as long as the hall; it had a big lake in the middle with a big cage over it; there were swans swimming around in it; there were large trees with rustic bird cages, and singing canary birds, and two fountains, stones and sand just like a natural park. Tiffany built the big golden cage; it was a sight. . . ." Ranhofer's book records the menu for this grand occasion, known as the "Swan Dinner." The eight courses ranged from *consommé impériale* and shrimp bisque through hors d'oeuvre, a fish course of red snapper and *paupiettes* of smelt, fillet of beef, chicken cutlets, canvasback duck and cold asparagus vinaigrette. After a pause for a palate-refreshing sherbet, the 75 diners forged on with saddle of mutton, truffled capon and various vegetables, winding up with a galaxy of desserts, glazed fruits and bonbons. Seldom can a tax refund have given so much digestion-taxing pleasure to so many.

The Delmonico panache set the tone, the style and the standards for all New York restaurants of the period. Delmonico alumni like Oscar Tschirky, who became famous as Oscar of the Waldorf, carried on the great tradition. Oscar was not a chef—his sole culinary foray was the Waldorf salad—but he was a superb maître d'hôtel who helped make his dining room the most celebrated in the land.

The peak of New York's lavish restaurant dining was reached in the Gay Nineties. Delmonico's and its great rival, Sherry's, which challenged each other across Fifth Avenue at 44th Street (the last of the Delmonico locations), were conservative and sedate compared to the new and flashier breed of "lobster palaces" like Rector's and Churchill's on Broadway, Shanley's, Bustanoby's and the Knickerbocker. Chorus girls with a taste for champagne, lobster and expensive trinkets were escorted to these plush hangouts by stage-door Johnnies, which may have been how the name "lobster palace," with its risqué connotations, came about.

One man above all epitomized that gay, gaudy, high-living epoch: Diamond Jim Brady, a fabulous character with an equally fabulous appetite matched only by that of one of his constant companions, the actress Lillian Russell. Among other tastes they shared a passion for corn on the cob, dripping with fresh farm butter.

Brady's meals were gargantuan (at his death, it was reported that his stomach was six times the normal size). The restaurateur George Rector called him "the best twenty-five customers we had," and described one of his "regular" dinners. It started with two or three dozen Lynnhaven oys-

Buffet Dansant

Per Person, Service sur Assiette

Oysters or Clams 30 Cocktail 40
Grapefruit Cocktail 60
Celery 30 Cantaloupe 40 Olives 30
Finest Malosol Caviar 1 50
Lobster Cocktail 60
Crab Flake Cocktail 60
Anchovy Canape 50
Hot or Cold en Tasse
Consomme Viveur 30 Chicken Broth 30
Strained Gumbo 30
Cold Crab Ravigote 60 Lobster Newburg 1 00
Crab Meat au Gratin 90
Breast of Chicken, Virginia 1 25
Breast of Guinea Hen, Ideal 1 50
Emince of Chicken a la King 1 00
Scrambled Eggs with Bacon 75
Filet Mignon, Parisian 1 25
Cold Virginia Ham and Chicken 1 00
Cold Boneless Squab Farci, Nerac 1 25
Chicken Salade 1 00 Lobster Salade 1 00
Chicken Sandwich 50 Club Sandwich 60
Ham or Tongue Sandwich 40
All Ice Cream or Ices 35
Biscuit Glace 35 Biscuit Tortoni 35
All Parfaits 35
Melba Peach 60
Petits Fours 25
Lady Fingers 25 Macaroons 25
Cheese 35
Cafe Noir 25
Large Cup Coffee and Cream 35

ters, six inches long, giants specially shipped for Brady's pleasure by Maryland dealers. After this, he might have half a dozen crabs, two portions of green turtle soup and "a deluge of lobsters," perhaps six or seven. Then he would consume a couple of portions of terrapin, two canvasback ducks, a steak and vegetables, and dessert—not just one French pastry, but a platterful. All of this was swilled down with gallons of freshly squeezed orange juice or lemon soda, for with all his gormandizing, Diamond Jim was a teetotaller. Lastly, to appease any lingering pangs of hunger, he allowed himself a two-pound box of candy.

By the time Brady died, in 1917, the golden age of eating was already over (Prohibition was just around the corner). Dancing was now the rage and had been since 1910, when Irving Berlin's *Alexander's Ragtime Band* became a national hit. People preferred to bunny-hug and fox-trot between courses rather than to concentrate on the serious business of eating. One of the last of the great private parties was given by millionaire C. K. G. Billings at Sherry's in 1903, for his fellow members of the New York Riding Club. Formally dressed in white tie and tails, they dined on horseback in the grand ballroom, which had been transformed with plants and sodded floor into a facsimile woodland. Small tables were fastened to the saddles and champagne was piped from the saddlebags.

I wish I could have dined at Sherry's or the old Delmonico's, but by the time I arrived in New York Louis Sherry was but a name on an ice cream, and Delmonico's was long since gone, killed in 1923 by the dead hand of Prohibition; in any event by that time the great restaurant was just a pallid shadow of its past glory.

One old New York landmark that still survives, where I like to go whenever I'm in the mood for some really old-time atmosphere, is Lüchow's on 14th Street, only a short walk from where Delmonico's once flourished. Lüchow's has been in this location ever since 1882, when the street was a hub of Manhattan gaiety, a place of good hotels and restaurants, German beer halls and Italian wine parlors. Lüchow's, with its robust German cooking and imported wines and beers, was the favorite haunt of musicians and opera stars, including Paderewski, Caruso, Richard Strauss and Victor Herbert.

With its dark oak paneling, oil paintings and rows of steins, Lüchow's still calls up a vivid picture of that vanished era. I like to go there in the winter, when the restaurant continues its long-standing tradition of the November venison festival and the mid-January goose festival, and eat my fill of two of my favorite foods, venison steak with chestnut purée and roast goose with apples.

Nowadays, you can get any kind of food you could possibly hunger for in New York's international bazaar of restaurants, from American to Zen Buddhist, and the expense-account restaurants like the Four Seasons, La Grenouille and Le Pavillon are, in their own 20th Century way, no less a symbol of the elegant, expensive life than "Del's" and Rector's were in their day. For in the century and a half since the two Delmonico brothers launched their pioneer venture, New York City has never relinquished its preeminence as the nation's restaurant capital. It is still a great place to live, if you live to eat.

The Gilded Age of Dining Out in Not-so-little Old New York

By the start of the 20th Century, a host of glittering restaurants adorned New York City, but it was the Waldorf-Astoria Hotel that transformed the glitter into gold. While other temples of gastronomy were harried by rising operating costs, the hotel's famous impresario, Oscar Tschirky, elevated dining out to new heights of elegance and made it pay. From royalty *(below)* to *nouveaux riches,* everyone flocked. To handle the overflow, Oscar strung up plush restraining ropes and perfected the cool manner that has become the hallmark of the maître d'hôtel. In a further contribution to the art of dining, Oscar pruned the Waldorf's menu, thus lending his prestige to the then-subversive notion that one did not have to eat much in order to eat well.

MENU
—

TORTUE VERTE À LA WALDORF

CÉLERIS   AMANDES SALÉES   OLIVES

CRABES D'HUITRES À LA NEWBURGH

POITRINE DE PINTADE FARCIE, SAUCE DIABLÉE.
POMMES DOUCES À LA DIXIE   COEURS DE LAITUE À LA FRANCAISE.

PUDDING AU RIZ À L'AMÉRICAINE.

CAFÉ.

White Rock
Cigars
Cigarettes

In 1919 Oscar of the Waldorf arranged a memorable dinner for the visiting Prince of Wales, later King Edward VIII. The cover of the menu *(left)* ornately depicted the Prince's arrival in New York City by battleship, but the relatively sparse bill of fare *(above)* reflected Oscar's distaste for gormandizing.

169

On a summer night, the Waldorf-Astoria Roof Garden entertains a full house with good food and soft music in a casual atmosphere.

New York had a restaurant
for every mood. The
Waldorf-Astoria offered
choices ranging from the
informality of the Roof
Garden *(opposite)* to the
stately precincts of the
Palm Garden *(left)*. Less
stuffy but very fashionable
was Sherry's, where, in
1903, dining out achieved
a new high in frivolity
(below). In a ballroom
that had been sodded over,
36 mounted horsemen ate
dinner in their saddles.

On September 17, 1919, the Waldorf-Astoria produced a sumptuous banquet for a lofty visitor to New York City: Belgium's Cardinal Mercier. Re-created here by the FOODS OF THE WORLD kitchen, the original meal was put together under considerable difficulties. Because Prohibition had lately gone into effect, the "wine list" was reduced to apple cider and sparkling water. And because September 17 fell on an Ember day, when Roman Catholics could not eat meat, the meal was made with fish, vegetables, fruit and cheese. Its menu included meatless hors d'oeuvre, fruit-filled cantaloupe *(top right)*, potato soup, lobster thermidor *(bottom right)*, poached salmon steaks with *mousseline* sauce *(center)*, sautéed potato balls, hearts-of-lettuce salad *(left)*, Port Salut cheese, peach Melba and several varieties of little cakes.

To serve 4

4 live 1½-pound lobsters
3 tablespoons butter, plus
    4 teaspoons butter cut into
    ¼-inch bits
1 cup finely chopped fresh
    mushrooms
¼ cup brandy
2 cups heavy cream
6 egg yolks, lightly beaten
1 tablespoon Worcestershire sauce
1 tablespoon finely chopped
    pimiento
1 tablespoon finely chopped fresh
    parsley
¼ teaspoon ground hot red pepper
    (cayenne)
2 drops Tabasco sauce
1½ teaspoons salt
¼ cup freshly grated imported
    Parmesan cheese
¼ cup soft fresh crumbs made
    from homemade-type white
    bread, pulverized in a blender or
    finely shredded with a fork

Lobster Thermidor

Pour enough water into a 12- to 14-quart pot to fill it halfway, and bring the water to a boil over high heat. Plunge two of the lobsters headfirst into the pot. Both the lobsters should be entirely submerged; if not, add more boiling water.

Cover the pot tightly, return the water to a boil, then reduce the heat to moderate and boil the lobsters for 15 minutes. Regulate the heat if necessary to prevent the water from boiling over, but keep the liquid at a boil throughout the cooking.

To test for doneness, remove one lobster from the pot. Grasp the end of one of the small legs at either side of the body and jerk it sharply. If the leg pulls away from the body, the lobster is done. If the leg remains attached to the body, boil the lobsters for 2 or 3 minutes longer.

With tongs or a slotted spoon, transfer the cooked lobsters to a platter to drain, and boil the remaining 2 lobsters in the same water, adding more water if necessary.

One at a time place the boiled lobsters on a cutting board. Twist off the large claws at the point where they meet the body, crack each claw in two or three places with a cleaver, and pick out all the meat. Cut the lobster meat into ½-inch pieces and reserve it; discard the claw shells.

Twist off the antennae and the legs and discard them. Turn the lobster on its back and, with kitchen scissors, cut lengthwise through the soft tail and stomach shell. Remove and discard the gelatinous sac (stomach) in the head and the long white intestinal vein attached to it. Scoop out and save the greenish-brown tomalley (liver) and the red coral (roe) if any. Lift the tail meat out in one piece and cut it into ½-inch cubes. Set the lobster meat and body shell aside and prepare the three remaining lobsters in the same manner.

About half an hour before you plan to serve the lobsters, preheat the oven to 350°. In a heavy 10- to 12-inch skillet, melt 3 tablespoons of butter over moderate heat. When the foam begins to subside, add the mushrooms and, stirring occasionally, cook uncovered for 8 to 10 minutes, or until the liquid that accumulates in the pan has evaporated. Do not let the mushrooms brown. Stir in the reserved lobster meat.

Warm the brandy in a small saucepan over low heat, ignite it with a match, and pour it flaming over the lobster mixture a little at a time, sliding the skillet gently back and forth until the flames die. Stir in the cream and cook over moderate heat until it comes to a boil.

Reduce the heat to its lowest setting. Ladle about 2 tablespoons of the hot cream into the egg yolks, mix well, and pour the mixture into the skillet. Stirring constantly, simmer over low heat for 2 or 3 minutes, until the sauce thickens and is smooth. Do not let the sauce come anywhere near a boil or the egg yolks will curdle.

Remove the skillet from the heat and stir in the Worcestershire, pimiento, parsley, red pepper, Tabasco and salt. Taste for seasoning. Spoon the lobster-and-mushroom mixture and the sauce into the reserved shells, dividing the mixture evenly among them. Mix together the grated cheese and bread crumbs, and sprinkle them over the lobsters. Dot the tops with the 4 teaspoons of butter bits.

Arrange the lobsters side by side on one or two large baking sheets and bake in the middle of the oven for about 15 minutes, or until the sauce has begun to bubble and the crumb topping has become golden brown. Serve at once.

NOTE: After the lobsters are boiled, the lobster meat and body shells may be separately covered with foil or plastic wrap and safely kept in the refrigerator for up to 24 hours. Or, if you prefer, lobster thermidor may be completely assembled ready for baking, then tightly wrapped and refrigerated for up to 24 hours.

Sautéed Potato Balls

To serve 4 to 6

½ pound unsalted butter, cut into ½-inch bits
9 medium-sized boiling potatoes (about 3 pounds)

First clarify the butter in the following fashion: In a small heavy saucepan, melt the butter over low heat, turning the bits about with a spoon so that they melt slowly and completely without browning. Remove the pan from the heat and let the butter rest for a minute or so. Then skim off and discard the foam. Tipping the pan slightly, spoon the clear butter into a bowl. (There will be about 12 tablespoons.) Discard the milky solids left in the pan.

Peel the potatoes and, with a melon baller or small knife, cut them into balls about 1 inch in diameter. Spread the potato balls on paper towels, and pat them completely dry with fresh towels.

In a heavy 10- to 12-inch skillet, warm 8 tablespoons of the clarified butter over moderate heat. When the butter is hot, drop in the potatoes and brown them lightly. Slide the pan back and forth occasionally to roll the balls around and regulate the heat so that they color evenly without burning. Add more clarified butter by the tablespoonful if necessary.

Reduce the heat to low, cover the skillet tightly and cook for 12 to 15 minutes, still sliding the pan back and forth from time to time. The potatoes are done when they are golden brown and show no resistance when pierced deeply with the point of a small sharp knife. Serve at once.

Waldorf Salad

To serve 6 to 8

3 large firm ripe apples, cored and cut into ½-inch pieces (about 4 cups)
2 tablespoons strained fresh lemon juice
3 medium-sized celery stalks, trimmed and cut into ¼-inch dice (about 2 cups)
1 cup coarsely chopped walnuts
1 cup freshly made mayonnaise (*Recipe Booklet*), or substitute unsweetened bottled mayonnaise
½ cup heavy cream
1 or 2 heads Boston or bibb lettuce, separated into leaves, washed, patted dry and chilled

Oscar Tschirky, who was known as Oscar of the Waldorf and was the maître d'hôtel of the famous Manhattan establishment from 1893 to 1943, invented Waldorf salad. The original version was composed of apples, celery and mayonnaise, served on lettuce. Though chopped walnuts were added later, they have become an almost indispensable ingredient.

Combine the apples and lemon juice in a deep bowl and turn the apple pieces about gently with a spoon to moisten them evenly. Stir in the celery and walnuts. Then, in another bowl, mix the mayonnaise and cream and, when the mixture is smooth, pour it over the apples. Toss all the ingredients together gently but thoroughly.

Shape the lettuce leaves into cups on 6 or 8 chilled individual serving plates. Mound the Waldorf salad in the cups, dividing it evenly among them. Serve at once.

VIII

A New Search for Simplicity

Euell Gibbons, naturalist, author and food expert, plucks wild persimmons from a tree near his house in Troxelville, Pennsylvania. Gibbons' books have helped convince many Americans that natural foods, either found in the wild or raised organically (without the aid of artificial fertilizers and pesticides), taste better and are more nutritious than mass-produced frozen and processed foods.

When America was young, almost everyone was a farmer; now, less than one per cent of the population works the land. In the Eastern Heartland, which contains five of the country's ten largest cities, there are millions of urbanites for whom the taste of good, naturally grown food, the kind our grandmothers used to prepare, has become little more than a memory. Without the modern techniques of processing and distribution, we would undoubtedly go hungry. But where are the home-baked breads and pies, the homemade pickles and preserves of yesteryear? The hand is losing its kitchen cunning, and the palate its discrimination.

Look at many a packaged food label today and you wonder what on earth you are eating, for the unfamiliar terms far outweigh the familiar ones, the chemical content the natural. Already we are being fed mock meats made from protein substitutes such as soybeans; the protein content is chemically extracted, spun into fibers like yarn, then formed into meatlike textures—in short, meatless meats.

Only rarely now, when we bite into a home-baked pie made with freshly picked blueberries or into a chunk of bread just out of the oven, crusty and brown and exuding the sweet earthy smell of yeast, do we realize what we are missing—food the way it used to taste. This is more than nostalgia. To munch a home-grown tomato, vine-ripened in the sun, is a positive delight, a revelation after the pale, tasteless tomatoes that huddle under plastic wrapping in supermarkets.

Yet there are encouraging signs that a consumer rebellion has begun against nonfood—food with no taste, no texture and, all too often, minimal nutritional value. The supermarket is here to stay, of course. The convenience and variety it offers have become an accepted part of modern life. But more and more people are turning back to some of the old ways, baking their own bread, growing their own herbs and produce, insisting on food that is really fresh. Increasing numbers of shoppers are taking the trouble to buy naturally grown produce—that which has *not* been sprayed with pesticides or treated with chemicals—and a small but growing number of people are fervently embracing the pleasures of stalking and eating the many delicacies that still grow wild for the picking.

There is nothing faddish, cranky or newfangled about this interest in the quality of the food we eat. A hundred years ago, in many parts of the Eastern Heartland from upper New York State to Indiana, there were communities of farmers whose concern for the quality of the foods they raised has perhaps never been surpassed. These were the Shakers, members of a sect that in its heyday produced some of the most enlightened and successful farmers in America, with a deep feeling for the land and all that grew on it.

Of all the pietist sects that settled throughout America in the 18th and 19th Centuries, the Shakers have always seemed to me the most fascinating, and certainly they were the most influential, because of their great contributions to the development of the agronomy and economy of this country and its cooking and manufacturing skills. They originated one of the greatest native styles of furniture, with a spare, austere beauty that

A 19th Century print depicts the brothers and sisters of a Shaker community performing a formal dance intended to shake off worldly doubts and to purge them of lust. This dance step, the "square order shuffle," evolved in the 1780s from the disorganized frenzies of leaping, shouting and shaking that gave the sect its name. Ultimately, the Shakers' rule of celibacy succeeded only too well: the sect has all but disappeared for the lack of children.

has become a classic of functional design. They invented a rotary harrow and threshing machine, a circular saw, a cheese press and a clothespin.

In a day when most farmers looked no further ahead than the next harvest, the Shakers pioneered in the careful cultivation of orchards and vegetable gardens, developed new and better species of fruits, established plant nurseries. From their spotless barns came dairy products superior to those of the neighboring farms. Honey was gathered, nuts harvested and maple syrup boiled down in great quantity. The fields of the Shaker communities were painstakingly tended and they yielded bountifully; many vegetables were planted and harvested twice in a season. "A tree has its wants and wishes," a Shaker elder wrote, "and a man should study them as a teacher watches a child to see what it can do. If you love a plant, take heed what it likes, you will be repaid by it."

The Shakers were repaid, in fact, both by their satisfaction in work well done and by more material rewards. For all their isolation from The World, as they referred to everyone other than themselves, they were very shrewd businessmen. They grew much more food than they needed, so they canned vegetables and fruits, packaged seeds and herbs and sold them far beyond the boundaries of their communities. They were particularly expert at growing an extraordinary variety of herbs, some of which, such as peppermint and feverfew, were used medicinally; at one time they offered a selection of more than 350 medicinal herbs, barks, roots, seeds and flowers, which they sold as far away as Australia and India.

Their seed catalogues listed an astonishing diversity—four kinds of onions, six kinds of squash, eight types of beans and as many peas, six choices of carrots and beets, melons of all types, cabbage, collard, mustard and other greens, and all manner of root vegetables. They also originated the mix—a basic formula of flour, baking powder, salt and shortening, but with no preservatives or flavorings—that, with the addition of liquid, could be turned into muffins, biscuits or pancakes. They were, indeed, the original American food processors.

The first Shakers arrived in America from England in 1774—a band of eight religious dissenters and their leader and prophetess, Mother Ann Lee, who had seceded from the Quakers. They belonged to a sect called The United Society of Believers in Christ's Second Appearing and were dubbed Shakers or Shaking Quakers from their extraordinary manner of worshiping: they were given to dancing, shaking, whirling, falling down in trances, and experiencing religious ecstasies in which they saw visions and spoke in strange tongues.

They believed in communal living and the common ownership of goods, a precept that was the more easily followed because the order was strictly celibate and there was no question of inheritance. They were never idle. "Give your hands to work and your hearts to God," was the credo by which they lived, and they considered labor sacred, relative perfection within the reach of everyone, and the functionalism of an object more important than its appearance.

Their celibate ranks were swelled by converts attracted to their peaceful, industrious way of life; and there were children, too—abandoned or orphaned youngsters taken in from nearby communities and reared with love and kindness. By the end of the 18th Century the Shakers had established prosperous communities in New York—the parent community was in New Lebanon, not far from Albany—and throughout New England. They went west during the great push across the Alleghenies into Ohio and Indiana, and by the last half of the 19th Century there were 19 settlements in all, most of them in the Eastern Heartland.

These Shaker communities were organized into "families" of between 30 and 100 members, each under the supervision of elders and elderesses, who directed the spiritual life, and deacons and deaconesses, who were charged with temporal matters: farming, building, making furniture and clothing, and preparing food. Meals were eaten in a common dining room with several long tables; each table was set with jugs of milk or cider and large baskets of bread, and the meat, fish, fowl and vegetables were brought from the kitchen in large bowls and platters. The food was plentiful, but waste was frowned upon. "Shaker your plate" has passed down to us an admonition against leaving a plate with untouched food. The families ate in silence, not from a lack of amiability but because talking whiles away time, and they knew the sisters working in the kitchen had little enough time to prepare three meals a day for as many as a hundred people.

As their communities grew, the Shakers became adept at large-scale cooking, and devised many inventions and innovations to speed food preparation. They had one kitchen for general cooking, another for baking, a third for canning. The kitchens had running water, stone sinks and such niceties as an oven from which finished loaves or pies could be removed by rotating the shelves. They invented a gadget for paring, coring and quartering apples, a pea sheller, a water-powered butter churn. While most early American written-down recipes were on the vague side—a "pinch" of this, a "handful" of that, "enough" of the other—the Shakers worked out an exact system of weights and measures based on pounds, quarts, cups and tablespoons. (Some of their formulas were less scientific but equally effective. In advising when apples were ready for the cider mill, one elder wrote: "Place the apples on the grass on the north or shady side of the barn to mellow. When at thirty feet distance you catch the fragrant apple aroma, they are ready for the press.")

In days when the national diet was stodgy with starch and heavy on salted meats and fish, the value of fresh vegetables and fruits was recognized by the Shakers. They scrubbed vegetables and boiled, baked or steamed them in their skins, saving the nourishing "pot likker" for soups, stews and sauces. And they did not overcook the vegetables. "The long boiling of any vegetable in water extracts the salts that are so beneficial," wrote one sister, evincing a wisdom that eludes many cooks even today.

Shaker cooks were skilled at cooking with herbs, using rosemary and summer savory, borage and basil, chives and chervil, mint and thyme in their recipes and instructing non-Shakers in the gentle art of herb cookery through the circulars sent out with orders of packaged herbs. The spacious Shaker outbuildings where herbs and wild roots were dried, ground and distilled, then boxed and labeled at long counters, were fragrant with the pervasive scent of rosemary and lavender and the petals of the

180

Continued on page 186

Round Stone Barn, at Hancock Shaker Village in Massachusetts, has a high central hayloft directly handy to the 52 cow stalls.

A Graceful Heritage of Simple, Useful Treasures

For the Shakers, true beauty consisted of a perfect union of simplicity and efficiency, and in pursuit of this ideal they made elegantly austere furniture and fabrics, clocks and baskets that were functional masterpieces. The Shakers not only grew all their own food, but canned much of it for sale to the outside world. And their ingenious practicality even showed in the few things they did not make for themselves. When ordering crockery containers for canning and cooking *(right)*, they standardized their purchases and identified each size and type of container by a specific color and pattern. Thus their recipes could indicate a precise quantity by merely calling for "buttermilk in the blue and white pitcher," or for beating "eggs in the yellow bowl with blue stripe."

The Shaker name on preserved foods guaranteed excellence.

A woman in homespun worsted kneads dough in the well-equipped kitchen where the Hancock Village community cooked its meals.

Imaginative planning and superb craftsmanship went into the Shaker kitchens, even to the smallest details. The communal kitchen in Hancock Village had a row of pegs *(right)* where chairs were hung at cleaning time. Baking was facilitated by the circular oven's rotating shelves, shown at left with two cherry pies *(top)*, a tea loaf and mince tarts. Another dessert baked in this oven was Mother Ann's birthday cake *(right)*, served March 1 to honor Ann Lee, who led the first Shakers to America in 1774. *(See the Recipe Index.)*

Shaker cookery made superb use of herbs. This meat-stuffed flank steak boasts rosemary, basil, savory and sage; asparagus with lemon cream sauce has mint, and Shaker salad a thyme-and-savory dressing. For all these dishes see the Recipe Index.

The beautifully polished tables in the central dining hall at Hancock Shaker Village were left bare at mealtimes, but the napkins were ample enough to be spread under the plates as well as over the diners' laps. To enhance their tables, the Shakers relied upon food alone, using the appeal of "neatly dished" victuals to good advantage. This typical menu includes golden-brown roasted chicken with gravy, mashed squash ornamented with chives and tomato wedges, pickles and a bowl of crimson cranberry sauce.

heavy-headed, deep-red damask roses from which the sisters made rose water and rose extract, used not only for food flavoring but in unguents and lotions as well.

For 18th and 19th Century America, Shaker cooking showed a remarkably epicurean touch. Spinach was flavored with rosemary *(Recipe Index),* apple pie with rose water. A delicate, fragrant herb soup combined chives, celery, sorrel, chervil, tarragon, nutmeg and chicken stock *(Recipe Index).* There was even a recipe for *dolma,* which an enterprising Shaker sister of the community of North Union (now Shaker Heights) near Cleveland must have culled somehow from Middle Eastern cooking in order to make use of the leaves from the grape vines the Shakers cultivated on the shores of Lake Erie for medicinal wines and unfermented grape juice. In their early days the Shakers had nothing against the use of alcoholic drinks—hard cider and peach brandy from their orchards, fruit wines and cordials. But in 1828, in a sudden access of strictness, the mother community in New Lebanon banned the use of "beer, cider, wines and all ardent liquors . . . on all occasions; at house-raisings, husking bees, harvestings and all other gatherings."

Still, for all their abstinence and piety, the Shakers were not dour folk, and took much delight in simple pleasures. One 19th Century Shaker reminiscence recalls a picnic enjoyed by the women of one of the Ohio communities: "The little band of sisters left their dwellings and crossed the fields singing like a flock of young blackbirds on a bright morning . . . they swing on tangled ropes of grapevines, gather wild dew-berries and wintergreens and the younger group rides bareback on the old horse. . . . The older sisters now spread their humble feast under a blooming red-bud tree. It is more than a feast—songs, mirth, good fellowship, and ample spread combined! . . . a spotless white cloth is spread on the green turf; great loaves of fresh-baked bread, plump rolls of golden butter, eggs, delicate cakes, and crusty cookies with fruit shrub and creamy milk emerge in abundance from the wide hampers."

I feel a distinct nostalgia in reading Shaker recipes. The names ring like a chime of old, sweet bells: Sister Lottie's Shaker gems (little muffins), Sister Abigail's strawberry flummery, Sister Abigail's blue-flower omelet and Sister Lizzie's sugar pie *(Recipe Index).* The blue flowers were chive blossoms and, as I always seem to have an excess of them in my garden in the summer, I tried Sister Abigail's trick of putting them in an omelet. The result was most appealing—the crunchiness of the blooms, with their strong oniony taste, makes a good contrast to the blandness of the eggs. Sister Lizzie's sugar pie, described as "a toothsome pie, especially beloved by children and a good recipe to fall back on when the apple-bins are empty in the spring," couldn't be simpler: just a pie shell spread with layers of creamed butter and maple or brown sugar with a sprinkling of flour, then filled with vanilla-flavored cream and baked. But toothsome it decidedly is—rich and creamy and sweet.

I found sugar pie on the luncheon menu of Ohio's oldest inn, The Golden Lamb in Lebanon, which is not far from the site of the Shaker community of Union Village north of Cincinnati. (This, like many other Shaker communities, was dissolved in the first decade of the 20th Century as the Shakers gradually died out and new converts could not be attracted. Now relics of the old Shaker community life are cherished in museums or reconstructed villages, such as those at Chatham, New York, and Hancock, Massachusetts.) The owners of The Golden Lamb, Lee and Michael Comisar, who also run two fine restaurants in Cincinnati, have laudably included some of the fine old Shaker recipes in the inn's bill of fare—notably the sugar pie and Shaker stuffed flank steak *(Recipe Index)*, with a filling of sausage meat, bread crumbs and spices that resembles a coarse pâté when the dish is served cold.

I wish there were more menus that boasted Shaker dishes. Simply but imaginatively prepared with the freshest ingredients, they typify the highest standard country-style cooking of the America that was. It would be a loss were they to vanish, as the communities themselves have done.

Yet it is heartening to find people here and there who share the Shakers' love of the land and of honest, wholesome food. An article in a Shaker magazine of the 1870s complained that millers were discarding the live germ of the grain, and the writer deplored the adulterated result, adding that "what had for countless ages been the staff of life has now become a weak crutch." I heard the echo of those words recently, standing by a wheat field in the rolling country west of the Susquehanna River in central Pennsylvania. The farm is called Walnut Acres and its owner, Paul Keene, was speaking: "The cheapening of products for the mass market has damaged the food and health of the people. Unless there is some kind of reversal now, in 10 years there will be no quality left, because everything will be raised for the machine. Nature is being bent to meet the fancied needs of man, no matter what suffers in the process."

For more than a quarter of a century Mr. Keene has been doing his best to bring about a reversal of this trend. His 400-acre farm is one of the largest producers and distributors of natural foods in the country. It ships grains, vegetables and a variety of prepared foods to customers wherever the demand for natural foods has taken hold. No chemicals, herbicides or pesticides are used on the plants at Walnut Acres. This is particularly important for root vegetables such as carrots and potatoes, which are in closest contact with DDT and other poisons in the soil. As we walked by a large, carefully groomed vegetable plot Paul pulled up a carrot from the ground and rubbed it clean for me to eat on the spot. It looked pretty much like a carrot anywhere, but the taste was a world apart from that of the bland, woody carrots I had last bought in a city market. Crisp and juicy, it had an intense, earthy sweetness that I had almost forgotten about.

Paul Keene thinks many more people are beginning to see the importance of all this care. "The trend to organic farming and natural foods is really becoming a tremendous movement," he says. "So many of the younger generation are reverting to the old ways; they want to get their feet in the soil and work with their hands." I am sure he is right about younger people learning to appreciate the earth's bounty at its purest and freshest, for it is among the children of my friends that I have found the greatest concern with the origin of the foods they eat. And certainly among many of the older generation, particularly those with European backgrounds, there is still a deep feeling for the natural foods that the earth brings forth. I can think of no better example than my friends Joseph and Wanda Czarnecki, who live in another part of Pennsylvania.

The Czarneckis' particular passion is mushrooms, which grow in great profusion all across the Eastern Heartland, including thousands of edible varieties. In Michigan's Upper Peninsula, for example, mushrooms flourish in the forests and amid the hardwood slashings left by the lumber industry, and the small but mixed ethnic population there has very definite preferences. The Italians gather the honey, or stump, mushroom *(Armilaria mellea)*, which grows on tree stumps, and pickle it, can it and use it in *antipasto*. If an Italian woman doesn't have a hundred quarts canned, I was told, she doesn't feel ready for the winter. The French pick morels in May and June, chanterelles in August and early fall. Germans and Poles, by tradition, gather the *Boletus edulis*, which is one of the most popular and flavorful of mushrooms.

But of all the mushroom lovers I have met, the Czarneckis (who are of Polish descent) are the most dedicated. They operate a restaurant in Reading called Joe's, which is, so far as I know, the only place in the country where wild mushroom dishes, soups, sauces and stuffings are always on the menu. (Serving wild mushrooms in a restaurant is illegal in some states—Michigan, for one—but not in Pennsylvania.)

Furthermore, I could have found no more experienced, patient and enlightening mentors in the art of mushroom hunting. My previous experience with mushrooming had been limited to the familiar, smooth-capped, white field mushroom, *Agaricus campestris*. (Once, on a summer weekend on Long Island, I spotted some on my host's smooth green lawn. He was less confident than I. "You eat one tonight," he said dubiously, "and if you're still alive in the morning, I'll try them.") But the Czarneckis' knowledge is encyclopedic; Joe can identify most edible mushrooms he finds from various characteristics visible to the naked eye that are giveaways to the expert. Like all experienced mycologists, Joe is careful to preserve intact for later study mushrooms he cannot immediately identify; they must be dug up so the base of the stem can be seen. A swelling cup or bulb, known as a volva, may indicate a deadly species.

Joe and Wanda go out on their forays at 4:30 or 5 in the morning, two days a week, nine months of the year, even in deep snow; and while she is picking, he is often stretched out on the ground with his camera, painstakingly photographing a new discovery for his records. I made two excursions with them, one in late August, when some of the more spectacular mushrooms appear, the other in October when Joseph and Wanda pick most of the mushrooms to be canned and dried for the restaurant.

For the first trip we met early in the morning, piled into the Czarneckis' Japanese-made jeep and headed for a spot in the Blue Mountains near Hawk Mountain Sanctuary. Serious mushroom hunters keep secret the location of their picking grounds, as fishermen do their trout pools, and they bristle visibly when they find anyone else in their territory.

The day was cool, cloudy, hinting at showers. Heavy rainfall had brought out the mushrooms but many of them were wormy and not fit to eat. We deposited the picnic gear at a shelter and fanned out with our

 Continued on page 193

Tiny bluegills *(above and below)* are tasty samples of the wild food Gibbons finds within an hour's walk of home.

The Bounty of Wild Land and Open Water

Beyond man's tilled fields and stocked fish ponds or oyster beds, nature offers delicacies that never appear on supermarket shelves. Sport fish, game animals and birds, and edible "weeds," all fascinating to hunt or track down, can provide the makings for a feast as lavish as the one shown on page 192.

Though master forager Euell Gibbons *(above)* once found 15 edible wild plants in a Chicago vacant lot, the most promising hunting grounds for roots, berries, nuts and leaves *(overleaf)* are old fields and farms, fence rows, roadsides and overgrown woods. Gibbons does his stalking around his Pennsylvania home, and there are literally thousands of other places in the Eastern Heartland where man can live off the land.

American persimmon trees grow wild in most states east of the Rockies. The ripe fruit, orange and grape-sized, tastes rather like fresh apricot. (Cultivated Oriental persimmons are large and red.)

Ground cherries grow in the Eastern, Southern and Southwestern U.S. A papery husk protects the half-inch berry, which is yellow to orange when ripe and tastes like a blend of strawberry and tomato.

Burdock, a "weed" of the Northern United States is cultivated by the Japanese in Hawaii. Young plants yield flavorsome leaves, seed stalks and roots; in older plants, the pith of the bloom stalk is edible.

The Jerusalem artichoke, sometimes called a Canada potato, is a variety of sunflower that grows both wild and under tillage. The edible tuber looks like a small sweet potato, but has white flesh. Eaten raw or boiled, it tastes like artichoke heart.

Wild hickory trees are found in most states east of the Rockies, and several species produce excellent nuts that can be used in pies, bread and cookies. The nuts are about an inch in diameter, with smooth shells best cracked with a hammer.

Chokecherry trees, common everywhere from Newfoundland to Texas, bear a dark-red "cherry" about the size of a pea when fully ripe. Highly astringent and just barely palatable, the fruit is very well suited for making jellies.

Raw wintergreen berries are a tingling treat; the leaves add zest to tea.

baskets. In an incredibly short time we had seen, identified and picked at least a dozen different kinds of mushrooms, admiring but avoiding the glowing orange jack-o'-lantern and the red-capped *Russula emetica,* both of which are poisonous. Our haul was diverse and fascinating—among other varieties the *Russula viriscens,* with a beautiful pale-green cap; the little *Clavaria,* or coral mushrooms, with delicate white or pale-yellow fronds that look just like a branch of coral; the charcoal-colored, funnel-shaped horn of plenty, or *Craterellus cornucopiodes,* sometimes called the poor-man's truffle; and the bright yellowy-orange *Cantharellus floccosus,* one of the most gorgeous of the trumpetlike chanterelles. The differences of form, color, even of flavor among these edible mushrooms were amazing. One we picked, *Lactarius piperatus,* exuded a milky liquid when the cap was broken and Joseph told me to touch it with the tip of my tongue. It was as burning hot as a chili pepper.

Joseph identified and reserved or discarded the mushrooms we had collected according to their edibility (some mushrooms, though not poisonous, do not make particularly good eating), and he washed in a stream the ones he had kept. Then he sliced them and tossed them into a big iron skillet, sautéed them in butter over our picnic fire, seasoned them, sprinkled them lavishly with shallots and, when they were almost done, stirred in lots of sour cream. The mushrooms tasted like food for the gods. We ate them with a thick charcoal-broiled steak and sourdough bread—baked by Wanda the day before—and it was one of the most gloriously satisfying meals I have ever had, indoors or out.

Our second safari into the woods was much more businesslike. We were hunting for the winter's supply of *Boletus* and three kinds of *Tricholoma: equestre,* which has a pale yellow or deep cream cap and gills, and *portentosum* and *terreum,* which have gray caps with white gills. These mushrooms grow in pine forests, and Joseph told me to work up the slopes so I could better see the spots where the emerging mushrooms, pushing their way up through the thick carpet of pine needles, leave telltale mounds. "Look for the hump, not the mushroom," he said.

If I had not learned this, I doubt I would have found many at all, for every time I came upon a clump, it seemed the deer and the rabbits had beaten me to it. I covered the ground slowly and with utter concentration, but at the end of the afternoon I felt like a flop, for my basket was only half full, while Wanda and Joseph had two or three big hauls. But that, after all, is the difference between the amateur and the expert.

When we got back to the restaurant, I realized what long, grueling work mushroom picking can be. There was still much more to be done, cleaning the fragile fungi and "cooking them off" before they spoiled. First Wanda soaked them in lukewarm water, until the dirt and pine needles were loosened, and rinsed them under a fine spray of water. Then she trimmed the stems off half an inch below the cap and cut any bad bits away. She brought the caps to a boil to dislodge any extraneous matter in the gills, and washed them again. She measured them into empty pots, covered them with water, with two tablespoons of kosher salt added for every quart of mushrooms, brought the water to a boil and cooked the mushrooms for 20 minutes.

Opposite: Wild foods can be cooked in as many ways as cultivated ones, and experimenting with them costs almost nothing. Euell Gibbons, who gathered and prepared this dinner for five guests, spent not much more than a dollar on it, for just a few store-bought items. Clockwise from top left, his menu included a carafe of tea brewed from a wild mint called pennyroyal; cream-cheese pie covered with glazed blueberries; wild-strawberry jam; ground cherries; boiled poke sprouts, which look and taste like asparagus; American-persimmon and hickory-nut bread *(Recipe Index);* boiled Jerusalem artichokes; batter-fried bluegill fillets *(Recipe Index);* wild fruit soup with sour cream *(Recipe Index)* and boiled burdock stalk.

Now the mushrooms were ready to be canned—put into Mason jars and sealed, but not too firmly. "Just give the screw-top lids a normal turn," Wanda told me. "They shouldn't be absolutely tight at the begin-ing." The jars are then immersed in boiling water, which should come an inch above the lids, and boiled for 45 minutes to an hour. All this takes time, and when Wanda told me that one day she had canned 38 quarts of mushrooms, I was staggered by this evidence of her energy.

I was even more impressed when I took my own haul of mushrooms back to New York and dutifully cooked them off, as instructed. I fell into bed at 2 a.m., aching all over with weariness. Mushrooming, I decided, was a bit too rugged for me.

I changed my mind the next day when I had friends to dinner and proudly served sautéed *Tricholoma equestre* with a rack of lamb. The mushrooms had a rare quality and a slightly gelatinous texture that slipped along the tongue like silk. My friends were enchanted and asked me end-less questions about how and where they were picked. I reveled in their interest and praise—and it made every minute of that backbreaking pick-ing and tedious cleaning and cooking worthwhile.

There are many wild foods besides mushrooms that most of us are familiar with: the nuts, greens and berries that grow thickly in fields and woods beyond the urban sprawl. It takes a more perspicacious eye to spot the edible foods that lie in hiding below the ground or concealed within a tough outer covering. It had never occurred to me that you could eat cattails or bulrushes or the root of the thistle—until I spent a day hunting wild foods with author and naturalist Euell Gibbons.

Euell, who lives in an old, remote farmhouse buried in central Penn-sylvania, probably has done more than anyone else in this country to make Americans aware of the bounty and the superbly fresh taste of the wild foods that surround them. His books, *Stalking the Wild Asparagus* and *Stalking the Blue-eyed Scallop,* one of which covers the plants and creatures of the countryside, the other of the shoreline, have been tre-mendously popular. When I first met Euell, a few years ago, he gave me a standing invitation to come and have a "wild" dinner. "I discover new wild foods around my place every year," he said. "About 150 to 200 at last count, although only 60 or 70 qualify as really good palatable things you'd enjoy eating."

So one crisp fall day when the countryside of Pennsylvania seemed in-finitely more desirable than the canyons of New York, I took him up on his offer. The air had a sharp edge, the sky was a cloudless blue, and a faint golden haze hung over the fields as we set out in the morning to for-age for our dinner. Behind the house, a tangle of woods encroached on the garden and nearby was a hackberry bush with reddish-purple berries from which Euell had made his first wild food at the age of five. "I took hackberries and hickory nuts and made myself a candy bar."

Beside the vegetable patch was a stand of sunflowers. These were the type whose roots are the tubers we call Jerusalem artichokes (the word Je-rusalem is a corruption of *girasol,* the Spanish for sunflower; the plant has no connection with the true artichoke, which is a member of the this-tle family). Euell dug up a good supply of the tubers to slice and put in the salad we would have that evening. Next came another salad ingredient, the small arrowhead-shaped bitter leaves picked from a patch of sheep sorrel. Then we crossed the road to a marshy stream thick with watercress. Great handfuls of this went into one of the plastic bags Euell always carries to cache his finds. "We get all the watercress we can eat right here," he said. "The water is perfectly pure; this is the head of the spring."

For the last of our salad pickings we drove up the road into Bald Eagle State Forest. There are no houses here, just woods from which deer made their way in front of us. We walked into the woodland to hunt for the glossy scarlet wintergreen berries that spark out from beneath the leaves underfoot. When I spied one, I picked it and bit into it—the wintergreen taste was very strong, so strong that Euell admitted he had had quite a time trying to find some way to use the berries until he had found that they add quite a zip to a salad. Local people, he told me, pick the leaves when they turn red to make a mild pink wine they call "women's wine."

Returning to the house, we deposited our laden bags and walked down the road to a field almost completely overgrown with vegetation. "I could live off this old field," said Euell. "There are loads of berries in the fence rows—black raspberries, blackberries, wild cherries, chokecherries, elderberries. You can make wine and jelly from the elderberries and if you half-dry them on a screen they make a very good pie filling. I dip the blossoms in batter and make fritters of them; they have a pleasant mild flavor, a little sweet."

With a spade he dug up the root of a thistle that when cooked is firm yet tender, with the flavor of an artichoke; then he uncovered the long fibrous brown root of the burdock, which I had last seen in Oriental food stores in New York. The Japanese slice it and cook it in sukiyaki, but the texture is very tough and stringy. The stalk is much more edible, and Euell had decided we should have this as the starchy part of our vegetable course. For the green part, we collected dandelions, just the tender crowns, the blanched leaf section above the root, since the outer leaves are strong and bitter so late in the year.

Bordering the road only about half a mile from the house were fallow cornfields, along the edges of which were trees burdened with tiny wild persimmons that we shook down onto a big sheet of plastic. The persimmons were sweet as honey, and Euell said that October is the best month for them. Sprawling along the ground were the plants of the ground cherry, which isn't a cherry at all but a member of the tomato family—it is, in fact, often called husk tomato or strawberry tomato (the Hawaiians call it *poha*). Inside the thin papery husk, which looks like a miniature Japanese lantern, is a small round yellow or orange fruit with a slightly acid bite. It is the basis for one of the most glorious jams I've ever tasted *(Recipe Index),* but you can also eat it like a berry, or make it into a pie, which was Euell's intention.

By now it was late afternoon, and time to catch the main course. We drove to a pond that lay at the bottom of a hill planted with apple trees, their boughs bent to the ground under the weight of huge red apples ready to be picked. The sun was low, the sky had paled and the air was definitely chilly. The motionless surface of the pond, like a dull dark green mirror, trapped the reflections of the sun's dying rays and of the trees across the water, their leaves mellowed to a soft gold. Euell fished for our supper, pulling out several wriggling bluegills and one or two ugly, tough little catfish that weren't going to give up without a struggle; I sat on the bank, letting the peace and beauty of the scene lap around me and wondering why people, myself included, ever chose to immure themselves in the drab concrete-and-steel jungles of cities.

Dinner was an adventure in new textures and tastes. Euell and his wife, Freda, had cleaned and prepared all the foods and then he did the cooking. Not everything was made on the spot, since he already had some things on hand; but most of the meal consisted of foods we had gathered that day. First we had a cold fruit soup made from fox grapes, which had a rich winy flavor. Then the fish, filleted and fried *tempura* style in a batter coating *(Recipe Index)*. With them came the burdock stem (which tastes rather like a potato), peeled, sliced and cooked in salted water, and the dandelion crowns (not bitter, but as mild in flavor as lettuce), boiled for 5 minutes, then drained, seasoned and dressed with butter. The salad was a brilliant composition of vivid red, white and green, with the wintergreen berries blazing against the leaves of the watercress and sheep sorrel, the creamy white of the Jerusalem artichokes.

Euell had taken from the freezer a loaf of persimmon-and-hickory-nut bread *(Recipe Index)*, which we ate with squaw huckleberry jam. The bread was utterly delicious: moist, nutty and tangy with the persimmon pulp. "I just took a recipe for banana-and-walnut bread and used persimmons and hickory nuts instead," Euell revealed. "That was one recipe that came out right from the beginning; I never had occasion to change it. Most years, hickory nuts aren't plentiful. But when they are, I bag them and put them in the freezer. They keep almost indefinitely."

For dessert, Euell had made a ground-cherry chiffon pie for which the tiny fruit had been puréed in the blender. It was an inspired idea—the fluffy lightness of the filling was a perfect base for the subtle undertones, at once sweet and sharp, of the ground cherries. To round out our wild dinner we had sassafras tea, an old American brew with a faintly medicinal, herblike taste that is strangely soothing and refreshing.

I had had some misgivings about a whole meal built around wild foods, expecting a collection of curiosities rather than good eating, but at this point my reservations had wholly vanished. From start to finish it had been a memorable and unusual dinner.

After such adventurous days with the Czarneckis and Euell Gibbons, shopping in the city now seems tame by comparison. More than ever I realize how much more there is to food than simply eating it. My encounters with friends throughout the Eastern Heartland who feel the same way have encouraged me to believe that all over the country people are rediscovering the great enjoyment and inner satisfactions that come from things as elemental as growing vegetables, baking bread or gathering berries. After all, what better way is there to spend leisure time than to hunt for wild foods in the countryside, thus sharing with the birds and animals the oldest and most basic of all searches—the search for food? It is truly a pursuit of happiness.

Ground-Cherry Jam

Ground cherries are not cherries at all, but the edible berries of low, sprawling, bushy plants that often appear wild although they may be grown from seed. Enclosed in a papery Japanese lanternlike husk, the berry is also known as a husk tomato, strawberry tomato or dwarf cape gooseberry. It is smooth, greenish yellow or orange when ripe, and about ½ inch in diameter.

Drop the ground cherries into a heavy 3- to 4-quart enameled saucepan and crush them lightly with the back of a wooden spoon. Add the lemon peel and water and bring to a boil over high heat. Then cook briskly, uncovered, for 5 minutes, or until a ground cherry can be easily mashed against the side of the pot with the back of the spoon.

Stirring constantly, add the sugar and boil vigorously for 1 minute. Remove the pan from the heat and immediately stir in the liquid pectin. Carefully skim off the surface foam with a large spoon. Ladle the jam into hot sterilized jars or jelly glasses and seal them at once, following the directions for home canning in the Recipe Booklet.

To make 1 pint

2 cups husked, fully ripe ground cherries, washed
1 tablespoon finely grated fresh lemon peel
¼ cup water
2 cups sugar
3 tablespoons liquid fruit pectin

Wild-Persimmon and Hickory-Nut Bread

Preheat the oven to 325°. With a pastry brush, spread 2 tablespoons of the softened butter over the bottom and sides of two 9-by-5-by-3-inch loaf pans. Add 2 tablespoons of the flour to each pan, tipping the pan back and forth to distribute the flour evenly. Invert the pans and rap them sharply on the bottoms to remove the excess flour.

Combine the 2 cups of flour, the baking soda and salt, and sift them together onto a plate or sheet of wax paper. Set aside.

Wash the persimmons gently under cold running water and let them drain in a colander. With a small sharp knife, cut them into quarters and pick out the seeds. Purée the persimmons through a food mill set over a bowl, or rub them through a coarse sieve with the back of a spoon. You will need about 1 cup of puréed fruit.

In a deep bowl, cream the remaining 12 tablespoons of softened butter and the sugar by beating and mashing them against the sides of the bowl with the back of a spoon until light and fluffy. Beat in the eggs, one at a time. Add 1 cup of the flour mixture and, when it is thoroughly incorporated, beat in about ½ cup of the puréed fruit. Add the remaining 1 cup of the flour mixture and then the rest of the purée, beating well after each addition. Stir in the hickory nuts.

Pour the batter into the two buttered-and-floured pans, dividing it equally between them and spreading it evenly with a rubber spatula. Bake in the middle of the oven for about 1 hour, or until the loaves begin to shrink away from the sides of the pans and a toothpick or cake tester inserted in the centers comes out clean.

Turn the loaves out on wire racks to cool. Serve the bread warm or at room temperature.

To make two 9-by-5-by-3-inch loaves

14 tablespoons butter, softened
4 tablespoons plus 2 cups unsifted flour
1 teaspoon baking soda
½ teaspoon salt
1 pound fully ripe wild persimmons (about 2 dozen)
1 cup sugar
2 eggs
1 cup coarsely chopped hickory nuts

To serve 6 to 8

A 2- to 2½-pound flank steak,
　thoroughly trimmed
8 tablespoons butter
4 or 5 slices homemade-type white
　bread, cut into ¼-inch cubes
　(2 cups)
1 cup finely chopped onions
1 cup finely chopped celery
¼ pound lean ground beef
¼ pound lean ground veal
¼ pound lean ground pork
1 egg
¼ cup finely chopped fresh parsley
¼ teaspoon crumbled dried
　rosemary
½ teaspoon crumbled dried basil
½ teaspoon crumbled dried savory
¼ teaspoon ground sage
1½ teaspoons salt
¼ teaspoon freshly ground black
　pepper
2 tablespoons vegetable oil
2 medium-sized celery stalks,
　trimmed, leaves removed, cut
　crosswise into ¼-inch-thick
　slices
1 medium-sized onion, peeled and
　cut crosswise into ¼-inch-thick
　slices
1 medium-sized carrot, scraped and
　coarsely chopped
1 cup beef stock, fresh or canned,
　or 1 cup water or a combination
　of the two

Flank Steak with Meat Stuffing, Shaker Style

Ask your butcher to cut a pocket in the steak, or do it yourself in the following manner: With a long, very sharp knife, slit the steak horizontally from one of the long sides, cutting through the steak to within about ½ inch of the other long side and to within about 1 inch of each short end.

Preheat the oven to 350°. In a heavy 8- to 10-inch skillet, melt 4 tablespoons of the butter over moderate heat. Add the bread cubes and, stirring frequently, fry them until they are crisp and golden brown. With a slotted spoon, transfer the cubes to a deep bowl.

Melt 2 more tablespoons of butter in the skillet, add the chopped onions and chopped celery and stir for about 5 minutes, until they are soft but not brown. With a rubber spatula, scrape the onions and celery over the bread cubes. Add the ground beef, veal, pork, egg, parsley, rosemary, basil, savory, sage, salt and pepper. Knead vigorously with both hands, then beat with a wooden spoon until all the ingredients are well blended.

Holding the steak upright on its long closed side, pack the stuffing tightly into the pocket, a handful at a time. Then lay the steak flat and close the open side by sewing it with a large needle and white thread.

Melt the remaining 2 tablespoons of butter with the oil in a heavy casserole large enough to hold the steak comfortably. Brown the steak in the hot fat, turning it with two spoons and regulating the heat so that the meat colors richly and evenly on both sides without burning. Transfer the steak to a plate and add the sliced celery, sliced onion and carrot to the fat remaining in the casserole. Stirring frequently, cook for 8 to 10 minutes, or until the vegetables are soft and delicately browned.

Pour in the stock or water or stock-and-water combination and bring to a boil over high heat, meanwhile scraping in the brown particles clinging to the bottom and sides of the pan. Return the steak to the casserole together with any juices that have accumulated around it. Cover tightly and braise in the middle of the oven for 1 hour, or until the steak shows no resistance when pierced deeply with the point of a small sharp knife. Place the steak on a heated platter. Remove the thread.

Skim off the surface fat and strain the cooking liquid through a fine sieve into a sauceboat or bowl, pressing down hard on the vegetables with the back of a spoon to extract all their juices before discarding the pulp. Taste for seasoning, and serve the gravy separately with the steak.

To serve 4

2 pounds fresh asparagus
1¼ teaspoons salt
1 cup light cream
2 tablespoons butter
1 teaspoon finely cut fresh mint
1 egg yolk, lightly beaten
1 teaspoon strained fresh lemon
　juice
½ teaspoon ground nutmeg,
　preferably freshly grated

Fresh Asparagus with Lemon Cream Sauce, Shaker Style

Line up the asparagus tips on a chopping board and cut off the ends so that the spears are the same length. With a small sharp knife, peel off the tough outer skin of each spear. At the end, the peel may be as thick as ¹⁄₁₆ inch but it will become paper-thin toward the tip. Divide the spears into four equal bundles and tie each bundle at both ends with string.

In a 4- to 5-quart enameled or stainless-steel casserole, bring 2 quarts of water and 1 teaspoon of the salt to a boil over high heat. Drop in the asparagus and cook briskly, uncovered, for 8 to 10 minutes, or until the stalks are barely tender and show slight resistance when pierced with the point of a small, sharp knife.

With two kitchen forks, lift the bundles out of the water by their strings. Cut off the strings, spread the asparagus on paper towels to drain, then transfer them to a heated platter. Drape loosely with foil to keep the asparagus warm while you prepare the sauce.

In a heavy 6- to 8-inch skillet, combine the cream, butter, mint and the remaining ¼ teaspoon of salt. Bring to a boil over high heat and, stirring frequently, boil for 5 minutes, or until the cream has reduced to about ¾ of a cup. Then reduce the heat to low. Add about 2 tablespoons of the cream to the egg yolk and mix well. Stirring constantly, gradually pour the mixture into the cream and simmer gently for a minute or so. Do not let the sauce come anywhere near a boil or it will curdle. Stir in the lemon juice, taste for seasoning, and pour the sauce over the asparagus. Sprinkle with nutmeg and serve at once.

Batter-fried Bluegills

Bluegills are a kind of sunfish, native to the Eastern Heartland, but now used for stocking lakes and ponds nationwide. A sought-after sport and food fish, sunfish are known as bream in the South.

Pour the vegetable oil into a deep fryer or large heavy saucepan to a depth of about 3 inches and heat the oil until it reaches a temperature of 375° on a deep-frying thermometer.

Meanwhile, prepare the batter in the following fashion: Combine the flour, cornstarch, salt and pepper, and sift them together onto a plate or a sheet of wax paper. With a wire whisk, beat the egg yolk and water to a smooth cream and then incorporate the flour mixture, a few tablespoons at a time. Just before using the batter, beat the egg white with a wire whisk or a rotary or electric beater until it is stiff enough to stand in unwavering peaks on the beater when it is lifted from the bowl. Scoop the egg white over the batter and fold it in gently with a rubber spatula.

Pat the fish fillets dry with paper towels. Pick up one fillet with tongs, immerse it in the batter, and drop it into the oil. Deep-fry 4 or 5 fillets at a time, turning them with a slotted spoon for 3 minutes, or until golden brown. As they brown, transfer the fillets to paper towels to drain.

Arrange the fillets attractively on a heated platter and serve them at once, accompanied by the lemon quarters.

Shaker Salad

Drop the string beans into enough lightly salted boiling water to cover them by at least 1 inch. Boil briskly, uncovered, for 4 to 5 minutes, or until the beans are tender but still somewhat crisp to the bite. Drain the beans in a sieve or colander and run cold water over them to cool them quickly and set their color. Spread the beans on paper towels to drain and pat them dry with fresh paper towels. Refrigerate until ready to serve.

Just before serving, combine the vinegar, onions, thyme, savory, dry mustard, salt and a few grindings of pepper in a serving bowl and mix well with a wire whisk. Whisking constantly, pour in the oil in a slow stream and stir until the dressing is smooth and thick. Add the beans, lettuce and scallions, and toss together gently but thoroughly. Serve at once.

To serve 4

Vegetable oil for deep frying
½ cup cake flour, not the self-
    rising variety
2 tablespoons cornstarch
½ teaspoon salt
½ teaspoon freshly ground black
    pepper
1 egg yolk
½ cup water
1 egg white
1 pound bluegill or other sunfish
    fillets, skinned
1 lemon, quartered

To serve 4 to 6

½ pound green string beans,
    trimmed, washed and cut into
    1½-inch lengths
3 tablespoons tarragon vinegar
1 tablespoon finely chopped onions
½ teaspoon crumbled dried thyme
½ teaspoon crumbled dried savory
½ teaspoon dry mustard
1 teaspoon salt
Freshly ground black pepper
½ cup olive or vegetable oil or a
    combination of both
2 firm heads bibb or Boston lettuce,
    trimmed, washed, separated in
    leaves and cut into 1-inch pieces
    (about 3 cups)
2 tablespoons finely chopped
    scallions, including 1 inch of the
    green tops

Recipe Index

NOTE: An R preceding a page refers to the Recipe Booklet. Size, weight and material are specified for pans in the recipes because they affect cooking results. A pan should be just large enough to hold its contents comfortably. Heavy pans heat slowly and cook food at a constant rate. Aluminum and cast iron conduct heat well but may discolor foods containing egg yolks, wine, vinegar or lemon. Enamelware is a fairly poor conductor of heat. Many recipes therefore recommend stainless steel or enameled cast iron, which do not have these faults.

More on Folk Wines

If your first experiments with making your own wine encourage you to more ambitious efforts, the finer points of the process can be found in two excellent books: *Folk Wines, Cordials and Brandies,* by M. A. Jagendorf (Vanguard Press, $10) and *Successful Wine Making at Home,* by H. E. Bravery (paper, Arc Books, 95 cents). The shopping guide at right lists stores that sell the wine-making equipment you need.

Below are additional recipes for two of the folk wines that appear in the picture on page 155. They, like two of the recipes on page 154, are old Pennsylvania Dutch recipes supplied by Mrs. Betty Groff of Mount Joy, Pennsylvania.

LOCUST BLOSSOM WINE

Place 3 quarts of freshly gathered locust blossoms (no stems) in a clean crock and scald with 4 quarts of boiling water. Let stand 24 hours and strain. Add 3 pounds of sugar, 1 sliced lemon, 1 sliced orange and bring to a boil. Cool, add 1 yeast cake and a well-beaten egg white (to clarify the wine). Let stand 15 days, then strain through cheesecloth into fermenting jug and insert fermentation lock. Let stand until fermentation ceases (about 3 months). For best results, keep the wine one year before drinking.

STRAWBERRY WINE

Crush 5 pounds of strawberries with 4 pounds of sugar in an enameled pot. Dissolve one package of dry active yeast in ½ cup of lukewarm water and add to fruit mixture. Stir in 1 gallon and 1 quart of cool water. Let stand 15 days and strain through cheesecloth. Add another gallon of water and 2 pounds of sugar, pour into fermenting jug and insert a fermentation lock. Let stand until fermentation has ceased, approximately 4 months. It can be drunk at this time or bottled and stored for a year.

Shopping Guide

Most of the ingredients called for in this book's recipes can be found at any grocery or supermarket. A few recipes include products that are not widely available, such as elderberries, wild American persimmons and hickory nuts, which grow in most states east of the Rockies, but seldom appear in markets anywhere. Sorrel and ground cherries grow wild in almost every state, and there are horticultural varieties of both that may be grown from seed. Sorrel is available fresh from May through October in Jewish, Polish and fancy vegetable markets and is sold bottled or canned in fine food stores across the country. Crab apples, grown wild or under cultivation, are sometimes sold at roadside markets or in specialty fruit stores in October.

If you want to grow your own foods, seeds for the sorrel and ground cherries, as well as American persimmon and crab-apple-tree saplings, are available by mail from R. H. Shumway Seedsman, Rockford, Illinois 61101. Planting-stock tubers for Jerusalem artichokes are available from Burgess Seed and Plant Co., P.O. Box 218, Galesburg, Michigan 49053.

Rehrücken, or mock saddle of venison, cake pans, used for a type of Austrian cake, are suitable for making the Moravian half-moon cakes *(Recipe Index)* and may be ordered from Paprikás Weiss Importer, 1546 Second Avenue, New York, N.Y. 10028.

WINE-MAKING EQUIPMENT

Milan Laboratories
57 Spring Street
New York, N.Y. 10012

Vino Corporation
Box 7885
Rochester, N.Y. 14606

WINE-ART OF AMERICA

The Wine-Art chain has more than 30 stores, which sell wine-making equipment. Those in major metropolitan areas are listed.

California
7357 Sunset Blvd.
Hollywood 90046

Colorado
705 East Sixth Ave.
Denver 80203

Georgia
1921 Peachtree Rd.
Atlanta 30309

Illinois
4016 Church St.
Skokie 60076

Minnesota
5308 Excelsior Blvd.
Minneapolis 55416

New Jersey
Blue Star Shopping Ctr.
Route 22
Watchung 07060

Ohio
819 West Market St.
Akron 44303

Washington
140 105th St. N.E.
Bellevue 98004

Chapman, John (Johnny Appleseed), 123, 124, 130; commemorative stamp, *130*

Charles II, 70

Chatham, New York, Shaker Community, 187

Cheese: Bismarck Schlosskaese, 125; cream-cheese pie with glazed blueberries, *192;* cup cheese, Lancaster market, 46; Liederkranz, 125; *Schmierkäse* (cottage cheese), 54; salad, 24

Cherries: cherry-apple wine, *155;* Michigan orchards, 124; ways to use, 124

Chesapeake Bay, 75

Chestnut Hill, Philadelphia, 81

Chestnuts, 126-127

Chew, Benjamin, Chief Justice of Pennsylvania, 70

Chicago, *map* 6, 12, 19, 148, 161; Great Fire of 1871, 19; stockyards, 19, 24

Chicago & Alton Railroad, 163, 164

Chicago & North Western Railroad, 163

Chicken: batter-fried, 131; -corn soup with egg noodles, 47, 54; and ham in sherried cream sauce, *71;* à la king (à la Keene), 166; pie, 47, 59; roasted, with gravy, *185;* Stoltzfus, 47, 59

Chokecherries, *190*

Chowchow, 65

Christmas tree, Moravian, *30*

Church suppers, 133

Churchill's Restaurant, New York, 167

Cider, 35, 36, 124, *128, 146,* 148, 149, 150; hard, 149, 150; making, Long Island, 1871, *149;* toast, 150

Cincinnati, Ohio, *map* 6, 12, 19, 24, 148, 161, 186, 187; hog killing foundation of city's fortunes, 24

Claiborne, Craig, 106

Clams: broiled, *99;* cherrystones, 101; chowder, Manhattan, *98-99,* 101; chowder, New England, 101; digging, Long Island, *94,* 95, 100-101; hard-shell, frozen, 101; littlenecks, 101; quiche or tart, 101; steamer or soft-shell, 101;

steamer, remoulade, *98,* 101; stew (Fire Island starve-to-death), 101; topnecks, 101

Clark & Brown's, Maiden Lane, New York, 166

Cleveland, Ohio, 12, 186

Clinton, De Witt, Governor of New York, 161

Cliveden, Germantown, 70

Coleslaw, *65;* Dutch *(kool sla),* 18

Colony in Schuylkill. *See* State in Schuylkill.

Comisar, Lee and Michael, 187

Confections: candied apple, how to make, *131;* clear toy candy, 10, *22;* mixed-nut brittle, *128;* sherried walnuts, *128;* spiced mixed nuts, *128*

Connecticut River, 13

Consommé Bellevue, *71, 77*

Constitutional Convention 1787, 71

Continental Congress 1774, 70, 71

Cookies: German Christmas cookies, 35; *lebkuchen,* 35; molasses animal cookies, *23*

Corn: chicken-corn soup, *47, 54;* cornmeal mush, fried, 35; dried, 50; Indian, *9;* raised in Indiana and Illinois, 135, *136-137;* -and-rivvel soup, 54; roast, Indiana, Illinois, 133-134; "strawberry," *9;* used by Pennsylvania Dutch, 59-60; yellow, *9*

Corncob jelly, 133, *139*

Cornish miners in Upper Peninsula, Michigan, 25, 27

Cornish pasties, 24-25, *26,* 27, 111; how to make, *28-29;* miner's way to heat, 27

Country Kitchen, Kutztown, Pennsylvania, *48*

Covered Bridge Festival, Parke County, Indiana, *138-139*

Crab-apple jelly, 65

Cracker pudding, 59

Cranberry sauce, *185*

Crefelders, 34

Crosby, Everett, 158

Crystal Lake, Michigan, 106

Cucumber salad, 106

Culinary influences of 19th Century immigrants, 19, 24

Czarnecki, Joseph and Wanda, 188, *193,* 196

Danckaerts, Jasper, 96

Dandelions, 152-153; leaves, 195; leaves cooked, with butter sauce, 196; salad for Maundy Thursday, 50; wine, 152, *153, 155,* how to make, 154

Davis, William M., 149

Declaration of Independence, 71

De Hart, Simon, 96

Delaware Bay, 75; whale fishing, 70

Delaware Indians, 95

Delaware River, 13

Delmonico, railroad dining car, 164

Delmonico, Charles, 166

Delmonico, John (Giovanni Del-Monico), Swiss wine merchant, 165

Delmonico, Lorenzo, 166, 167

Delmonico, Peter (Pietro Del-Monico), Swiss pastry maker, 165

Delmonico's, New York, 161, *164, 165,* 166, 167, 168; menu for Dickens, 166

Desserts: apple custard with Rhenish wine, 18; cracker pudding, 59; *Fastnachts* (doughnuts), 60, 61; floating island, 72, 77, to shape meringue ovals, *93;* funnel cakes, 10, *20, 21;* ice cream, 74, molded, Philadelphia style, 75, *82-87,* vanilla, with strawberry sauce, 79; *Oliebollen* (Dutch doughnuts), 18; peach custard, *142;* persimmon pudding, Indiana style, 129-130, 133; strawberry flummery, 72, *80,* 186; sugar doughnuts, *146;* syllabub, 72; trifle, 72. *See also* Cakes; Cookies; Pies

Detroit, Michigan, 12, 113

Dickens, Charles, 162, 166, 167

Dining car, *163, 164*

Dolma (stuffed grape leaves), Shaker, 186

Duck, domestic: industry Long Island, *102, 103;* roast, stuffed with apricots and rice, 102, *104-105*

Duck, wild, 113; roasted rare, with crushed peppercorns, 113

Dunkards, 34

Dutch. *See* Pennsylvania Dutch

Dutch influence on cookery of Middle Atlantic states, 12, 17-18

Dutch West India Company, 17, 148

Easthampton, New York, 106

Edgewater, New Jersey, shad bake, *14, 15*

Edward VIII, King of England (Prince of Wales), *169*

Eggs: blue-flower omelet, 186; red beet, *49, 54*

Elderberry: blossom fritters, 195; wine, 150, 195, how to make, 154

Engle, Mrs. Erma, 58

English influence on cookery of Middle Atlantic states, 12

Ephrata, Pennsylvania, 37

Epicurean, The, Charles Ranhofer, 166

Erie Canal, 161

Fairmount Park, Philadelphia, 81

Fancy Dutch (Moravians, etc.), 34, 35

Farmer's Club (Philadelphia eating club), 79

Fastnacht Day (Shrove Tuesday), 61

Fastnachts (doughnuts), 60, 61

Feinschmeckers (good eaters), Pennsylvania Dutch, 35

Filberts, 126, *127*

Finger Lakes, New York, 156

Fire Island, New York, 100, 101, 106

Fish: fresh-water varieties, Michigan, 12, 106-107. *See also* names of fish

Fish House (State in Schuylkill), Philadelphia eating club, 79, 81; punch, 79, recipe, 81

Flip (hot drink, pre-Revolutionary), 148

Floating island, 72, 77; to shape meringue ovals, 93

Flower wines, 150, 151

Flummery, strawberry, 72, *80;* Sister Abigail's, 186

Fort Wayne, Indiana, 124

Four Seasons Restaurant, New York, 168

Fox grapes, 156; soup, 196

Frank, Dr. Konstantin, 156

Credits and Acknowledgments

The sources for the illustrations that appear in this book are shown below. Credits for the pictures from left to right are separated by commas, from top to bottom by dashes. Richard Jeffery—Cover, 4—bottom right, 14 bottom, 16, 22, 23, 30, 47, 52, 53, 57, 65, 73, 80, 91, 98, 99, 104, 105, 117, 128, 142, 146, 155, 172, 173, 184. Costa Manos from Magnum—9, 26, 27, 28, 29, 108, 109, 110, 112, 114, 115, 122, 126, 127, 131, 132, 135, 138, 139, 190 bottom right. Enrico Ferorelli—68, 71, 76, 77, 78, 82, 83, 84, 85, 86, 87, 94, 176, 189 top, 190 except top left and bottom right, 191, 192. Other photographs: 4—Richard Meek, Monica Suder —Richard Henry, Walter Daran. 6—Map by Lothar Roth and Gloria duBouchet. 11—Culver Pictures. 13 —Brian Seed. 14 top, 15—Bill Binzen. 20, 21—Brian Seed. 32, 37 through 45—John Robaton from Camera 5. 48—Fred Schnell. 49—John Robaton from Camera 5. 56, 58, 59—Brian Seed. 93—Walter Daran. 96 —Museum of the City of New York. 102, 103—Brian Seed. 136, 137—John Zimmerman. 149—New York State Historical Association, Cooperstown. 152, 153 —Brian Seed. 158, 159—Charles Phillips. 160—Paulus Leeser courtesy The New-York Historical Society. 163—Bettmann Archive. 164—Brown Brothers. 165 —Bettmann Archive. 166, 167, 169—Paulus Leeser courtesy The New-York Historical Society. 170—Brown Brothers. 171—Bettmann Archive—Photograph by Byron from the Byron Collection Museum of the City of New York. 178—Robert S. Crandall for TIME courtesy Shaker Village, Hancock, Mass. 181—Robert S. Crandall for TIME. 182, 183, 185—Bud Lee. 189 bottom, 190 top left Richard Meek.

Betty Groff of Mount Joy, Pennsylvania, contributed some of the recipes in this book, and assisted in testing them in the FOODS OF THE WORLD kitchen.

For help and advice in the production of the book, thanks are extended to the following: in Illinois: Alice and Howard Alexander, Chicago; Ruth Ellen Church, Chicago Tribune; Dr. Herrell DeGraff, American Meat Institute, Chicago; Larry H. Simerl, United States Department of Agriculture, University of Illinois, Urbana; Reba Stagg, National Meat and Livestock Board, Chicago; in Indiana: Marjorie Ashby, Stokely-Van Camp, Inc., Indianapolis; Carl E. Betz and Betty BreedLove, Martinsville; The Covered Bridge Festival Committee, Parke County; Josephine and Marvin Maier, Bremen; Becky Surface, The Hoosier Farmer, Indianapolis; Miskel Wolfinger, Southern Indiana Gas and Electric Co., Evansville; in Massachusetts: Hancock Shaker Village, Pittsfield; in Michigan: Ingrid Bartelli, Michigan State University, Marquette; Ted Bogdan, Marquette; Pearl Brailey, Negaunee; Gus Colombe and Philip Houle, The Homestead Lodge, Toivola; Cleo and Lester Gruber, Detroit; Jack Imbs, St. Joseph; Nancy Kennedy, Ford Times, Detroit; Wallace Keskitalo, Michigan State University, Houghton; Lempi Laamanen, Trimountain; Frank G. Matthews, Negaunee; Jo Mishica, Calumet; Selma Sanford, Dollar Bay; Kay Savage, Detroit Free Press; Wilmer Savela, Portage; Dorothy Walkmeyer, Traverse City; in New Jersey: Albert Von Dohlm, Edgewater; in New York: Sam Aaron, Sherry-Lehmann, Inc., New York City; Terry Bisbee, New York City; John Bellini, Long Island Duck Farmers Cooperative, Inc., Eastport; Everett Crosby, High Tor Vineyards, New City; Louis DeMartino, New York City; John Von Glahn, Fishery Council, New York City; James Kaler and Jeff Zegal, The Great South Bay Farmers Cooperative Association, Inc., West Sayville;

Ruth McMorran, Troy; Gale Steves, National Marine Fisheries Service, United States Department of Commerce, New York City; Lillie Stuckey, Lewis/Neale, Inc., New York City; Walter S. Taylor, Bully Hill Vineyards, Hammondsport; Mary Tobin, New York State Department of Commerce, New York City; Richard P. Vine, Pleasant Valley Wine Co., Hammondsport; Elizabeth Wallace, Shellfish Institute of North America, Sayville; in Ohio: Mr. and Mrs. Carl V. Bailey, Green Springs Nursery, Green Springs; Lee and Michael Comisar, Cincinnati; Florence La Ganke Harris, Cleveland; Alma Kaufman, The Plain Dealer, Cleveland; Mr. and Mrs. Robert Lorenz, Fremont; Elizabeth Nord, Shaker Historical Society, Cleveland; Mr. and Mrs. Harvey Oaks, Fremont; Hazel Phillips, Warren County Historical Society Museum, Lebanon; Jerry N. Ransohoff, Cincinnati; in Pennsylvania: Sam Bookbinder Jr., Philadelphia; Kitty Brown, Marietta; Joseph and Wanda Czarnecki, Reading; Julie Dannenbaum, Sally Ellis and Vincent de Finis, Philadelphia; Freda and Euell Gibbons, Troxelville; Abraham Groff, Mount Joy; Clarence Herr, Strasburg; Kathryn Larson, Philadelphia; Claude Oldt, Sinking Spring; Harry and Lillian Prock, Philadelphia; Charles Regennas, Lititz; John Taxin, Old Original Bookbinder's, Philadelphia; Janette Turner, Bethlehem; Helen Sigel Wilson, Philadelphia; Constance Wolf, Blue Bell; Fred and Mollie Zendler, Zendler's Ice Cream, East Germantown; Edwin Zimmerman and family, Kutztown; in Washington, D.C.: United States Brewers Association.

The following shops and galleries supplied antiques, tableware and other objects used in the studio photography in this book: in Massachusetts: Henry Coger, Antiques, Ashley Falls; in New York: Michael Bertolini, Antiques, Goshen; in New York City: The American Collector, Antiques Center: Bardith, Ltd.; David Barrett, Antiques; John Gordon, American Antiques; James II Galleries, Ltd.; La Cuisinière; John-Lewis, Antiques & Decorations; H. J. Kratzer, Inc.; A. Morjikian Co., Inc.; The Peaceable Kingdom, Ltd.; James Robinson, Inc.; Terrestris Greenhouses, Inc.; R. Thibaut Co.; Wuthering Hollow, Antiques; in Virginia: Copper Lantern Antiques, Arlington.

Sources consulted in the production of this book include: Brewed in America, Stanley Baron; Penn Family Recipes, edited by Evelyn Benson, recipe reprinted on page 154 by permission of George Shumway, Publisher, York, Pa.; The Perennial Philadelphians, Nathaniel Burt; Life in America, Marshall B. Davidson; American Notes, Charles Dickens; The Evolution of Long Island, Ralph Gabriel; Stalking the Wild Asparagus, Euell Gibbons; The Lifeline of America, Edward C. Hampe Jr. and Merle Wittenberg; The Art of Pennsylvania Dutch Cooking, Edna Eby Heller; Folk Wines, Cordials and Brandies, M. A. Jagendorf; Travels in North America, Peter Kalm; The Martha Washington Cookbook, Marie Kimball; Shaker Recipes for Cooks and Homemakers, William L. Lassiter; The Best of Shaker Cooking, Amy Bess Miller and Persis Fuller; Luchow's German Cookbook, Jan Mitchell; History of the American People, Samuel Eliot Morison; Good Home Cooking, Nell Nichols; Turn of the Century Cooking, Marcia Ott; The Shaker Cook Book, Caroline B. Piercy; The Philadelphia Cookbook, Anna Wetherill Reed; Delmonico's, Lately Thomas; The Epicurean, Charles Ranhofer; Domestic Manners of the Americans, Frances Trollope; The Way Our People Lived, W. E. Woodward.

XX Printed in U.S.A.